T0303532

WHO *is* EQUAL?

The equality code of the constitution

WHO *is* EQUAL?

The equality code of the constitution

SAURABH KIRPAL

VINTAGE
An imprint of Penguin Random House

VINTAGE

Vintage is an imprint of the Penguin Random House group of companies whose addresses can be found at global.penguinrandomhouse.com

Published by Penguin Random House India Pvt. Ltd
4th Floor, Capital Tower 1, MG Road,
Gurugram 122 002, Haryana, India

First published in Vintage by Penguin Random House India 2024

10 9 8 7 6 5 4 3 2 1

ISBN 9780670100149

Typeset in Sabon LT Std Pro by Manipal Technologies Limited, Manipal
Printed at Thomson Press India Ltd, New Delhi

www.penguin.co.in

Contents

Introduction vii

1. Equality of What 1
2. Rule of Law 29
3. Education 59
4. Employment 88
5. Business 124
6. Democracy 150
7. Marriage 178

Epilogue 205
Notes 217

Introduction

In small-town India, one day a young Dalit mother decided that she had suffered enough caste-based discrimination. She belonged to the Bhangi caste, a term that has morphed into a casteist slur in India. She wanted to ensure that the centuries-old discrimination against people like her did not percolate down to her children and decided to do something different.

She decided to raise her children as upper-caste Brahmins, rather than the Dalits they were. She wanted friends and neighbours to see her children as part of the caste elite and not as beneficiaries of caste-based reservation. She wanted to stem the narrative that lower castes were stealing jobs and seats in universities from the upper castes. The Dalit woman's daughter, Yashica Dutt, was educated and spent a part of her working life hiding her identity through elaborate lies to mask her 'Dalitness'.[1] It took the suicide of a young PhD scholar, Rohith Vemula, for Dutt to break free from her cocoon and 'come out' and declare herself a Dalit.

This symbolic 'coming out' mirrors the agonizing decision that millions grapple with when they come out about their sexuality. Children, teenagers and some adults, late in life, recognize that they are different, and admitting to that difference by coming out potentially invites societal disapproval. But how can coming out about one's identity be so difficult in twenty-first-century India? One reason is that those coming out recognize that they will not be equal citizens of the country and will have to face constant and endemic discrimination. Some may have convinced themselves that the trajectory of the country is moving towards ever-greater equality, but the reality appears different, at least when viewed through the eyes of those suffering discrimination. This persistent inequality flies in the face of the promises made in the foundational document of our country—the Constitution.

In 1950, we, the people of India, gave to ourselves a Constitution that promised justice, liberty and equality. These ideals were supposed to lead to a fraternal society which would 'assure the dignity of the individual and the unity and integrity of the nation'.[2] These Constitutional values have been taught to many generations of schoolchildren in their political science textbooks and are regularly promised by politicians and the courts alike. But the ideal that was so easy to promise, has been very hard to achieve in practice. When we look around and ask, 'who is equal?', the short answer is, 'not very many'. Yashica Dutt's parents were compelled to seek a better life for their daughter by hiding an important part of their identity, therefore, essentially living a lie. While substantial progress has been made in the many years after Independence, there still exist multiple fault lines along which we are divided as a nation.

One possible reason why this seemingly simple idea of equality has been so elusive to achieve is because we have deep-rooted differences about what it means to be equal, and how best to achieve it. Yet, we cannot but help strive towards it, because an unequal society is usually a deeply unjust one. In fact, the first step towards remedying an injustice is to acknowledge it exists, and to understand it.

So how does one tackle the vast subject of equality? Or perhaps the question should be altered to ask, 'how does one address inequality?', because it is only when one confronts discrimination that the true need for equality is revealed.[3] Discrimination can be felt in many spheres of life and for many different reasons. For instance, someone can face discrimination at the workplace, at school or even within the family. Equally, there are multiple grounds on which the effects of inequality can be felt. In the Indian context, these are sex, gender, caste and religion.[4] While human ingenuity will find multiple reasons to hold someone unequal, to cast them as 'the other',[5] there are some grounds of discrimination that constantly recur in society.

To compound the complexities of discrimination, these biases can overlap and create a unique form of inequality. A Dalit, or a woman, may suffer discrimination at the workplace, but their experiences would not be identical. The experience of a Dalit woman would also be distinctive because it's an amalgamation of the two intersecting axes of discrimination. Sexual violence against women is not unusual in India, but in the case of Dalit women, it is used as a weapon by upper-caste men to assert their dominance.[6]

This violence against a Dalit woman is distinct and worthy of separate examination. What is required then, is some kind of mapping, an examination of the different areas of human existence, and how these inequalities affect them.

For instance, take the case of Bhanwari Devi, a lower-caste social worker, who worked to stop child marriages in the villages of Rajasthan.[7] Bhanwari Devi had informed the police that a nine-month-old girl belonging to the upper-caste Thakur community was being married. Incensed at the perceived interference by a lower-caste woman, the relatives of the infant bride decided to teach Bhanwari Devi a lesson, and accosted her and her husband in the fields, and gang-raped her. This violence was meted out to her only because she was trying to do her job and because the upper-caste men thought that they could get away with the violence. Indeed, that belief was nearly true, because the trial court held the men innocent of the rape, partly on the ground that it was inconceivable that an upper-caste man would rape a lower-caste woman. The toxic mix of caste and gender defined the experience of Bhanwari Devi, as it does countless lower-caste women, every day.

The book, therefore, aims to address different aspects of a person's existence and their interaction with the State and the community, in the context of equality. The chapters include a discussion about education, employment, democracy, economy and marriage. In each sphere, a special emphasis has been placed on the different grounds of discrimination. Thus, when speaking of education, the cause and effect of inequalities faced by the oppressed castes, and the poor, have been discussed. The focus is not on the unique forms of discrimination a person may face due to their disparate and intersectional[8] identities. Here, the attempt is to examine one aspect of life and determine how people suffer discrimination on the three common grounds of inequality, i.e. sex, caste and religion.

To add to this cocktail of issues, the overarching theme of this book, is the state of the law relating to equality. Thus, though the book begins by asking what equality means, both jurisprudentially and philosophically, it is ultimately about examining specific cases and legal provisions, which impact equality. The discussion seeks to give the reader the lay of the land of the law of the land. Jurisprudential theories, which are discussed in the first part of the book are discussed to enable one to appreciate the range of concerns that any discussion of equality poses.

The Fountainhead of Equality

The first provision that any lawyer, judge or a reasonably well-informed citizen will turn to in the context of equality is Article 14 of the Constitution, which promises the equal protection of laws to all persons. The pithily worded provision[9] captures public imagination through its promises of egalitarianism and justice. However, like most provisions of the Constitution, the exact import of the Article cannot be understood in a vacuum. The first chapter seeks to unpack some of the foundational aspects of the equality code in the Constitution by asking self-evident questions. For instance, we all assume that equality is a valuable goal, but is that actually the case? In turn, to decide whether something is important, it is usually necessary to ask what we mean by that concept. Therefore, the chapter examines what equality truly means (is it equality of opportunity or equality of result?) and why it is an important ideal to strive towards. The answers to these questions lie partly in the domain of human biology (why do we instinctively seem to want to be equal?), moral philosophy (what does equality ethically imply?) and political pragmatism (how do we formulate policies that foster equality?).

While this discussion might appear esoteric in a book that claims to be an explainer of the law, it is still essential to address these issues because the answers to the questions posed have a real-life impact on how judgments are delivered. What the court imagines its task to be, is shaped deeply by the judges' understanding and their views on the right to equality. For instance, two common, and allegedly contradictory, views of equality are the formal and the substantive theories. The former looks at the text of the law and is satisfied if the law, on the face of it, does not discriminate. The latter theory inquires into the actual impact of the law rather than its formal language. A more conservative judge who ascribes to the formalistic theory would be more reluctant to intervene, even when the effects of the law are palpably discriminatory, as long as the law is worded neutrally. On the other hand, a progressive judge would be emboldened in taking more interventionist decisions by pointing out that the Constitutional obligation of equality requires her to ensure equality, and not just on paper. One example of this would be Section 377 of the Indian Penal Code which criminalized sexual activity against 'the order of nature'. Two judges of the Supreme Court, adopting a rather formalistic reading of Article 14, initially held that the provision was Constitutional. They wrote, 'Section 377 IPC does not criminalise a particular people or identity or orientation. It merely identifies certain acts which, if committed, would constitute an offence. Such a prohibition regulates sexual conduct regardless of gender identity and orientation.'[10] There was, in their view, no hostile discrimination against the queer community because what was criminalized was a sexual act and not any particular gender-identity, orientation or sexuality—a clear case of formal equality.

This view was subsequently reversed by a unanimous five-judge bench of the court which had a different vision of what equality implied. In that judgment, the Supreme Court held that 'the effect of Section 377, thus, is not merely to criminalise an act, but to criminalise a specific set of identities. Though facially neutral, the effect of the provision is to efface specific identities. These identities are the soul of the LGBT community'.[11] As per this judgment, even if the law was, on the face of it, equally applicable to all persons, its impact on the queer community was overwhelmingly negative and therefore the provision was Constitutionally suspect. This view of equality was thus shaped by the judges' vastly different interpretation of the equality clause—one that requires judges to intervene when the effects of a law were disproportionately adverse to a community, even if they appeared at first blush to be neutral.

Of course, the attempt to understand the basis for a judicial decision is not solely philosophical or ideological but is also intimately connected to the evolution of the relevant jurisprudence and history. The Constitutional imperatives of equality have evolved over the years and judges often justify decisions by pointing to what the founding fathers of the Constitution meant when they adopted the text.[12] The first chapter therefore also traces the historical trajectory of the right to equality in the country, both before Independence and thereafter. The Constituent Assembly debates as well as the statements of political leaders during the struggle for independence provide rich, source material for a pre-Independence approach to issues relating to equality. Post-Independence, this examination moves to the judgments of the courts, and particularly the jurisprudence of the Supreme Court.

In the initial years after the enactment of the Constitution, Article 14 was interpreted very narrowly by the courts. If discrimination was alleged between two groups, the court adopted the narrow 'classification' test. Here, the court would reject the argument based on discrimination if a basis for classification between two groups, howsoever tenuous, could be demonstrated. All that was required to be demonstrated was that the classes had been made on the basis of some 'intelligible differentia' which had a rational nexus with the object that the Act purportedly sought to achieve.[13] This was a test that had been developed in the jurisprudence of the American courts and offered only the most tenuous protection against discrimination. Further, there was a presumption in favour of constitutionality of any statute with considerable leeway being given to the government in determining and classifying the subject of its laws.[14]

Over the years, this view of equality was abandoned in favour of a more robust form of equality. This was an interpretation where historical and structural disadvantages of the past were taken into account to determine whether any legislation passed Constitutional muster. Thus, the Supreme Court ruled that reservations for the oppressed castes were not really an exception to the equality clause but were actually part of it.[15] This was on the reasoning that to treat unequally placed people, which the scheduled castes and tribes were, on par with their far more socially and economically competitors, amounted to a violation of equality.

Around the same time, other than a change in judicial attitude and willingness to consider equality realpolitik, the courts also adopted a new test to determine violations of Article 14. Rather than relying on the traditional classification test, the courts developed a new rubric under which legislative as well as administrative acts would be put under Constitutional scrutiny. This was a test against arbitrariness where the court held that any decision which appeared to be palpably irrational logically, (as well as legally), automatically violated the equality clause in the Constitution.[16]

These tests and approaches to equality closely mirror the language of the rule of law. This is not a surprise because the rule of law has often been understood to be as fundamental a feature of a liberal democracy as equality, justice and liberty. The exhortations to the rule of law in judgments as well as in the public domain are often couched in the language traditionally used in the context of equality.[17] Thus, the chapter on the 'Rule of Law' examines this close link between the two concepts with the aim to establish that each concept gives meaning and substance to the other.

After examining the general facets of equality, the book moves on to specific areas where the right to equality has been elaborated upon by judgments of the courts. The first chapter looks at how the demands of egalitarianism manifest themselves in the field of employment, particularly in reservations. The balancing act required by the court, in matters of public employment, provides a sharp relief to the competing values of a Constitutional democracy. The need to provide reservations for the disadvantaged are juxtaposed with the idea of 'merit' that general category candidates allegedly have. Therefore, a commonly asked question is, 'How far should the law go in ensuring that public employment reflects the social composition of the country without sacrificing the needs of efficiency?'[18] Reservations also bring into question an important facet of equality—are promising jobs to oppressed castes a vindication or a suppression of the idea of equality? This area of law has seen constant amendments to the Constitution followed by judicial determinations. The chapter on employment also examines other facets of inequality by relying upon the data as well as the law—most strikingly in the sphere of gender discrimination. Data reveals that women routinely earn less than men, violating the principles of equal pay for equal work. They also face service conditions, which make it hard for them to participate in the workforce. This is partly by allowing insufficient leeway for unique concerns women face, including motherhood and family responsibilities. Though the law has attempted to remedy these issues, the problem remains sticky and resistant to change.

The theme of reservations carries on in matters relating to education. Education has a transformative potential in the lives of the underprivileged and deprived. It offers a means to overcome historic and systemic deprivations, the most obvious of which are economic class and caste. The chapter on education deals with how the law and the courts have sought to address this imbalance. In the case of economically weaker classes, the legislature has sought to even the playing field through the enactment of the Right to Education Act as well as providing for reservations in public and private institutions through Constitutional amendments. These legislative interventions have both been upheld by the courts but remain highly contested. The chapter also examines the more contested aspects of reservations. In particular, it seeks to answer who are the beneficiaries of reservations and the institutions that are required to provide reservations. It considers whether the equality clause permits the exclusion of a 'creamy layer' of beneficiaries, i.e. a subset of persons who are comparatively more socially developed than other members of their peer caste group. The chapter also explores the law in relation to reservations in minority-run private educational institutions. This discussion seeks to highlight that the conflict in the context of reservations is not only between the general category and reserved category students, but also between the oppressed castes and religious and cultural minorities.

From divisive ideological battles, the book moves on to survey the equality jurisprudence of the courts in the more prosaic area of economy. In fact, the equality clause has been pressed into service most often by businesses. Relying on the new test of arbitrariness mentioned above, a host of governmental actions affecting the economy have been challenged before the courts of law. These include how governments enter into contracts with private parties (i.e. how bidders are selected) and make substantive policy decisions. The concept of natural justice, i.e. the requirement that any person should be heard before a judgment is passed, also has its origins in the law relating to businesses. This chapter discusses how equality is a potent economic tool even for economic entities, which are otherwise focused largely on profits. Even in the case of the economy, the courts have had a varying attitude to the Doctrine of Equality and the extent of its jurisdiction. Before the days of economic liberalization, the courts had begun to demand a great amount of accountability from the State in matters relating to its commercial transactions. However, over the years, the courts started giving the government more free play in the joints and took a more hands-off approach. This also matched a trend in recent years when the courts have generally been more deferential to governmental decision making.

The discussion in the book thus far might have led a reader to believe that fair outcomes can be obtained only by using the constitutional provisions concerning equality. This, of course, is not true. Perhaps the most potent way to achieve the constitutional ideal of egalitarianism is through having a sensitive government and legislature, which actively seeks to achieve them through economic and social policies. However, to have a responsive government, and keeping aside fears of majoritarianism, the process of choosing one's representatives must itself be fair. The chapter on democracy examines whether that is in fact the case. Thus, issues of the weight of each vote within a constituency, the equal rights of any citizen to contest elections, and the very right to be a citizen are examined in the chapter.

The discussion about equality in the areas of education, employment, business, and elections is largely about the actions of the State when it acts as a public entity. However, some of the greatest inequalities are to be found not in public but in private spaces. In particular, sex, gender and sexuality are some of the areas where inequalities within families manifest themselves. This is partly because women and sexual minorities have to face the patriarchal power structure. The law too, reinforces these structures by institutionalizing discrimination in religious personal laws. Inequality manifests itself not only in the black letter of the law, but also how the law is applied within the power structures in a marriage. These imbalances cause some feminists to question the very worth on the institution of marriage. That, of course, leads one to ask—if marriage is inherently problematic—why do so many people want to marry? In particular, why do non-heterosexual persons seek to get married under an institution that is patriarchal? The answer to this question, which is discussed in the chapter on marriage, lies partly in the legal benefits that the institution of marriage endows upon a couple, and partly the legitimacy that State recognition bestows on a non-heterosexual marriage. In most areas discussed in this chapter, the courts have been reluctant to intervene in the ideal of equality. While different reasons are given for this reticence, patriarchy is at least part of the reason for the decisions made in the context of the family.

Having examined various substantive questions in relation to equality, the final chapter seeks to draw together the themes of the previous chapter to speculate, to an extent, on the unique challenges that lie ahead. In the case of employment, the focus in the coming years may shift to reservations in the private sector. In education, the question of reservations on grounds other than caste will also arise. In particular, the question of reservations based on religion will also arise. In the field of family law, the Uniform Civil Code is being touted as a means to ensure gender equality. The chapter will examine whether there is any legal and political basis for such a claim, or whether incremental reform in personal laws is a better idea. Finally, the chapter examines the consequences of not having a general anti-discrimination law in the country and therefore its impact on fair play in the everyday lives of citizens.

Equality: The Courts, Parliament and the People

We live in deeply polarized times. In the multiple conflicts which surround us, there is also a struggle for the control over that most sacred of texts—the Constitution. Parliament claims for itself the power to amend the Constitution, arguing that it represents the will of the people.[19] The judiciary has, on the other hand, asserted its prerogative as the ultimate interpreter and protector of Constitutional values and ideals. This debate is most trenchant when the discussion moves to the 'basic structure' of the Indian Constitution.[20] At its heart, the basic structure of the Constitution comprises those rights and features which makes the Constitution recognizable. The proponents of the doctrine argue that amending something which is the very essence of the document would no longer be an amendment but would repeal it. For instance, one could amend the Constitution to provide for hereditary, dynastic rule. The Constitution would technically still exist but would not be recognizable in any form. This, the courts have held, is not permissible.

Relying on the basic structure doctrine, the courts have held that the power to amend the Constitution is limited and reserved for themselves the authority, to determine how much of the Constitution can be amended. On the other hand, the government has accused the courts of disturbing the delicate balance of power enshrined in the Constitution by using this doctrine to strike down Constitutional amendments passed by Parliament, charging them with usurping the domain of the legislature.

What forms part of the Constitution's basic structure is a deeply contested issue. While the courts, over the years, have held different facets of the Constitution to be integral to it, they have decisively also held that certain fundamental rights guaranteed to citizens form part of this basic structure.[21] These are the rights to equality, freedom and life. Together, these three rights have been held to constitute the 'golden triangle' of fundamental rights. Chief Justice Y.V. Chandrachud wrote in 1980 that:

> Three Articles of our Constitution, and only three, stand between the heaven of freedom into which Tagore wanted his country to awake and the abyss of unrestrained power. They are Articles 14, 19 and 21. Article 31-C has removed two sides of that golden triangle which affords to the people of this country an assurance that the promise held forth by the preamble will be performed by ushering an egalitarian era through the discipline of fundamental rights, that is, without emasculation of the rights to liberty and equality which alone can help preserve the dignity of the individual.[22]

The words of the judgment exhort us to remember that in any tussle between the executive and the legislature, it is the individual who is at the heart of the Constitution.[23] The 'egalitarian era' cannot be achieved by trampling upon rights in the name of equality. Instead, it is only through safeguarding her right to equality that a citizen's dignity can be assured. The Constitution provides an elaborate structure which seeks to promote a robust form of equality, both in terms of the substantive rights as well as institutional mechanisms to operationalize the rights.

However, no Constitution, no matter how well and laboriously drafted, will ensure fairness and equity. Dr B.R. Ambedkar, in his last speech to the Constituent Assembly, said, 'I feel, however good a Constitution may be, it is sure to turn out bad because those who are called to work it, happen to be a bad lot. However, bad a Constitution may be, it may turn out to be good if those who are called to work it, happen to be a good lot. The working of a Constitution does not depend wholly upon the nature of the Constitution. The Constitution can provide only the organs of State such as the Legislature, the executive and the Judiciary. The factors on which the working of those organs of the State depend are the people and the political parties they will set up as their instruments to carry out their wishes and their politics.'[24]

The Constitution ultimately belongs to the people of India and its efficacy depends on how we act upon its principles. It is only when we, a collective of citizens, conform to Constitutional values and follow the spirit, as well as the text of that document, that the promises made in the preamble can be accomplished. There is, therefore, a great responsibility on us to pursue constitutional values—after all the price of liberty is eternal vigilance. To be vigilant pre-supposes a need to be aware, and that is what this book seeks to achieve. The exact contours of how the equality code has been interpreted over the years is something only lawyers and Constitutional experts are aware of. This book aims to be a bridge between the abstractions of the law and the realities of lived experiences with the fond hope that an educated electorate would also be a wise one.

1

Equality of What

In 2008, researchers in California conducted an experiment to determine how people would react to inequality.[1] A website maintained a record of what employees working for the state earned per month. The researchers first sent an email to employees alerting them about the existence of this website, which was apparently not that well known. This caused a spike in people visiting the site to compare the salaries that they were drawing versus their colleagues. Shortly after the first email, researchers asked the employees a rather leading question—how satisfied were they with their jobs? The people who found out that they were being paid less than their peers consistently reported being dissatisfied with their jobs (as opposed to a control group who did not know their colleagues' income). This was an example of what economists call the relative-income model, where people react to income inequality emotionally, rather than rationally. You feel unworthy and unappreciated when you find out that you are paid less than a person doing an identical job to yours even if you earn as much as you think you deserve.

Thus, there seems to be something special about equality. Most of us react angrily if we feel that we are being treated unequally.[2] While the rhetoric of equality is often used as a mere slogan by politicians, most people intuitively feel that it captures something truly important about the human essence. Forget academic debates concerning the distribution of government benefits and historic patterns of inequality, even very young children will reject the idea of being treated unequally.[3] Thus, equality seems to capture something unique, almost primeval, about us as persons. So, it is not surprising that most countries claim to promote equality in their foundational documents.[4] India is no different in this regard with the preamble proudly declaring that the goal of the Constitution is to ensure 'equality of status and opportunity'.

But does simply declaring ourselves to be equal guarantee that we achieve equality? Are we really equal? What does it, in fact, mean to be equal? To answer this, one needs to dig deep into the very meaning of the concept of equality. It requires us to address many questions which have engaged the attention of philosophers and jurists for centuries[5]. Before we can ask ourselves, 'are we equal?', we must first ask ourselves, 'what is equal?'. Or to put it another way, what does equality really mean? Does equality refer to the equality of opportunity (i.e., a level playing field for all participants) or an equality of outcomes (i.e., an equal distribution of resources, regardless of the starting position of parties)? Finally, if after all this, we can agree on what equality means, there still remains the question of how best to achieve it. For instance, is equality best achieved through quotas or by giving the disadvantaged some other form of a head start (like a lower qualifying mark)?

However, this is not solely a book on jurisprudence or moral philosophy. It is, as stated in the introduction, a book which seeks to describe the current state of the law of equality under the Indian Constitution. So, why are these questions relevant? It is partly because the answers to these queries have a practical impact on how the law and the courts deal with the enduring inequalities in India. The players—lawmakers in Parliament or even judges—may not always explicitly refer to these philosophical issues. However, their judgments are often related to their own understanding of what equality entails. A judge committed to the idea of equality of results would be more liable to uphold legislation that transfers wealth from the richest to the poorest in a society. On the other hand, a more conservative judge concerned only with formal equality, might strike down such legislation if it can be shown that there are no legal barriers for anyone to do business in a country. For such a judge, once every citizen is equally free to work, there is no reason to play Robin Hood. Thus, questions about the nature of equality have to be examined before conducting a meaningful discussion of the status of equality jurisprudence in India.

This chapter will seek to not only examine the nature of equality, but also place it in a historical context. This is because what courts do cannot be seen in an ahistorical vacuum. The decisions judges take are shaped by past precedent as well as the conditions and problems of the times that they are delivered in. Since the basis of equality jurisprudence in India starts with our Constitution, a study of how those provisions were incorporated is essential. The argument is not that what history was must determine what the future should be. It is essentially that we cannot understand the present without looking at the past.

Why Is Equality Important?

Perhaps the most fundamental question one can ask is whether equality is a valuable goal at all.[6] Most theories of moral and political philosophy seem to argue that equality is an important virtue, and therefore, a goal worth achieving. But that does not answer whether it's correct to seek equality as opposed to some other ideal. Indeed, some schools of thought, on the face of it, reject the idea of equal distribution of resources. Someone might say that it is perfectly justified to have an unequal society if the poorest people still have a good life.[7] In other words, it is better to be unequally wealthy than equally poor.

However, even these ideologies appeal to some form of equality, though this may be hidden in the formulation rather than being explicitly evident. For instance, a utilitarian believes that the goal of society is to maximize happiness. In such a philosophy, whatever increases the total happiness of all its members is preferred. It is almost a mathematical model where every person's happiness (typically called 'utility') is measured and added up to determine the total utility of society. Any measure that increases the net utility of society should be adopted and that which lessens it, has to be spurned.[8] If some citizens end up extremely unequal (and that too for no fault of theirs) so that the overall happiness of society increases, so be it. It would appear that such a philosophy has no room for claims about fairness and equality. Yet, if we scratch beneath the surface, we realize that equality is a central tenet even of such a belief system. This is so because when aggregating the total happiness of all members of society, the value of each person's happiness is equal to any other person's. When calculating the total utility in a society, the happiness of each person is accorded the same worth—an idea in which equality is deep rooted.

It would thus appear that equality is a deeply cherished value and is intrinsically worthwhile. There are several reasons for this near-universal belief in the worth of equality. They could be moral, political, pragmatic and even human. As stated earlier, there is an innate human belief in the concept of equality, which is explicit from a very young age. It thus appears to be something that is hard-wired in the human brain and would appear to serve some evolutionary purpose. One possible explanation is that since humans are social animals, a commitment to equality was a good way to ensure social stability (even within hierarchies). Thus, counter-intuitive though it may seem, research shows that even in hunter-gatherer communities, where the brute strength of the male would seem to outweigh the power of females, a semblance of equality between the sexes was necessary to ensure a diverse and stable social structure.[9] The road to forming ever-larger communities based on mutual co-operation thus seems to require at least some facets of equality to be accepted by the group.

Importantly, equality is also a facet of one's individual identity and dignity. Research has shown that high self-esteem results in better life outcomes.[10] Thus, a person with self-worth is more likely to find success in work, relationships and even health. Equality increases self-esteem. Human beings generally see themselves as equal to their peers and being treated unequally lessens their self-worth.[11] Thus it is important to ensure equality in a society,[12] if we want to maximize the chances of its members to have successful lives.

There is also a pragmatic reason for demanding equality. A system which did not concern itself with equality would require two identically situated persons to be treated differently in an arbitrary manner. No person in such a State can be certain how the law would visit upon her. Life would be unpredictable and such a situation hardly lends itself to stability. Life in such a society would be, 'nasty, brutish and short'.[13] To have a governable polity, there is an implicit requirement that the citizens consider systems to be just and fair.

In the realm of moral philosophy, the justification for equality is slightly more complex. As economist and Nobel Laureate Amartya Sen points out, 'the demand for some form of equality is intrinsic to all major theories of social arrangements. This is possibly because to be accepted as valid, a political theory must have an element of universality and acceptability'. Sen says, '[T]he absence of such equality would make a theory arbitrarily discriminating and hard to defend . . . perhaps, this feature relates to the requirement that ethical reasoning, especially about social arrangements, has to be, in some sense, credible from the viewpoint of others—potentially all others.'[14] Thus, a coherent political and moral philosophy, which aims to have a broad reach, necessarily requires a commitment to equality.

Given the innate human faith in equality, (or, at the very least, fairness[15]), it is unsurprising that there is a near-universal acceptance of the requirement of equality in most countries, even in the most autocratic ones. With the widespread acceptance of universal adult franchise in most democracies, i.e., the right of all adults to be able to vote regardless of sex or any property restrictions, the concern for equality also makes political sense. Of course, it is also in the political sense, where inequalities most often arise, particularly with marginalized and oppressed communities being treated unequally by the more powerful. But this is usually acknowledged as a failure of the application of the principle of equality rather than its inapplicability per se.

Equality of What?

It appears that a consensus exists that equality, in some form or the other, is a valuable goal. But this consensus cannot be further translated into an agreement about what the object of equality should be. In other words, even if we can agree that equality is a central tenet to be followed by any polity, there still remains the question, what 'equality' means or 'equality of what?' The premise behind this question is that there are multiple and often competing visions of what it means to be equal and how best to achieve that goal. It would thus be worthwhile to consider some of these different views to understand how contested a notion equality really is.

For one, there is a distinction between the idea of 'equality of outcome' as opposed to the 'equality of opportunity'. Equality of outcome would describe a state where all citizens have the same amount of goods, income and standard of living as other citizens[16]. Equality of opportunity, however, focuses on the process rather than the result. It implies that society must be organized in such a manner that each person has the same chance to acquire any resources as any other person. In such a situation it is not the end result that matters as much as the initial position of everyone in society.

Each of these ideals of equality has their pros and cons. In the case of equality of outcome, there is a fundamental problem about how to distribute inadequate resources. For instance, if ten students seek admission to five seats in a college, there can never be any equality of outcome. There is no way that each student will have equal resources since five students will get seats, and five will not. Even in the case of goods which can be distributed equally, there is a concern of excessive state intervention and efficiency. To ensure that every person has the same assets in society, constant and intrusive government intervention would be required. It would be useful to consider an example to see the level of government meddling required in such a case. The present system of taxation envisages different bands of income earners who must pay differential rates of tax. This collected tax is then distributed amongst those who earn less. This system will not achieve equality of income. To take 40 per cent of tax from a person who earns Rs 1 crore or a person who earns Rs 100 crore, would still leave them unequally wealthy—the former would have Rs 60 lakh and the latter Rs 60 crore. To avoid such a situation, the government would have to calculate the amount of tax for each person separately so as to determine the exact amount to be taxed. This will ensure that each person enjoys the same income. This is, to say the least, a Herculean task.

Similarly, even when distributing wealth to the poor, the government cannot give a fixed amount to the poorest of the poor. To achieve an equality of outcomes, a detailed examination of the resources and income of each person needs to be undertaken and only thereafter can money be transferred to a person to achieve income parity. This requires massive data collection by the government, one that most societies may not be willing to do. Whether the government is at all capable of collecting this data given the huge administrative cost of collation is another matter.[17]

Thus, there are clear problems with the application of 'equality of outcomes' in an absolute manner. It is equally difficult to completely disregard the effect any social ordering has on outcomes. For instance, if the result of a redistribution exercise is deemed irrelevant, one could end up with a very unjust society where individuals would have very vast differences in wealth and income. Such a society could be socially unstable and would hardly foster a spirit of fraternity as required under our preamble.[18] Even if such a society were stable (for instance if it were run by a dictator[19]), a large income inequality is intrinsically unfair.

Equality of opportunity is often placed as an alternative to equality of outcome. Rather than focusing on how resources are distributed in any society, the primary concern of such philosophies is the manner of distribution. The idea is that justice requires that no person should be disadvantaged from competing for scarce public resources and that everyone should have a fair shot in seeking to improve their lot. Such an argument, at least at first glance, would overcome the problem a theory of equal outcomes faces in distributing scarce public resources. Here, every individual would have the same chance of getting admission into a college or a job. In the example discussed above, the ten students would all have the same chance to compete for the five seats. The best students would get the five seats and that would be a fair outcome. Another advantage of such an approach is that it makes good economic sense. Research shows that income inequality falls in countries with a high degree of equality of opportunity.[20] Such countries are also more stable and democratic. One of the greatest proponents of such a moral philosophy has been John Rawls, who contends that all persons should be entitled to the same basic goods and that inequality can only be permitted if it complies with the 'differencc principle'.[21] This principle accepts that inequality can be justified only when the distribution of resources results in the maximum advantage to the least well off.[22]

However, there are several problems and disagreements with equality of opportunity as well. This would appear unfair to a section of society because it would fail to take into consideration historical injustices. For instance, can it really be argued that the daughter of a Dalit from a rural area has equal opportunity, to get admission in a school or a college as the son of a rich city dweller? The answer is no. Equal opportunity could, over time, lead to a society where there is a disproportionate amount of inequality in wealth distribution and status, which is undesirable.

To overcome these difficulties providing equal opportunity, another binary is often suggested. This is the difference between 'formal' and 'substantive' equality. Formal equality would imply that all persons have the same opportunity to receive public resources. This would imply equal opportunity without regard to their caste, creed, race, sex or any other characteristic. However, as noted above, this system would perpetuate historical inequalities. To ignore caste, for example, is a privilege of the upper castes.

Thus, a more robust account of equality, the so-called substantive equality, is often suggested to overcome these problems. Such a philosophy would reject formal equality as being an illusion that hides systemic injustices and ends up treating persons who are otherwise unequal in status, in an identical manner. Since this approach perpetuates inequality, proponents of substantive equality contend that everyone must have real and equal opportunity to obtain resources. As per the proponents of such a theory, adequate adjustment is required to be made for immutable or acquired characteristics like poverty, race, caste, gender etc. In other words, one must account for injustices which are beyond the control of a person in order to determine the fairness of granting equal opportunities. Such a formulation of equality seems to tie-in with moral intuition since it accounts for both disadvantages beyond the control of an individual, as well as the merit, skill and effort of a person.

However, such a substantive conception of equality also has its share of critics—both from the left and the right. On the right is a libertarian philosopher, who would reject any attempt to equalize resources or opportunities. For a libertarian, the actions of the State involve balancing the concerns of equality with freedom.[23] Each person 'owns' her labour and is entitled to use it to generate as much wealth as she can. Any attempt to tax her for the purposes of redistribution (to cure any perceived inequalities) would amount to an unfair impingement on her freedom to earn and retain the fruits of her labour.[24] The other side of the attack is from the left, which argues that the doctrine merely seeks to legitimize systemic inequalities that exist in society.

It is not surprising that there is so much disagreement about the content of equality. Many normative ideals in a free society are deeply contested, simply because different people have different understanding of public good.[25] Politically there is increasing polarization where a person holding a particular opinion tends to exalt his own view and berate the beliefs of others. However, at least in academic and legal circles, these debates have nurtured further thought and reflection leading to refinement and the elaboration of different ideas.

Similarly, the discussion about the 'equality of what' is not merely an academic exercise but one that has real-life consequences. From a public policy perspective, it is ultimately an aid to enable administrators and politicians to frame policies. Different forms of equality would require different strategies for implementation. Thus, before we realize how to achieve equality, we must agree on what it actually means. But given the trenchant disagreements about what equality means, there is an equal amount of debate about how equality should be achieved.

If one focuses on the equality of outcomes, one might argue in favour of reservations in jobs and seats in educational institutions. Such a system would be effective in ensuring that the distribution of resources in a society reflects, among other things, its socio-economic makeup. Even here, the question about the quantum of reservations would still arise. If a strong model of the equality of outcomes is to be achieved, there would have to be a proportional representation of the caste, gender, and economic break-up of society. Some other model, which would take into account an idea of efficiency or merit, might still provide for reservations, but may not be strictly proportional to the makeup of society. Equal opportunity, on the other hand, might require that there should be no reservations but some other method to level the playing field between disparate groups. Thus, such a system might envisage variable qualifying marks for different groups.

Another idea that is often bandied about as a counterpoint to equality is the idea of merit. Of course, what merit means is far from controversial.[26] Can merit be determined without accounting for advantages some candidate might have had because of reasons beyond her control? There is also the question of moral luck, that is a situation where a person is born with a particular skill set, which society values over others. Thus, a person who is a gifted Kabaddi player may by unlucky to be born in a country that is mad about cricket. Expecting the star Kabaddi player to compete in cricket, with even an above-average cricketer, might seem unfair.

This discussion can seem dizzying. There appear to be multiple, and often contradictory, views on what constitutes equality, and what measures to adopt to ensure that we become a more equal society. Of course, in a largely legal treatise, one can hardly endeavour to provide the 'correct' formulation of equality, particularly when these questions have caused forceful disagreements between the finest minds in the world. The attempt is only to state that the very idea of equality is controversial.

The debate about the nature of equality takes place both in ancient philosophy and contemporary political and moral thought. These questions have also been the subject of a lively debate in the history of Indian Constitutionalism. When we examine the question of what equality means and requires in the Indian context, we find that the same disagreements about the nature of equality, and how best to eliminate inequality, fuelled the debates in the time leading up to the framing of the Indian Constitution. Even after Independence, the debates in the Constituent Assembly reveal that while the Constitution speaks clearly about the ideal of equality, the specifics of what that goal meant, was different for different people. While there was a consensus on the ideal of equality, what that required and how it was to be achieved split the members of the Constituent Assembly and the freedom fighters before them.

Colonization, Equality and the Tryst with Destiny

The history of India,[27] at least its Constitutional history, cannot be understood without addressing the issue of colonization and the Independence movement. The fight for Independence was ultimately about equality—the demand for the right *not* to be treated as second-class citizens.[28] It is therefore not a surprise that there was a fair bit of writing during the period of the freedom struggle on the question of equality. This was enhanced by the fact that the country was deeply unequal, even within itself. Years of colonial oppression had caused massive poverty while simultaneously encouraging vast wealth in the hands of a few.[29] If Independence was to be secured, most of the poor would also have to be drawn into the struggle for freedom.

In the case of discrimination based on sex, the voices in favour of egalitarianism were finding expression in political discourse. With the increasing clamour for self-rule and Independence, it was suggested that a draft Constitution for India be framed. To that end, 'The Commonwealth of India Bill, 1925' was drafted by the so-called 'National Convention'. This was a body of some 256-different persons including legislators and representatives of the India Women's Association with Sir Tej Bahadur Sapru[30] as its head. The report had a clause guaranteeing fundamental rights, including the statement that, 'there shall be no disqualification of discrimination or disability on the basis of sex'.[31] This report was followed by another report submitted by Motilal Nehru in 1928, called the 'Nehru Report', which also stated that 'men and women shall have equal rights as citizens'.[32]

In 1938, under the joint initiative of Jawaharlal Nehru and Subhash Chandra Bose, the Congress Party set up a National Planning Committee.[33] One specific sub-committee was set up to look into, 'women's role in the workplace'. The report by the committee was presented before the plenary session of the National Planning Committee in 1940.[34] Though the report may seem rather tame today, it was revolutionary for its time. As the report noted, '[a] woman should be recognised as an equal unit in the social order with man, and that she should gain the same political rights, civic and legal status, social equality and economic independence . . . For, woman cannot be free until the means and training for economic liberty have been assured to her, and until the functions which nature and society impose on her are organised in such a way that while fulfilling them woman still retains the right to mould her social and economic life in any way she chooses'.[35] Though this passage seems to recognize some kind of 'separate but equal' theory (by promising equality but segregating the roles of a woman by reference to the functions assigned to her by nature), there is a clear reference to the dignity, autonomy and freedom of choice of a woman.[36] In fact, one member of the sub-committee felt that the report did not go far enough and issued a dissent where it was stated that it was not sufficient to empower women without fundamentally altering all the other social, political and economic institutions which held her down.[37]

The appeal for equality, in the case of women, was based on a moral imperative. However, in the case of religion and caste, the movement for equality was also political. The Commonwealth of India Bill, 1925, as well as the Nehru Report had provisions promising citizens equality regardless of religion.[38] However, with the growing strength of the Muslim League and the call for a separate Muslim state, there was also a question about political representation for the religious minorities in the country.[39] One controversial attempt to seek equity for religious minorities was to ensure that the numerically greater Hindus should not overwhelm the Muslim minorities in matters of political representation. This was a demand of the newly formed Muslim League, which felt that it would go unrepresented (or represented in a proportion unequal to their population) if some provision for reservation or a separate electorate was not made in the elections. Thus, in 1909 the British Parliament enacted the Indian Councils Act[40] where the elections to the provincial and state councils were first envisaged.[41] The rules under the Act provided for separate electorates for religious minorities. As opposed to simply reserving seats for candidates from different religions, the system envisaged the splitting of the electoral college where members of a minority community would vote for the candidates from their community. This was in addition to the right to vote for a candidate in the general category—the so-called double vote.

However, when the question of equality for the oppressed castes was concerned, the route adopted prior to independence took a different course. Since the depressed castes were underrepresented in the legislatures, an attempt was made to have separate electorates for them in the same manner as for religious minorities. In 1932, British Prime Minister Ramsay MacDonald delivered what is known as the Communal Award. The award envisaged separate electorates for the depressed castes in the same manner as they had existed for religious minorities. Fearing that the provision of separate electorates would cause fissures within Hindu society, Mahatma Gandhi decided to oppose the award by going on a 'fast unto death', while he was incarcerated in Yerawada prison in Poona.[42] Fearing that the Mahatma would die as a result of the fast, Dr Ambedkar was forced to give up the hard-fought right to separate electorates.[43] Dr Ambedkar and Gandhi entered into an agreement called the Poona Pact under which while there would be no separate electorates for the depressed castes, the number of seats reserved for them in the provincial legislatures would increase from seventy-one under the communal award to 148. Though this might be seen as a victory, Dr Ambedkar saw this as a setback to Dalit upliftment and noted that 'the increase in seats was no recompense for the loss of separate electorate and the double vote'.[44]

The Poona Pact also had a deleterious impact on the depressed castes in areas other than elections. The government provided reservations for minorities in public services in 1934 but excluded the depressed classes. The gazette notification made a specific mention of the Poona Pact and read, 'in regard to the depressed classes, it is common ground that all reasonable steps should be taken to secure for them a fair degree of representation in the public services. The intention of the caste Hindus in this respect was formally stated in the Poona Agreement of 1932 and His Majesty's government in accepting that agreement took due note of this point. In the present state of general education in these classes the government of India considers that no useful purpose will be served by reserving for them a definite percentage of vacancies out of the number available for Hindus as a whole, but they hope to ensure that duly qualified candidates from the depressed classes are not deprived of their opportunities of appointment merely because they cannot succeed in open competition'.[45] The right to equality, as so often happened post-Independence, was replaced by mere hope. Despite noting the poor 'present state of education' of the depressed castes, there was no plan to improve their lot in life, both socially and economically. Backwardness, it seemed, begat backwardness.

Things might well have remained the same for the scheduled castes and tribes in the country. However, events were to develop that would empower them politically. This political empowerment transformed a moral obligation into a political necessity. In the 1930s, Dalits became more powerful politically by virtue of having reserved seats under the Government of India Act, 1935. Dalit leaders started using religious conversion (other than to Hinduism), to secure greater political and social equality.[46] With time, their voices and demands for a just and fair treatment gained greater acceptance, a fact that would be translated into Constitutional promises.

This discussion does not establish that all political parties and leaders of the time were great liberal supporters of equality in all its forms. There are plenty of historical records which show that there was still resistance to the idea of equality between the sexes, castes and religions.[47] However, the material does show that there was a growing acceptance of the innate equality of all human beings. This is not surprising, for as noted above, the recognition of equality was a fundamental driving force of the freedom struggle, as well as the mood in most fights for Independence during the colonial era.

The Framing of the Constitution

The increasingly impassioned calls for equality soon found a new venue—the hallowed halls of the council house,[48] where the Constituent Assembly met and discussed the draft of the new Constitution of India. Nevertheless, even though the forum of discussion shifted, the focus on ensuring equality and dignity to all Indian citizens remained the same. As the historian Aditya Nigam puts it, '[T]he whole history of the anti-colonial struggle can be read as an intricate process of the writing of the Constitution. The various landmarks of the freedom struggle . . . are episodes in the writing of the text that emerged, with significant embellishments, of course, from the Constituent Assembly.'[49]

For a body that was sowing the seeds of democracy, the Constituent Assembly was not an entirely democratic or representative body. The transfer of sovereignty to the people of India had been preceded by a Cabinet Mission Plan of 16 May 1946. The plan envisaged a united India and therefore proposed elections to the Constituent Assembly by way of indirect elections. The legislators of the provincial assemblies (who were elected by a narrow electorate) were to elect members of the Assembly through a single transferable vote,[50] which was designed to ensure proportional representation. The Cabinet Mission Plan had specifically stipulated that 'the cession of sovereignty to the Indian people on the basis of a Constitution framed by the assembly would be conditional on adequate provisions being made for the protection of minorities'.[51] Elections to the assembly were held in on the basis of separate electorates with members of the Muslim, Sikh and Hindu communities voting for candidates of their religion. In the elections that ensued, the Congress got an overwhelming majority of seats. Shortly thereafter and caught up with the promise of a separate Islamic state, the Muslim League stopped participating in the deliberations of the Assembly. The Congress party therefore constituted almost 82 per cent of the seats in the assembly. It was, therefore, almost a one-party system with Muslim and Sikh members nominated by the largesse of the Congress party. However, this did not stop the Assembly from discussing the concerns of various marginalized communities.

Dr Ambedkar had supported the 'annihilation of caste',[52] seeking to extinguish its very existence as a concept. Given the pivotal role of Dr Ambedkar in the drafting of the Constitution, as well the general consensus on the pitiable states of the 'harijans' in the country, there was substantial discussion in the Assembly about how to address the social and economic deprivation that the community faced.

One method of improving the social and political condition of the oppressed castes was through the provision of reservations. This was duly accepted by the Assembly without much resistance. However, there was also a fear that reservations on the ground of caste would perpetuate the very idea that was sought to be annihilated. To compensate for these contradictory demands, the Assembly decided to use more neutral terminology in the form of reservations for the 'backward classes',[53] commonly accepted to be a euphemism for Dalits and Shudras.[54] Interestingly, the scheduled castes were seen by some members not as a separate group but as part of the Hindu community. Reservations, therefore, were meant to be temporary 'till they are completely absorbed in the Hindu community'.[55] Pandit H.N. Kunzru was of the view that reservations should be limited for a period of ten years after the promulgation of the Constitution.[56] To this suggestion, a peeved T. Channiah said, 'I am really sorry that the honourable Pandit Kunzru should have felt that the backward class should be given this opportunity only for a period of ten years. Sir, I want this reservation for 150 years which has been the period during which opportunities have been denied to them.'[57] Ultimately, the Constitution provided for a time limit for reservations in Parliament and legislatures but not in public employment.

In the case of minorities, the Assembly was of the view that quotas were not appropriate. This was quite a change from colonial times when quotas in elected bodies as well as in public employment had been provided for religious minorities. Even the early drafts of the Constitution contained provisions for reservations in favour of minorities. However, when it came to the matter being discussed in the Assembly, the provisions were dropped. One possible reason for this exclusion was that the nation had undergone a painful Partition and there was a feeling that quotas would further split the polity along religious lines. The Muslim League was also considerably weakened and was unable to sufficiently push its interests. Thus, the dominant Congress party did not feel the need to alter its own agenda.[58] The discussion about equality in the context of religion was focused more on the idea of ensuring a secular state, where no member of any community would be discriminated, on the basis of faith. K.M. Munshi stated that 'a secular state is used in contrast with a theocratic government or a religious state. It implies that citizenship is irrespective of religious belief, that every citizen, to whatever religion he may belong, is equal before the law, that he has equal civil rights and equal opportunity to derive benefit from the state and to lead his own life and nothing more'.[59]

While Muslim members of the Assembly initially sought to be recognised as 'backward' and hence entitled to reservations,[60] they came to argue that they should be treated on par with other religions. No special reservations were necessary since all they wanted was to be treated equally.[61] This was also a time of Partition where communal tensions were high. There was a felt need to ensure that all followers of different religions come together under one rubric as 'Indians'. To ensure this, the State promised the ideal of secularism, which allowed religion to be kept out of public domain. However, foisting matters of faith in the private domain came at the cost of the Constitution failing to publicly acknowledge the very real differences between religions, and not affording special treatment to minorities.[62] Indeed, one member of the Constituent Assembly rued, 'it seems as if in this Constitution, the Muslims as a community, have no place in politics'.[63]

Muslims were not the only minorities in India. There were also a sizeable population of Christians who could have demanded reservations for themselves. In the case of Dalit Christians, it has been argued that there were two separate conflicting strands of thought during the debates.[64] One was a 'right to be a member of a minority', which was essentially a 'right to be left alone', to a 'right to autonomy'. On the other hand, there was a claim to be a member of the scheduled castes which entailed making demands of the state. Far from asking to be left alone, this claim required the patronage of the State. During the debates the elite class of Christians in the Assembly focussed more on the former—autonomy and freedom—at the expense of reservations and therefore conceded any claims to reservations.

A similar concession, though for slightly different reasons, was made in the case of women. The fifteen 'founding mothers', i.e. women members of the Constituent Assembly, used to work together to achieve their goals.[65] They chose to construct the identity of women as 'sexless citizens', prioritizing the idea of women as equal to men and therefore not requiring separate reservation. Perhaps, as research notes, this was a tactical move. As Annie Devenish notes, 'the question of whether to accept or reject reservations for women was linked to the broader strategy deemed to be most effective in the struggle for equality'.[66] In other areas, the Assembly was divided on matters of equality for women, particularly in relation to the idea of the Uniform Civil Code. The female members of the Assembly urged the assembly to adopt a fair and just, codified system of personal law.[67] On the other hand, some members of the Muslim minority were opposed to any Constitutional intervention in matters of personal law.[68]

In economic matters, the desperate poverty of the vast majority of Indians was, ultimately, a compromise in the form of Article 44 was reached which only required the State to enact a uniform civil code at some point in the future, kicking the can down the road.

In matters of economic inequality, the discussion in the Assembly was largely about the endemic poverty in the country and the concentration of wealth in the hands of a few. There was a general agreement that the only way to achieve economic equality was through adopting a socialistic form of economy. One of the greatest chroniclers of the framing as well as the working of India's Constitution has said, 'nearly everyone in the assembly was Fabian and Laski-ite enough to believe that "socialism is everyday politics for social regeneration"' and that 'democratic constitutions are . . . inseparably associated with the drive towards economic equality'.[69]

These discussions on caste, religion, gender and economic status also reveal another story. The Assembly had multiple persons putting forth their points of view. There were discussions held and compromises reached. There are two schools of thought about how the decision-making in the Assembly proceeded—the discursive and the political.[70] In the former model, the Assembly is a place for exploration and exchange of ideas to enable the adoption of the best idea. In the latter, the Assembly is a forum of realpolitik.

Whatever the true nature of the Constituent Assembly, there was no unanimity as to what equality meant or how it was to be achieved. The discussion was often fraught with disagreements frequently being aired in the Fundamental Rights Sub-Committees as well as the main Constituent Assembly. There was, however, a commonly shared understanding that striving towards equality was imperative and that the security and integrity of the nation could not be achieved without securing equality for all. One of the most eloquent expositions of this idea is to be found in a speech made by Dr Ambedkar when he introduced the draft of the Constitution to the Constituent Assembly on 4 November 1948. In his address he noted, 'on the social plane, we have in India a society based on the principle of graded inequality which means elevation for some and degradation for others. On the economic plane, we have a society in which there are some who have immense wealth as against many who live in abject poverty. On 26 January 1950, we are going to enter into a life of contradictions. In politics we will have equality and in social and economic life we will have inequality. In politics we will be recognizing the principle of one man, one vote and one vote, one value. In our social and economic life, we shall, by reason of our social and economic structure, continue to deny the principle of one man, one value. How long shall we continue to live this life of contradictions? How long shall we continue to deny equality in our social and economic life? If we continue to deny it for long, we will do so only by putting our political democracy in peril. We must remove this contradiction at the earliest possible moment or else those who suffer from inequality will blow up the structure of political democracy which this Assembly has so laboriously built up'. Equality was thus not just an end in itself, but also seen to be a guarantee against despotism and a failed State. This statement finds echo in the preamble to the Constitution when it states that the object of the Union is to secure freedom, justice and equality and promote fraternity so as to assure the 'dignity of the individual and the unity and integrity of the nation'.

Conclusion

This chapter has shown that equality means different things to different people. It also means different things at different times. Yet, the text of the Constitution remains the same, guaranteeing all people equality before the law at all times. Thus, there seems to be tension at the core of the idea of equality. However, as many Constitutional scholars would point out, this is hardly unique to the equality code in the Constitution. Foundational texts often use broad and deliberately ambiguous language so that future generations can adapt the words to changing needs. What is different about equality is that the stakes for a just society could not be higher. Whichever formulation of equality one considers valuable, it is apparent that the larger goals of the Constitution require the fulfilment of the right to equality because this right is not merely an independent Constitutional imperative but is also a means of securing the ideals of justice and the dignity of the individual.

The Constituent Assembly debates as well as the text of the Indian Constitution show that it marked a clear break from the past, at least in the field of fundamental rights. The colonial concept of the master-servant relationship between the State and the citizen was abandoned and a more egalitarian power structure was adopted. Every person was equal in the eyes of the law—a statement that sounds trite today, but was truly revolutionary, even internationally, for its time. In this, India was part of a global movement of dramatic change after the Second World War when decolonization had started and the spirit of egalitarianism was slowly gaining ground globally.

The renowned economic historian Thomas Piketty states that the fight against inequality was a result of multiple struggles across the world.[71] Another, more controversial thesis, is that the world is becoming increasingly equal with the passage of time. He says that 'the long term movement towards equality . . . is the consequence of conflicts and revolts against injustice that have made it possible to transform power relationships and overthrow institutions supported by the dominant classes, which seek to structure social inequality in a way that benefits them with new institutions and new social, economic and political rules that are more equitable and emancipatory for the majority'.[72] It is his view that the move towards increasing equality globally, is by revolution, rather than incremental change. This is because historic inequity is so strongly entrenched in the power structures that the real way to bring about change is not to merely tinker at the edges but to approach them head on.

The freedom struggle and the drafting of the Constitution was just such a revolution. There is a growing body of work which seeks to show that the Indian Constitution was a transformative document, one which made a radical break with the past.[73] Indeed, the discussion above shows that the members of the Assembly envisaged just such a role for the Constitution. The Constitution in one swoop declared all to be equal. Unfortunately, equality cannot be achieved in practice by mere declarations, no matter how sanctified the declarant is. To most observers, it would seem that the task of achieving true equality is unfinished. Given the fact that we are today a Constitutional democracy, change today cannot be brought about by the same means as were adopted in the years leading up to Independence. Equality has to be sought for and obtained within the confines of the Constitution. Not many would advocate a fresh revolution. Yet, the way that the courts have interpreted the Constitution and the fundamental right relating to equality, has been nothing short of revolutionary. The story of the equality code in the Constitution is one of judges rejecting the hidebound status quo and of using novel means and ideas to ensure that substantive equality is achieved for all persons living in the Indian republic.

2

Rule of Law

In the 1970s, British postal trade unions decided to boycott mail and telecommunication services with South Africa in protest against that country's apartheid policies. A public-spirited citizen wanted to file a case against the unions to stop the boycott. The Attorney General, whose consent was mandatory before any court case was brought, refused permission to sue the trade unions. When the matter reached the Court of Appeal, a rather miffed Lord Denning rapped the Attorney General.[1] In the opinion of the celebrated judge, failure to grant permission to sue would imply that an illegal act[2] would remain unchallenged in court. Holding that every citizen was required to obey the law, Lord Denning quoted the words of Thomas Fuller, 'be you ever so high the law is above you'.[3]

Over the years, this phrase has entered the Indian legal lexicon[4] and is seen as encapsulating a fundamental principle of the rule of law. The idea is that in a modern democratic society, general laws are meant to be consistently applied to everyone. No citizen is supposed to have immunity from the law and all persons, including government officials, are meant to be equally accountable for any violation of the law. This epitomizes the idea of equality and if there is any provision in the Constitution which embodies this idea of the rule of law, it is the guarantee of equality contained in Article 14.[5]

However, the rule of law, like equality, has many layers and nuances, and to compare the two, one must closely examine what each means. Given the close alliance between the rule of law and the ideal of equality, it is not surprising that there are as many readings of Article 14 as there are of the rule of law. While the philosophies underlying these concepts have engaged scholars for centuries, judges and legal practitioners have no option but to explore them to some extent. The reason is that different readings of these concepts have a practical implication on how the courts determine whether any legislative or executive act violates the provisions of the Equality Clause.

While the concept of equality has been fleshed out in the first chapter of the book, the meaning of the rule of law is a bit more elusive. It has almost become a slogan with policymakers regularly appealing to the concept to justify their actions.[6] It is also a contested subject since its exact content is not always clear. On one end of the spectrum is the narrow idea of the rule of law which simply implies that the law, whatever it may be, must be obeyed by all.[7] On the other extreme, the doctrine imposes a requirement on the State to adhere to a host of liberal and democratic values.

Mirroring the narrow view of the rule of law, a formal reading of the Equality Clause mandates a strict adherence of rules by similarly placed individuals. This has given rise to a vast body of jurisprudence where the courts have held that the Constitution permits reasonable classification but not class legislation. To put it in terms comprehensible to a non-lawyer, this means that the Constitution permits the law to treat people differently, provided that the distinction in treatment is reasonable having regard to the object of the legislation.

On the other hand, at a more substantive level, the equality clause imposes a requirement to act in a rational or non-despotic manner. Thus, the court has held that both legislative as well as executive action can be struck down as violating Article 14 if it can be shown that the decision is 'manifestly arbitrary'. Clearly, there is a value judgment in such a judgment because what is patently unreasonable to the judge may be completely reasonable to the decision-maker. In this sense, this test of equality resembles a more robust understanding of the rule of law.[8]

Other than the formal and substantive versions of the rule of law, there also exists a third, procedural aspect. In fact, this is probably what a lay person would have in mind when talking about the rule of law. Such an understanding includes the concept of an impartial judge deciding matters in an open court according to well-established and fair procedures. It is at first blush, difficult to understand what this has in common with the idea of equality. However, Indian courts have included such procedures under the rubric of 'natural justice' and traced them to the Constitutional guarantee contained in Article 14.

Thus, it can be seen that there is a neat identity between each of the three versions of the rule of law and the Doctrine of Equality. This suggests that the two concepts have a deep, underlying jurisprudential link. Unfortunately, this link has not been adequately discussed in case law. One unfortunate consequence is the confusion over which test is applicable when a violation of equality is posited. This chapter will endeavour to more closely examine the different meanings of the rule of law and how they impact with how the court has interpreted the equality code under the Constitution.

Rule of Law and Equality

The debate about the true meaning of the term exists not only between members of society today but has also caught the attention of ancient philosophers as well as contemporary ones. Aristotle stated that an ideal republic should be governed by law and not by the rule of men. Writing in 350 BCE, he offered a rationale for his view stating, 'for in democracies which are subject to the law the best citizens hold the first place, and there are no demagogues; but where the laws are not supreme, there demagogues spring up'.[9] These words still ring today possibly because people have changed their character far less over the centuries than our modernist anthropomorphic tendencies would have us believe. Equally, the disputes about what the term means continues to be as disputed today as it was in ancient times.

One reason as to why the meaning of the rule of law is so contested is because of its sheer democratic reach. Legal philosopher Jeremy Waldron notes that what the rule of law requires is controversial 'partly because the Rule of Law is a working political idea, as much the property of ordinary citizens, lawyers, activists and politicians as of the jurists and philosophers who study it. The features that ordinary people call attention to are not necessarily the features that legal philosophers have emphasized in their academic conceptions'.[10] Each citizen would presumably wish to live in a society governed by the rule of law, but not everyone can agree what they mean by it.

Even though there are a multitude of views put forth by various scholars, the idea of the rule of law can be roughly divided into three broad areas. These areas are formal, substantive and procedural. Each of these aspects informs of a different view of the idea of equality and hence each needs to be fleshed out in further detail.

The least controversial sense of the rule of law is a formal one, partly because it is the common denominator in almost all theories. Most people would agree that at the minimum, the concept must include a set of rules, which define how the legal system operates. These rules do not necessarily describe the content of the law (for instance what act should or should not be a crime), but how the law ought to operate and be applied so as to have a modicum of fairness. The most well-known list of these requirements was made by Lon Fuller in a book that has become mandatory reading for any student of law and philosophy.[11] In the book, Fuller describes a fictional king who wishes to reform the legal system in his country and sets about to make a new legal code. Fuller describes the eight errors that the king makes while drafting the code, each of which was anathema to setting up a coherent legal framework under which people could lead normal lives. These eight errors mirror the corresponding virtues that any system governed by the rule of law should have, which are described briefly below.

(i) Generality: This principle requires the enactment of a general legal code or a set of rules rather than deciding each issue on a case by case or ad hoc manner. Thus, decisions should be made for the population as a whole rather than vary from individual to individual.
(ii) Promulgation: The applicable laws should be publicly known and available rather than being secret.
(iii) Retroactivity: Laws when enacted should generally operate prospectively. Conduct which is legal on a particular day when it is done, should not be declared illegal by changing the law, and making it applicable to past conduct.
(iv) Clarity: Laws should be intelligible, i.e., capable of being understood. They should not be so arcane as to be incomprehensible.
(v) Consistency: The comprehensive code of law should be internally coherent. Thus, if one provision of law declares certain conduct to be legal, there should not be another provision which simultaneously declares the same conduct to be illegal.
(vi) Impossibility: The law should not require a person to perform tasks which are impracticable or impossible.
(vii) Constancy: The laws should be stable and not subject to constant amendments or repeals. This constancy enables people to plan their lives for the future and live without fear of violating the law unknowingly.
(viii) Congruence: This principle requires that officials follow the law and obey it—that there is a congruence between what the law says and how it is applied. There is no point in having a clear, prospective and a comprehensible general law if it is simply not applied.

These rules do not appear to require any particular content of the law but are formal requirements of a legal system.[12] This can be explained by a reference to a few of the features listed above. For instance, the requirement of 'generality' simply states that the law ought not to be ad hoc but does not require it to be just. Therefore, such a requirement would not stop the enactment of a law that, for example, mandates that all women must sit at the back of the bus. All that the rule of law prohibits is that there should not be a whimsical application of the principle with officials deciding on a case-to-case basis as to whether some women should be required to sit at the back, while others can sit wherever they want. This example shows that the formal requirement of generality permits classification (between women who are mandatorily required to sit at the back) but does not permit individuals with the class to be treated differently (i.e. it is not possible for some women to sit in the front of the bus withal other women being forced to sit at the back).

Rejecting a mere formal reading of the rule of law there are those who suggest a more substantive one. The proponents of this school of thought argue that the form of a law alone is not important. A state which regularly and viciously oppresses its citizens, denying them freedom and equality, cannot be said to be governed by the rule of law. They point out that Nazi Germany may well have complied with the formal attributes of a system of law but cannot be called a country governed by the rule of law. Of course, the danger in this concept lies in the conflation of the idea of the rule of law with a host of other values a modern state ought to possess, such as respect for liberty, democracy and freedom. Nevertheless, it is argued that there is a core component of the rule of law which is distinct from these ideas.[13]

But what is this 'core component'? Perhaps the Latin phrase, '*lex unjusta non est lex*' captures the intention of this idea of the rule of law[14] that, an unjust law is not law at all and therefore a system of unjust laws cannot be said to be a legal system. But justice is an elusive concept and surely the idea of the rule of law captures something distinct. For instance, a country which does not levy any income tax and does not transfer money from its richest citizens to its poorest might be unjust but might still adhere to the rule of law. Some theorists have suggested that the rule of law is linked to the idea of human dignity where people are seen as autonomous agents capable of living and making decisions for themselves.[15] Such a system would imply that the people have a right to non-arbitrary treatment. A political theorist says on non-arbitrary treatment, 'that the state must have a moral justification for its laws and judicial decisions that is consistent with the free and equal status of individuals. This does not mean that the law must be fully just, but it does guarantee against coercion that cannot be justified by reasons consistent with free and equal citizenship'.[16] The substantive rule of law is thus a rule of reason and every government act must be informed by reasons which are compatible with the dignity of its citizens. An unreasonable law would therefore violate this substantive conception of the rule of law. This 'thicker'[17] view of the rule of law permits greater interference by judges to avert a violation of the rule of law if the substance of the law, as opposed to its mere form, is pernicious.

The substantive concept of the rule of law is often juxtaposed with the formal reading of the same concept.

However, some academics point out that most ordinary citizens have something else in mind when they speak of the rule of law.[18] This is the third model of the rule of law—the procedural version. Like the formalist reading of the rule of law, here too, the concern is not with the substance of the law. Instead, the issue is how the law is to be applied in a fair and impartial manner. The procedural idea of the rule of law posits that adjudication of legal disputes in any country governed by the rule of law must be in accordance with well-established and fair procedures. Judges are not supposed to decide matters arbitrarily and in secret, but after hearing parties in an open court. There are multiple views on what the exact procedural requirements imposed by this formulation of the rule of law are. Accordingly, many laundry lists, akin to the eight principles of the formal rule of law mentioned above, have been suggested. One such list on the procedural requirements of a system governed by the rule of law can be described below:

(i) A hearing by an impartial and independent tribunal that is required to administer existing legal norms on the basis of the formal presentation of evidence and argument.
(ii) A right to representation by lawyers at such a hearing.
(iii) A right to be present, to confront, and question witnesses, and to make legal arguments about bearing the evidence and the various legal norms relevant to the case and,
(iv) A right to hear reasons from the tribunal when it reaches its decision, which are responsive to the evidence and arguments presented before it.[19]

These rules resonate with the basic sense of fairness that most people expect from a robust legal system. This can be demonstrated by examining how one would react if these elements were not present in case of a judicial determination. Therefore, we would be appalled if a judge decided a case in which she had a direct financial interest (for instance, decided a property dispute where she herself was a claimant). Equally, if the judge decided a matter by taking evidence and hearing only one side of the dispute, we would instinctively reject the correctness of such a decision, regardless of the outcome. This revulsion is nothing other than a manifestation of the procedural aspect of the rule of law, based as it is on the value of human dignity.[20]

There is a substantial amount of academic writing about each of these formulations and famous debates between different philosophers arguing that theirs is a better description of the concept. However, one caveat must be noted. While the chapter has examined all these meanings of the term, it is important to remember that different people have different ideas in mind when they use the term. Therefore, the answer to the question 'which of these three concepts of the rule of law are correct' might well be 'each of the above'. This is not a cop out, but a very plausible way of understanding the concept.[21] Many different beliefs and philosophical theories can be amalgamated in the overarching ideal of the rule of law.

Like the rule of law, equality also means different things to different people. If one has to have conceptual clarity, these different strands have to be teased out and examined. In particular, the relation between the idea of the rule of law, and equality, deserves special consideration because in a way each of these concepts bleeds into the other. As one academic points out, the rule of law is morally valuable because it 'fosters vertical equality between officials and non-officials and horizontal equality among non-officials . . . When states achieve vertical equality, their legal institutions guard against hubris, officials' use of their powers to claim certain kinds of superior status . . . When states achieve horizontal equality, their legal institutions prevent legal caste, the state's support of hierarchies among individuals, particularly along ascriptive group lines. They also serve the obligation of reciprocity individuals have, to one another, to share alike the cost to produce the public good of law and order'.[22] In other words, the rule of law is, at the very least, a measure to determine whether a society is an equal one. It is only when the formal, substantive and the procedural dimensions of the rule of law are satisfied that, the society can be truly labelled an egalitarian one. As mentioned earlier, nothing encapsulates this ideal of equality better that Article 14 of the Constitution.

The Equality Clause: A Brief Biography

Article 14 has become almost ubiquitous. It is spoken of so often that it has almost taken on a life of its own with little reference to its actual wording. It is also true that judicial decisions have expanded the meaning of the Article to almost unrecognizable limits. However, it would do well to remember the exact words of the provision, as they contain at the least, a basis for understanding what the equality code, as well as the rule of law, require. The words of the provision stated that 'the State shall not deny to any person equality before the law or the equal protection of the laws'.

At the outset, one can notice that the Article has not one, but two separate portions. First, is the injunction on the State to, 'not deny to any person the equality before the law'. It is then that the more familiar, second command comes, i.e., the State shall not deny any person 'equal protection of the laws'. While there are two distinct commandments contained in the Article, there is remarkably little academic commentary on the exact implication of the first phrase.[23] International opinion does seem to indicate that the first part of the Article enacts the formalistic conception of the rule of law. In this view, the phrase, 'equality before the law' only means that the laws must be applied in the same manner to all those to whom the law applies. Another way of expressing the idea is that the words in the clause are not concerned with the merits of the legislation but in the manner of its enforcement. Judges and officials are required, perforce the Article, to act uniformly and apply the law in the same manner to all subject to them.

The best interpretation of the first part of the Article is that it embodies a formal conception of the Rule of Law.[24] In one judgment of the Supreme Court, the origin of the words 'equality before the law' was traced to the Irish and the Weimar Constitutions as well as the language of the Universal Declaration of Human Rights. The same verdict then stated that equality before the law implied that there would be no privileged classes who would be above the law, i.e. the classic sense of the rule of law discussed above.[25]

This then brings one to the second part of the Article, i.e., the promise that no person shall be denied equal protection of the laws. This phrase, coupled with the guarantees stipulated in Article 15, contains the Constitutional promise against discrimination and has been the subject matter of most judicial interpretation. This part of Article 14 is usually read in a negative manner, i.e., as containing a prohibition restricting the State from treating any person adversely for no good reason.

It is on the battleground of non-discrimination jurisprudence that the different ideas about the nature of the rule of law as well as equality have been discussed. The Courts have employed different tests and standards to determine whether a particular act does, or does not, discriminate. These tests closely mirror the various readings of the rule of law, i.e. the formal, the substantive, and the procedural, and it is these that will now be examined.[26]

A Formal Reading of Equality and the Rule of Law

Shortly after the adoption of the Constitution, citizens started challenging pieces of legislation on the grounds of violation of fundamental rights. As the legal historian Rohit De notes, '[T]he Indian Constitution profoundly transformed everyday life in the republic. Moreover this process was led by some of India's most marginal citizens rather than by elite politicians and judges. It shows that the Constitution, an elite document in English that was a product of elite consensus, came so alive in the popular imagination that ordinary people attributed meaning to its existence, took recourse through it, and argued with it.'[27]

De refers to a case filed by a Parsi journalist, Fram Nusserwanjee Balsara, as an example of a public-spirited citizen using the newly-minted right of equality to challenge Prohibition era laws in the State of Bombay. Under the Indian Constitution, the State has been enjoined to 'bring about prohibition of the consumption of . . . intoxicating drinks'.[28] With the same sentiment in mind, the Congress party-led, State of Bombay, enacted the Bombay Prohibition Act, 1949 ('The Prohibition Act'). The Prohibition Act criminalized the act of drinking liquor without obtaining a special permit. The government was authorized to issue permits to foreign nationals who were visiting Bombay (but not Indian visitors) as well military personnel. Balsara, who had in his possession 'one bottle of whisky, one bottle of brandy (both partly used), one bottle of wine, two bottles of beer, one bottle of medicated wine'[29] was aggrieved by the fact that he could not be issued a permit to drink the contents of those bottles. Therefore, he moved the High Court of Bombay challenging the permit system on several grounds. In particular he argued that treating military personnel and foreigners as a distinct class and allowing them access to liquor while denying him the same right amounted to a violation of Article 14.

The Bombay High Court agreed with Balsara and held that he had been discriminated against. The high court was of the view that there was no ground to treat military personnel and foreigners visiting Bombay differently from ordinary citizens of India. However, the Supreme Court took a different view, when the matter was taken in appeal, and held that there was no violation of the equality clause.

Quoting prior precedent,[30] the Supreme Court ruled that the doctrine of equality did not mean that a legislature could not create different classes of people—in this case military personnel and civilians. Without any hint of irony the court noted that the military constituted a separate class which should be allowed to drink since they followed special rules which 'enable them to face dangers and perform unusual tasks of endurance and hardship when called upon to do so-qualities such as dash and courage, unbreakable tenacity and energy ready for any sacrifice which should be unfaltering for long days together'. How alcohol would imbue the armed forces with such courage was not quite made clear in the judgment.[31]

Effectively the court held that the exercise of classifying people into separate classes and treating them differently was permissible. Therefore, there was no unconstitutionality in distinguishing between military personnel and civilians by permitting the former, but not the latter, to drink alcohol. The underlying rationale of the court was that classification of people was permissible, and on occasion even necessary, because the legislature had to cater to a wide variety of people not all of whom were in the same position. Thus, the different needs of different classes of people warranted classification so that they could be treated in a manner conforming to their varying needs. This power to classify people for legitimate purposes inevitably meant treating them unequally. The court held that 'mere production of inequality is not enough . . . While reasonable classification is permissible, such classification must be based upon some real and substantial distinction bearing a reasonable and just relation to the object sought to be attained'.

Breaking down the above analysis, what the court held was that 'mere production of inequality' was not a ground to allege a violation of Article 14. If any person claimed discrimination, the State only had to show that there was a 'well-defined' classification based upon a 'real and substantial distinction'. This principle of law has also been repeated in other cases where the court has held that Article 14 permits classification if the classification is based on intelligible differentia, which has a rational nexus to the object sought to be achieved by the Act.[32] But what does 'intelligible differentia' and 'rational nexus' mean and what do they have to do with the rule of law? That is something that deserves further exploration.

Intelligible Differentia

The phrase 'intelligible differentia' literally means a 'distinguishing mark or characteristic' which is 'able to be understood'.[33] Unfortunately, this dictionary definition does little to explain what it actually means. The concept is more easily addressed in the negative, i.e., by examining what is the effect if there is no intelligible differentia. The absence of intelligible differentia in classifying people means that the State can form groups of citizens randomly, and without any commonality, and proceed to treat them differently. Such a system permits arbitrary classification, i.e., failure to include people who are identically placed or, as a corollary, inclusion of people who do not belong in that class. The way such a restriction works in practice is subtle. It is generally not likely (though not impossible) that the government would be so wanton in its attempts at classification, as to include a motley group of unrelated persons for special treatment. The effect is usually felt in single-person laws or in matters of executive discretion.

A single-person law is one where a particular individual is targeted for a special privilege or disadvantage. In 1950, the Nawab of Hyderabad gave his assent to a law which dealt with the personal estate of Nawab Waliuddowla, a wealthy nobleman and a high dignitary of Hyderabad. The estate was embroiled in litigation with multiple family members making a claim to the properties. The law rejected the claims of the two wives of the nawab, Mahboob Begum and Kadiran Begum, and their children, and forbade them from approaching the courts for any relief. Unsurprisingly, the begums moved the court alleging that they had been singled out for discrimination. They argued that there was no difference between them and the other claimants to the property, and yet only their claims had been rejected by the law. The Supreme Court agreed with the argument of the wives and held that there was no Constitutionally-valid reason to single out the wives, and their children, and treat them differently from all the other heirs to the property.[34] As per the court, the Act targeting 'specific individuals, who are deprived thereby of valuable rights which are enjoyed by all other persons occupying the same position as themselves, does, in our opinion, plainly come[s] within the Constitutional inhibition of Article 14'. No law which singles out a person for special treatment for no good reason can be said to meet the criteria of intelligible differentia.[35]

There is another way in which people can be treated arbitrarily and that is by conferment of excessive executive discretion. A classic example is that of a statute that confers substantial discretion to those applying the law to determine whom to apply the law to. This too can be explained by reference to a judgment delivered by the Supreme Court. In 1949, some communists raided a munitions factory and the airport at Dum Dum in Kolkata. During the course of the raid, five people were killed. A member of the revolutionary, Communist Party of India, Anwar Ali Sarkar, was arrested for the robbery. His trial was conducted by a special court constituted under the West Bengal Special Courts Act, 1950 ('the Special Courts Act') and he was sentenced to transportation for life.

After the conviction, Sarkar challenged the provisions of the Special Courts Act. While the procedures under the Special Courts Act were different and slightly more onerous than the normal Code of Criminal Procedure, it was not his case that they were unconstitutional. He rested his claim on the ground of discrimination under Article 14. Sarkar alleged that there was no reason why his case had been picked and referred to the Special Court as opposed to other cases which were dealt with under the ordinary law of the land. At the heart of the dispute was Section 5 (1) of the Special Court Act which laid down that, 'a Special Court shall try such offences or classes of offences or cases or classes of cases as the state government may, by general or special order in writing direct'. This section empowered the Executive, i.e., the state government, to decide at its absolute discretion, which matter to refer to the Special Court and which matter to retain to be dealt by the ordinary courts. This power vested in the executive created a situation where two identically placed people could be treated differently at the mere whim of the government. Therefore, if two people were accused of the same offence, it was possible for the government to send one to the Special Court and another to the ordinary courts. The court held that this was contrary to Article 14 as the statute conferred an unguided power to classify to the government. Justice M.C. Mahajan, who would go on to become a chief justice of India, put it in the following manner, 'Classification thus means segregation in classes which have a systematic relation, usually found in common properties and characteristics. It postulates a rational basis and does not mean herding together of certain persons and classes arbitrarily. Thus the legislature may fix the age at which persons shall be deemed competent to contract between themselves, but no one will claim that competency to contract can be made to depend upon the stature or colour of the hair.'[36]

Another learned judge, Justice Mukherjea, who was part of the majority in the case, pointed out the problem when he stated that 'the selection is left to the absolute and unfettered discretion of the executive Government with nothing in the law to guide or control its action. This is not a reasonable classification at all but an arbitrary selection. A line is drawn artificially between two classes of cases. On one side of the line are grouped those cases which the State Government chooses to assign to the Special Court; on the other side stand the rest which the State Government does not think fit and proper to touch'. The court therefore ruled that this conferment of discretion made the law unconstitutional as it violated the Equality Clause.

The two cases are violation of the intelligible differentia, single-person laws and unguided executive discretion, and are also the antithesis of the rule of law. The formal understanding of the rule of law requires that everyone should be treated in accordance with the same law, without fear or favour. If the government is permitted to choose persons upon whom it wishes to impose legal disabilities arbitrarily, it not only treats them unequally but also violates the concept of the rule of law. Granting special exemptions to a privileged class of persons, something which this formulation of the rule of law frowns upon, is just a corollary of imposing disadvantages on an arbitrarily selected class of persons. This is formal and not substantive in the sense that the substantive content of the law does not matter as much as the act of classification. Thus, in the case of Anwar Ali Sarkar, the procedures prescribed under the Special Courts Act were not, by themselves, unconstitutional. In other words, Sarkar would have been subjected to a fair trial even if he was proceeded against under the Special Courts Act. His complaint was formal in the sense that whatever be the nature of the procedure, there was no reason to single him out.

Rational Nexus

The second requirement to satisfy the requirement of Constitutionality in the case of an alleged violation of equality is that the suspect classification must have a rational nexus with the object sought to be achieved by the Act. In other words, the reasons for the classification must align with the reasons for enacting a particular piece of legislation. This is nothing but a test to ensure that the alleged reason given by the State to justify its decision to classify (the intelligible differentia discussed earlier) is legitimate and not a ruse to discriminate against people.[37] One controversial example of an absence of a rational nexus was in the case of illegal migrants from Bangladesh into India. After the Bangladesh War, there was an influx of migrants from to India. To curb that migration, the government enacted a special law called the Illegal Migrants (Determination by Tribunals) Act, 1983 ('the IMDT Act'). This Act was made applicable only to the State of Assam, while in the rest of the country, the provisions of the Foreigners Act, 1955 were applicable. Sarbanada Sonowal, a citizen who would go on to become the chief minister of Assam, filed a petition before the Supreme Court arguing that the IMDT Act was too lax and that a large number of illegal migrants were being given Indian citizenship leading to widespread demographic shifts. He urged that the more stringent provisions of the Foreigners Act should be applied in Assam and that there was no reason to apply the IMDT Act in that state.

The court accepted Sonowal's argument and struck down the IMDT Act. The Act classified people on a geographical basis. i.e. those who lived in Assam and those who lived elsewhere in India. This geographical classification had been upheld in earlier judgments as conforming to the test of intelligible differentia. However, the court held that there was no rational nexus between the intelligible geographical classification and the object that the IMDT Act purportedly sought to achieve. In the judgment, the court noted that the object of the IMDT Act was to identify and eject illegal immigrants. Upon examination of the provisions of the IMDT Act, it was apparent that the Act made it easier for illegal immigrants to gain Indian citizenship. This was thus, exactly contrary to the professed purpose of the Act. The court ruled that 'the mere making of a geographical classification cannot be sustained where the Act instead of achieving the object of the legislation defeats the very purpose for which the legislation has been made' and on that ground struck down the Act.

Like the intelligible differentia test, the rational nexus test is also formalistic in nature and closely aligned to a similar conception of the rule of law. This is because while the court examines if there is a rational nexus between the classification and the object of the Act, it does not further examine the extent of the nexus. For the judges, it is sufficient that there is a link between the two. It is not necessary to show that the classification is particularly efficacious in achieving the object of the Act. Further, like the formalistic reading of the rule of law, the rational nexus test does not impose any independent moral requirement. In other words, the test can condone an unjust classification if it can be shown that there is a rational nexus between the measure and the purpose sought to be achieved by any Act, no matter how tenuous the link[38] or immoral the purpose of the Act. Thus the court has upheld provisions of an Act that gave immunity to a tax defaulter, as opposed to an honest taxpayer, holding that 'immorality by itself is not a ground of constitutional challenge and it obviously cannot be, because morality is essentially a subjective value, except insofar as it may be reflected in any provision of the Constitution or may have crystallised into some well-accepted norm of social behaviour'.[39]

In summary, it can be said that the classification test, as applied traditionally by Indian courts, is highly formalistic and unconcerned with the merits and morality of the substantive content of the law.[40] Nevertheless, it imposes a substantial curb on legislative and executive action by restraining them from creating special classes of citizens who are treated differently from the rest of the populace. In this manner, the rigours of Article 14 ensure that the State does comply with the formal understanding of the rule of law, even if in individual cases the results may not always be fair. Of course, judges are also human and do not readily wish to condone an unjust outcome. Therefore, there are instances when the test has been misapplied to achieve a just result.[41] However, this is at the cost of internal consistency of the law or, to use the terminology of the formal reading of the rule of law above, it leads an incongruent or unpredictable result.

A Substantive Reading . . .

Inconsistent application of the law is not the only way that judges can remedy perceived injustices in the law. Another way of ensuring that the test of equality is not purely formal is to abandon the classification test and adopt a more substantive one. This is exactly what the courts did in the mid-1970s when they felt constrained by the rigid requirements of the classification test.[42] While dealing with the true effect of Article 14, the court found a novel way of ensuring equality. In a celebrated passage the court held that Article 14 'must not be subjected to a narrow pedantic or lexicographic approach. We cannot countenance any attempt to truncate its all-embracing scope and meaning, for to do so would be to violate its activist magnitude. Equality is a dynamic concept with many aspects and dimensions and it cannot be "cribbed, cabined and confined" within traditional and doctrinaire limits. From a positivistic point of view, equality is antithetic to arbitrariness. In fact equality and arbitrariness are sworn enemies; one belongs to the rule of law in a republic while the other, to the whim and caprice of an absolute monarch. Where an act is arbitrary, it is implicit in it that it is unequal both according to political logic and constitutional law and is therefore violative of Article 14'.[43]

This was a dramatic shift from the classification test. The court now held that executive action which was manifestly arbitrary would also be hit by Article 14. There was no need to show any classification, intelligible differentia or rational nexus. All that is now required is to show that the Act being challenged was so whimsical or arbitrary that it violated ordinary norms of rationality. While there was some debate as to whether the newly minted arbitrariness test would also apply to laws passed by the legislature[44] or only to executive decisions, the issue now seems to have been settled. In the case dealing with the practice of triple talaq amongst Muslims, the Supreme Court has unequivocally held that even an act of Parliament can be struck down through the application of this test.[45] Specifically, the court held that 'The thread of reasonableness runs through the entire fundamental rights chapter. What is manifestly arbitrary is obviously unreasonable and being contrary to the rule of law, would violate Article 14'.

Nevertheless, the question that keeps on cropping up is what is the content of this new test of manifest arbitrariness. It has for instance been pointed out that arbitrariness and unreasonableness are not the same thing. An action can be arbitrary without being unreasonable and vice versa.[46] One of India's foremost Constitutional scholars, H.M. Seervai has trenchantly criticized this formulation of the test stating that it 'hangs in the air' because 'it is propounded without reference to the terms in which the guaranteed right to "the equal protection of the laws" is conferred'.[47]

However, at least some part of the criticism of the new test is probably exaggerated. An argument that equality only implies an erroneous classification ignores the substantive reading of the concept. The right against inequality speaks not only to the difference in treatment between different persons, but also addresses the underlying causes for it. As Professor Sandra Fredman postulates, the substantive doctrine of equality aims 'to redress disadvantage; address stigma, stereotyping, prejudice, and violence; enhance voice and participation; and accommodate difference and achieve structural change. This reflects the principle that the right to equality should be responsive to those who are disadvantaged, demeaned, excluded, or ignored'. This view aims to imbue the right to equality with a content that highlights the dignity of the individual. Whenever a person is treated without regard to her particular needs and circumstances, she is not treated as a complete human deserving of all State action that someone in her position deserves. Thus, any government act that permits prejudice that a historically disadvantaged class of citizens continues to face, would violate the right to equal treatment that inheres in that group of persons. Such an action arguably would also be, as per the new doctrine of Article 14, manifestly arbitrary and unreasonable. Adopting this mode of reasoning, permits the court to reach out and cure injustices that any person or class of persons faces, without being confined by the technicalities of the classification test.

In this, one can find close parallels with the substantive theory of the rule of law. As discussed earlier, the core component of the rule of law is based on the idea of human dignity.[48] All government action must be informed by reasons and those reasons should be consistent with the free and equal citizenship of all persons. An act which violates either of these precepts and is not informed by any reason or if the underlying rationale is to treat people as inferior, it would be violative of both the rule of law as well as the requirements of the equality code of the Constitution.

While it is true that the substantive concept of the rule of law has close links with equality, there is a fundamental problem. How do the courts determine which test to apply to ascertain whether the right to equality has been breached? There are no clear guidelines as to when the classification test should apply and when the manifest arbitrariness test should prevail. Often, judges simply state that there are two facets of the Article 14 test, without clarifying why one, and not the other, is being adopted in a particular case.[49] The uncertainty as to, which of the two tests will be applied, at which point of time, is an example of the very inconsistency that undermines the rule of law.

. . . and a Procedural Reading

To compound this uncertainty, there is another facet of equality that has been applied by the courts. Judges have interpreted Article 14 to require compliance with the principles of 'natural justice'. These are rules of procedure which ensure basic elements of fairness while taking decisions, both by the courts as well as administrative authorities. However, this manner of looking at the equality clause is not readily apparent from a reading of the text of the Article. It is, instead, a result of a creative reading of the Article by judges whose aim appear to have been to give a Constitutional foundation to the valued principles of natural justice, or procedural due process.[50]

There is a romantic belief that the British gave us the concept of the procedural rule of law, at least at the minimal level of a neutral application of the law to all citizens.[51] This view, other than ignoring the obvious power disparity between the colonial master and its subjects, is also ignorant of facts which show that, there was hardly any uniform application of the laws in the colonial era.

Given the egregious violations of the principles of natural justice by the British-run courts in India,[52] there was greater pressure to accept these principles in the Indian courts. The early judgements of the courts achieved this by following the principles of common law, which was basically a series of prior judgments that had crystallized into certain set principles of law.

When the courts discovered the 'activist magnitude'[53] of Article 14 in the 1970s, it gave an opportunity to judges to lay the foundation of the principles of natural justice within the expanded meaning of Article 14. One of the earliest cases where this doctrine was developed was in the case of Maneka Gandhi, daughter-in-law of the late Prime Minister Indira Gandhi. After the Emergency imposed in 1975 was lifted and the Janata Party government came to power, it impounded Maneka's passport. A petition was filed in the Supreme Court challenging the impounding on several grounds including the fact that Maneka was given no notice or hearing before the decision to impound her passport. A failure to issue a notice and hear the affected party, the court said, was a violation of the principles of due process, which in turn implied a violation of Article 14.[54]

The manner in which the principles in natural justice were incorporated in the right to equality has been explained by the use of deductive reasoning. The Supreme Court ruled that 'violation of a rule of natural justice results in arbitrariness which is the same as discrimination; where discrimination is the result of State action, it is a violation of Article 14; therefore, a violation of a principle of natural justice by a State action is a violation of Article 14'.[55] This form of reasoning is known as a syllogism conceived by Aristotle[56] where a major premise (all men are mortal) and a minor premise (Aristotle is a man) overlap and lead to a conclusion (therefore Aristotle is mortal). What is important is that this form of reasoning does not testify to the correctness of either the major or the minor premise. In the explanation offered by the Supreme Court, it is assumed (without explaining why) natural justice results in arbitrariness. After all, a decision could end up being completely fair even if one party is not heard. The better foundation for the link, between natural justice and Article 14, is possibly through the ideal of the rule of law.

In Indian jurisprudence, the rules of natural justice mandate a decision by an unbiased authority[57] which passes a reasoned order[58] after hearing all parties to a dispute.[59] It can be seen that this view of equality neatly dovetails with the third facet of the rule of law—the procedural aspect. As noted earlier, there are at least four principles which embody the procedural vision of the rule of law which are virtually identical to the requirements of natural justice as deduced from the case law. So, an adapted syllogism might well be that Article 14 embodies the rule of law. The rule of law requires adherences to natural justice. Therefore, Article 14 requires compliance with the principles of natural justice. This form of expressing the argument reveals not only the strong connect between equality and natural justice but each of the three formulations—substantive, formal and procedural.

Conclusion

The rule of law is intimately connected not only to the ideal of equality. The rule of law as a concept is akin to a skeletal framework, around which other normative values necessary for a modern state, must adhere. Thus democracy, justice and liberty are all values which can be more easily expressed in a society that follows the rule of law. These ideals form the foundation of Indian democracy as expressed in our Constitution. That same document arguably mandates that the ultimate guardians of each of these principles are the courts.[60]

There is a great debate among academics about the nature of the Constitution. Some conservative philosophers argue that the Constitution is part of a pre-existing legal tradition. They believe that the meaning of the equality code must be determined with reference to the standards that existed prior to Independence. Other academics argue that the Constitution marked a radical departure from the past. They argue that the Constitution is a transformative document which completely undermined the earlier conception of the State being the master dispensing rights to its citizens.

What cannot be lost sight of is that, conservative or radical, in practice the Constitution is what the judges say it is. Regardless of the criticism that the judgments on Article 14 are not true to its text, with time judges have decisively held that the equality code embodies multiple different hopes, ideas and inspirations. The ideal of the rule of law, with its moral as well as political appeal, has proved to be a valuable ally of the courts. To understand the vision of the courts in their quest to ensure equality, the concept of the rule of law cannot be ignored.

Just as equality can have conflicting meanings, this chapter has argued that the rule of law mirrors these arguments. The case of the striking post office workers in Britain, referred to in the beginning of the chapter, brings out in sharp relief how the rule of law and equality can vary depending on the situation of the actor. From the point of view of the judge, nothing was more important than the formal idea of the rule of law, i.e., the belief that even the highest officer of the land was bound to ensure that the laws of the country were diligently obeyed by all. However, from the perspective of the striking workers, the reality was different. They believed that a country like South Africa, with its systemic discrimination against the Black community and people of colour, was an anathema to the rule of law. Boycotting South African mail as a form of civil disobedience would help ensure the triumph of equality and the rule of law. This was an assertion of a more robust, substantive version of the rule of law. Both the judge as well as the workers claimed to be upholding the same ideal; it is just that what that required, depended on the worldview of the player.

3

Education

In 2019, the FBI stormed into the house of Emmy Award-winning actress Felicity Huffman.[1] The charges against her were that she had conspired with university officials to illegally secure admission for her daughter to a prestigious college. There was an uproar in the media with commentators saying that the position of a more meritorious student had been bought by the actress. Ultimately, Huffman had to undergo a prison sentence as well as pay a fine. Closer home, there was a little less furore when Priyanka Panwar submitted a false caste certificate claiming to be a scheduled caste member. Using that certificate, Panwar got admission into Mahatma Gandhi Mission Medical College in Navi Mumbai on a reserved seat. The college cancelled her admission when the certificate was discovered to be fake. Panwar moved the Bombay High Court which upheld her expulsion by holding that permitting such a student to continue in that seat would amount to usurpation by those not entitled to it.[2] This was not an isolated case. Every year, multiple students submit fake caste certificates to obtain admission in colleges. These incidents show that parents (or perhaps students themselves) will go a long distance to ensure admission to a top-tier college. This is because college degrees are seen as a necessary gateway to a secure and stable future which any parent would want for their child.

Even if we believe that all people are born equal, we cannot but accept that they do not remain equal for the rest of their lives. A variety of forces, some which may be hereditary, and some, a matter of choice, lead different people to have different life experiences. For those who are committed to the cause of equality, education may be the way to mitigate disadvantages of being born without privileges.[3] It is believed that members of the elite classes get substantial advantages in life through the medium of their education while those with poor or no education find it difficult to rise to their full potential. One way to remedy this systemic disadvantage is through education. Education can substantially improve the life prospects of an individual and even overcome barriers of caste, sex and religion.

While education is seen as an antidote to the effects of discrimination, it is also a battlefield. Precisely because education is so important, those with the greatest privilege want to retain their hold over it, while those who are the victims of prejudice fight for greater and better access to it. Those from the oppressed castes seek reservations in educational institutions to ensure that they will have fulfilling careers, while those from the upper castes see reservations as going against the principles of merit, and paradoxically, equality. Arguments for and against reservations are most shrill when taking place in the field of education, particularly reservations on the basis of caste.

Yet caste-based reservation is not the only area where educational inequality manifests itself or becomes controversial. Unequal access to education is a deeply problematic concern for the poor, women, and religious minorities, as well.[4] The discrimination faced by these groups may not be immediately obvious,[5] but is no less serious. This is so because if the very starting blocks on which one builds a life are uneven, there can be little hope in building a stable future and an egalitarian society. Thus, this chapter will focus extensively on the problems of caste in education but will also examine the issue from other perspectives including religion, sex, and economic status. However, even in these areas, the sceptre of reservation looms large. It is because the main way by which the agency of the law can intervene and help ameliorate inequalities is through the provision of quotas. And whenever quotas are provided, those who are ousted from consideration claim that their right to equality is infringed and that they are being discriminated for not belonging to the oppressed caste, gender or religion. There is then a clash about competing claims to equality. An examination of this issue illuminates not only the specific issues in relation to the regime of quotas but also the debate about the nature of equality under the Indian Constitution.

Quotas and the Vulnerability of the Constitution

As mentioned in Chapter 1, the demands of equality depend on the questions asked. Different conceptions of equality yield often inconsistent and incommensurable answers to a social problem. It is no surprise that in a matter as important as education, these questions and their answers are extremely vexed and contentious. Opponents of reservations say that quotas violate their right to equality, because they are discriminated against on account of their caste or other factors. The proponents, on the other hand, argue for a substantive form of equality. They point out that given the historic inequalities, expecting a lower-caste person to compete in an open examination against a person who has all the advantages of wealth and education is unfair. In effect, by expecting two dissimilarly positioned people to compete in the same way, we end up treating unequally situated persons equally. In this formulation of inequality, quotas are a way to ensure equality so that systemic disadvantages are removed and everyone is placed on a level playing field.

In arguing for their positions, both sides point to Constitutional provisions to make their case. What the Constitution says unfortunately, is not always very clear. Interestingly, the Constitution as drafted initially, did not make any provision for reservations to educational institutions. It was only because of a judgment of the courts that the Constitution was amended and a provision for reservations added. The very first amendment to the Constitution, made even before the first elections to Parliament were held, was in a case relating to quotas and a judgment which went contrary to the established political views of the time. In fact, a pattern would soon emerge where when faced with an inconvenient judgment, Parliament would amend the Constitution to undo the judgment.

Underscoring the importance of education, one of the first cases in which a claim of fundamental rights was made, was in the context of admission to an educational institution. From the 1920s, the State of Madras used to divide seats available for admission in technical colleges to members of various communities.[6] These reservations were provided in documents called the Communal GOs (Government Orders) which had their origin in the anti-Brahminical movements in south India.[7] The Communal GO which was in existence in 1950 provided that for every fourteen seats to be filled in an institute of higher education, the candidates were to be selected in the following proportion:

Non-Brahmin (Hindus)	...	6
Backward Hindus	...	2
Brahmins	...	2
Scheduled castes	...	2
Anglo-Indians and Indian Christians	...	1
Muslims	...	1

Shortly after the promulgation of the Constitution, some upper-caste students sued the State of Madras claiming that the Communal GOs were discriminatory. Two Brahmin students claimed that they were more qualified than members of the other castes and communities and would have been selected had it not been for the reservations that existed in favour of the non-Brahmins. Evidence was filed which showed that because of the Communal GO some seventy-seven Brahmins, 224 non-Brahmins and twenty-six SCs were selected for admission to the Engineering College. Had there been no reservation, and selection had been made solely based on the marks obtained in the qualifying examination, 249 Brahmins, 112 non-Brahmins and no scheduled caste candidate would have been selected.[8] Thus, a large number of Brahmin students were excluded by virtue of their caste, while twenty-six SC students were admitted solely on the ground of their caste.

The High Court of Madras ruled in favour of the students and struck down the communal GOs as being contrary to the equality provisions of the Constitution. A particular telling quote by one of the learned judges was 'It would be strange if, in this land of equality and liberty, a class of citizens should be constrained to wear the badge of inferiority because, forsooth, they have a greater aptitude for certain types of education than other classes. It would be very unjust - it is now unconstitutional - to deprive deserving youths of a particular community of a right of so elementary a character, that deprivation of its enjoyment in common with and on the same footing as others, is a deprivation, in the competition of life, of one of the most essential means of existence ; and this for no sin or fault of theirs and for no other reason than that they belong to a particular caste or religion.'[9] The fact that a system was so rigged that no member of the scheduled castes would have qualified, but for the reservations, did not occur to the learned judge. Instead, he lamented that those with a 'greater aptitude' could not secure a seat. The implication of this mode of reasoning is that those with no aptitude, i.e., scheduled castes, got admission in place of the meritorious because of reservations alone, an argument that is heard all too often even today.

The matter travelled to the Supreme Court of India where the judgment of the high court was affirmed, though on very narrow grounds. In the case titled 'State of

Madras v. Champakam Dorairajan',[10] the court held that the system of reservations was unconstitutional as it was violative of Article 29(2) of the Constitution. The provision stipulates that 'no citizen shall be denied admission into any educational institution maintained by the State or receiving aid out of State funds on grounds only of religion, race, caste, language or any of them'. In the opinion of the court, since Brahmin students were excluded from securing admission only on the ground of their caste, the communal GOs were unconstitutional.

The reaction to this judgment was fast and furious. On the urging of politicians, particularly from southern India where the anti-Brahmin sentiment was strong, the Constitution was amended.[11] The first amendment to the Constitution inserted a new provision which permitted the State to provide for reservations in educational institutions[12] in the same way that the Constitution provided for reservations in matters of public employment.[13] The then prime minister, Jawaharlal Nehru, while introducing the bill laid bare his vision of equality when he said, 'it is all very well to talk about the equality of law for the millionaire and the beggar but the millionaire has not much incentive to steal a loaf of bread, while the starving beggar has. This business of the equality of law may very well mean, as it has come to mean often enough, the making of existing inequalities rigid by law'.[14] The intent behind this statement is a clear rejection of the formalistic framing of the idea of equality, that is the sense that any two persons are equal before the law while ignoring their innate differences. The amendment to the Constitution, thus sought to achieve this vision of equality, and undo the judgment of the Supreme Court.

After the amendment, the place of reservations in educational institutions was firmly established in Indian law. The Constitutional validity of the amendment was upheld, and with it, the place of quotas in matters relating to government-run educational institutions. With time, the quota debate has achieved a modicum of political consensus inasmuch as no mainstream political party argues against them. The only opposition to the political necessity of accepting reservations appears to come from the court. Among the other judicial decisions, two clear areas where the courts have intervened, is to ask who the beneficiaries of reservations can be, and in which institutions can reservations be provided. Each of these questions has implications about the judicial interpretation of the idea of equality.

Reservations for whom . . .

The first question that the courts have ruled on is who the beneficiaries of reservations can be. Article 15 (4) of the Constitution enables reservations for scheduled castes and tribes as well as other backwards classes. The text of the provision reads:

> Article 15 (4): "Nothing in this article or in clause (2) of Article 29 shall prevent the State from making any special provision for the advancement of any socially and educationally *backward classes* of citizens or for the Scheduled Castes and the Scheduled Tribes".

A debate has always raged around whether the term 'backward classes' can be synonymous with 'backward castes', i.e., whether caste can be the sole determinant of backwardness.[15] This issue gained even more attention following the adoption of the Mandal Commission report which provided for 27 per cent reservations in matters of public employment. The validity of quotas for the 'Other Backward Castes' (OBCs) was decided by a nine-judge bench of the Supreme Court in the case of Indra Sawhney v. Union of India.[16] In the case, the court upheld the reservations for the OBC on the basis of caste,[17] but made an important exclusion. The court excluded people who had advanced socially and educationally by the passage of time from the ambit of reservation. This group of people were called the creamy layer of individuals who were not entitled to the benefits of reservation.

After the Indra Sawhney judgment, it was judicially established that a caste could constitute a backward class. However, not all members of a caste were necessarily backward. There would be certain members of the caste who would have progressed sufficiently, both socially and economically, to cease to be backward. For instance, an IAS officer who was OBC, could hardly be said to be backward because once he joins the services 'his status in society (social status) rises; he is no longer socially disadvantaged. His children get full opportunity to realise their potential. They are in no way handicapped in the race of life. His salary is also such that he is above want. It is but logical that in such a situation, his children are not given the benefit of reservation. For by giving them the benefit of reservation, other disadvantaged members of that backward class may be deprived of that benefit'.[18] For the purpose of identifying who had sufficiently advanced socially, income could be used as a test or a measure but could not be the sole determining factor. What this means is that the extent of reservations cannot be decided on the basis of income. However, a backward caste family's earnings would be a measure of their social status, which would have risen independently of their wealth. It was plausible that an extremely wealthy backward caste person would be unlikely to suffer from the ills of social exclusion and hence it was appropriate to assume that a rich person from a backward caste was no longer in need of reservations. Thus, the court directed that the socially and educationally advanced members of backward castes, the so-called 'creamy layer', would have to be excluded from the benefits of reservations.

This principle of excluding the privileges of members of a backward caste was extended to members of the scheduled castes and tribes by a judgment of the Supreme Court in the case of Jarnail Singh v. Lachmi Narain Gupta.[19] In the case, the court ruled that 'the whole object of reservation is to see that Backward Classes of citizens move forward so that they may march hand in hand with other citizens of India on an equal basis. This will not be possible if only the creamy layer within that class bag all the coveted jobs in the public sector and perpetuate themselves, leaving the rest of the class as backward as they always were'. The net result of these judgments is that in case of any reservations, the socially advanced creamy layer of the oppressed castes is not entitled to preferential treatment.

While this decision feels intuitively correct, there is an issue of jurisprudence. The effect of the exclusion of the creamy layer from the beneficiaries of reservation has a clear implication on how the courts view the idea of equality. The question is whether reservations are meant for the individual in her own capacity or whether they are for the benefit of the group as a whole. The effect of the exclusion of the creamy layer is to make the equality provision focussed more on the individual than the group, though that is not always reflected in the judicial consciousness when ruling upon the issue.

The judgments of the courts seem to suggest that the purpose of reservations is to remedy 'group backwardness and not individual backwardness'.[20] Yet, excluding the creamy layer does militate against this principle. The focus shifts from membership of a group to the relative backwardness of the individual concerned. After all, if exclusion of a member of the scheduled caste on a test of economic well-being is permitted, it follows that even caste is merely a test for membership of a backward group, rather than being an independent ground of discrimination.[21] If reservations are to be limited to poor members of a lower caste, is the basis of reservations poverty or caste? If wealth is sufficient to evict a beneficiary from a reserved class, why not include an extremely poor person from an upper caste as well? Ultimately, if the focus of the inquiry is the individual, can it not be said that the upper caste Hindu man who is excluded from securing admission in a medical college because of seat reservations, has a point, when he complains about discrimination on the basis of his sex/caste/religion? These questions are important because they reveal that reservations are more easily justified when reference is had to group inequality, the causes for which may be historic or systemic. When the debate shifts to individuals, this reasoning becomes harder to maintain. This controversy does not appear to have been sufficiently addressed by the courts in their judgments.

. . . and Where?

The courts have also had to answer the question of which institutions can reservations be permitted. The issue was initially settled by an eleven-judge bench of the Supreme Court in the case of TMA Pai v. Union of India.[22] While the main issue before the court was extent of permitted government intervention in minority-run institutions, the judgment held that there could be no reservations in private, unaided institutions, whether run by minorities or otherwise. After some controversy about the exact import of this judgment, this view was further cemented by a seven-judge bench of the court in the case of P.A. Inamdar v. Union of India.[23] Interestingly, the basis of the judgments of the court was that an unaided private institution had a fundamental right to engage in its occupation guaranteed under Article 19(1)(g) of the Constitution, and that the institution could not be foisted with the burden of the State policy of reservations. The right to reservation would, if at all, be limited to state-funded institutions. There was no discussion in the cases about the right of the oppressed classes to seek reservations in private institutions, possibly because the courts have held that there is no right to reservations.

By restricting quotas to the public sphere, the court clearly meant that the duty to ensure equality rests upon the State and not the private sector. This is commonly known as the vertical, as opposed to the horizontal application, of the principle of equality. The vertical relationship between the State and the individual embodies the idea that fundamental rights are inherent in an individual and impose a corresponding duty on the State to ensure that those rights are not violated. This is opposed to the horizontal application of rights where one individual can claim a right to non-discrimination against other individuals or private entities.[24] In such a case there would be a parallel obligation upon the private entity or person not to discriminate against any person on the basis of their caste/religion etc. Whether a right can be horizontal or vertical has a great impact on people's lives especially in a time when more and more educational institutions are becoming private.[25]

As a contrast, the US Supreme Court has held that there can be no quotas or racial preference given to minority communities on the basis of their race in public or private institutions[26]. In the opinion of US Chief Justice John G. Roberts 'many universities have for too long wrongly concluded that the touchstone of an individual's identity is not challenges bested, skills built, or lessons learned, but the color of their skin. This Nation's constitutional history does not tolerate that choice'. The view of the majority required the Constitution to be neutral on issues surrounding race, holding that any discrimination on the basis of race would be subjected to the strictest scrutiny. The minority was scathing in its dissent. Justice Ketanji Brown-Jackson, the first Black woman appointed to the court ruled, 'With let-them-eat-cake obliviousness, today, the majority pulls the ripcord and announces "colorblindness for all" by legal fiat.' Justice Sonia Sotomayor wrote that the majority opinion 'cements a superficial rule of colorblindness as a constitutional principle in an endemically segregated society'. Rather than focusing on the rights of the educational institutions, the US Supreme Court focused on the rights of the excluded candidate.

These bitter exchanges between judges may be something that Indian lawyers are not used to, given the largely convivial style of writing judgments. Yet, such exchanges do bring out in sharp relief the issues at hand. As with other cases of dissent, the opinion of the minority judges also offer the losing side the assurance that their point of view was at the very least considered by the court even if it did not ultimately prevail.[27] On the other hand, in the T.M.A. Pai case, the core issues, i.e., whether equality requires the court to be blind to systemic injustices in society, and whether the fundamental right to do business can trump the claims of the historically disadvantaged groups, do not appear to have been adequately addressed.

However, before these academic issues could be debated further, Parliament intervened. By way of the ninety-third amendment to the Constitution, Article 15 (4) was added. The new clause reads:

> (5) Nothing in this article or in sub-clause (g) of clause (1) of article 19 shall prevent the State from making any special provision, by law, for the advancement of any socially and educationally backward classes of citizens or for the Scheduled Castes or the Scheduled Tribes in so far as such special provisions relate to their admission to educational institutions including private educational institutions, whether aided or unaided by the State, other than the minority educational institutions referred to in clause (1) of article 30.

There was a clear attempt to undo the judgment of the Supreme Court where private educational institutions were given immunity from reservations. Interestingly, the amendment did not include minority institutions in its fold. However, the Constitution now included the power to provide for reservations in private non-minority-run educational institutions. The validity of the amendment was challenged, but the Supreme Court upheld it by ruling that Article 15 (5) could not be said to be an exception or a proviso overriding Article 15 of the Constitution, but was 'an enabling provision to make equality of opportunity promised in the Preamble in the Constitution a reality'.[28] The net result is that today, as the law stands, reservations for backward classes, as well as scheduled castes and tribes, can be provided in all educational institutions, save for those run by linguistic or religious minorities which are protected under Article 30 (1) of the Constitution.[29]

The removal of the creamy layer raises questions about whether the individual or the group is properly the subject matter of the reservation regime. But what is the effect of excluding minority educational institutions from quotas meant for backward castes and the scheduled castes and tribes? This exemption of minority educational institutions raises an interesting issue about the claims for equality raised by different groups of people in society. Now, the competing claims of equality are not between an individual and a group, but between two separate groups—the minorities and the backward castes.

A Conflicted Inequality?

In a discussion about equality, it is also important to remember that a guarantee of equality is also a potent way to entrench protection for minorities.[30] A Constitution that guarantees general equality would also imply that no member of a minority community can be discriminated against on the basis of religion. However, this guarantee of equality cuts both ways. Thus, while affording protection against hostile discrimination by the State, the idea of equality also makes demands of the minority community to ensure that the members of the majority are not discriminated against by them.

At first blush it might seem odd that it is possible for a minority to discriminate against a majority. After all, political power most likely would vest with the majority. But this confusion can be resolved when we look at the other provisions of the Constitution which give special rights to minorities. Under the Constitution, it is not only an individual who has a right to freedom and equality[31] but also the rights of a community have also been recognized. Article 29 of the Constitution promises 'any section of citizens'[32] who have a distinct language or culture, the right to preserve the same. Similarly, Article 30 gives the right to all minorities, whether based on religion or language, the right to establish and administer educational institutions of their choice. These rights can then be exercised by the minority community and are, in a way, a protection against creeping majoritarianism.

However, the right given by these provisions, comes with a sting in its tail.[33] Article 29 (2) states that 'no citizen shall be denied admission into any educational institution maintained by the State or receiving aid out of State funds on grounds only of religion, race, caste, language or any of them'. It may be recalled that it was Article 29 (2) that had been used by the Brahmin student, Champakam Dorairajan, to get the Communal GOs issued by the State of Madras be declared unconstitutional.

The question then, is how the right of minorities to administer their institutions, fits in with the right not to be discriminated against when the individuals are from another religions/linguistic group. There is, in effect, a pitting of the individual right to equality (of a member of the majority community) against the right of a minority community to preserve its social, cultural, and educational institutions. In some cases, the conflict is between two groups, i.e. the right of the minority community to administer its own affairs with the right of an oppressed caste to get quality education through reservations.

The Supreme Court has answered that question by holding that the exclusion of minority educational institutions from the ambit of Article 15 (5) is not violative of the principle of equality. Counsels arguing the matter had challenged the insertion of Article 15 (5), saying that failure to include minority educational institutions in the ambit of reservations was violative of the equality clause in the Constitution, and was therefore contrary to the basic structure of the Constitution. This argument was rejected by the court. The judgment of the court noted that 'the minority character of the minority educational institutions referred to in clause (1) of Article 30 of the Constitution, whether aided or unaided, may be affected by admissions of socially and educationally backward classes of citizens or the Scheduled Castes and the Scheduled Tribes and it is for this reason that minority institutions, aided or unaided, are kept outside the enabling power of the State under clause (5) of Article 15 with a view to protect the minority institutions from a law made by the majority'.[34]

This passage explains how the court justified the exclusion of minority institutions and why the amendment to Article 15 was Constitutional. It was pointed out that if socially and backward castes were to gain admission by way of compulsory reservations, the members of the minorities would have to give up their seats. This could well change the status of the minority institution—for instance, a Tamil-medium school operating in Delhi would be forced to take in a large non-Tamil speaking population of backward castes leading to alteration of its character. Thus, the court held that the decision not to include minority educational institutions from the quota regime was valid as the rights of minorities to maintain their own heritage, religion, and culture would be undone if quotas were to be imposed on them. In drawing this balance, the court seemed to value the ideal of protection of the rights to minorities rather than the right to equality of the members of the backward castes. While some hierarchy is inevitable in any ordering process wherein members of some classes get benefit of reservations and others don't, it is important that the court make that decision explicit.

A clash between caste and religion (or language) is just one possible example of how different group identities can be at loggerheads with each other. Another area where the competing claims of equality manifest themselves is in the case of single-sex educational institutions. There is ample evidence to suggest that women, particularly young girls, perform better in single-sex educational institutional rather than co-educational ones.[35] However, just because an idea is good does not automatically imply that it is legal. The law in relation to single sex education unfortunately is not as clear as one would expect given the ubiquity of such institutions.

While there is no authoritative decision by the Supreme Court, various high courts across the country have weighed in on the issue as to whether boys can be admitted into all-girl institutions and vice versa. In a pattern that is becoming all too familiar, the judgments are hardly clear and seem to contradict each other. Roughly speaking, it appears that boys can be excluded from all-girls school and colleges,[36] but excluding girls from all-boy educational institutions may be unconstitutional.[37] This, perhaps, follows from a reading of Article 15 (3) of the Constitution which permits the State to make 'special provision for women and children'. Thus, an all-female institution would be protected as a special provision under the constitution, but not an all-male one.

The law in the case of a minority educational institution is a bit more complex. In one case, a Christian-run all-boy school in Kerala wanted to start inducting girl students as well. However, this permission was denied by the State authorities on the ground that there was already an all-girl school in the neighbourhood, albeit one run by the Muslim community. The Supreme Court held that such an action would be violative of the fundamental rights of minorities under Article 30 of the Constitution.[38] The court has ruled that Constitutional considerations permit minority-run educational institutions to determine issues of single sex education differently than from non-minority institutions. In that case, the school wished to run a co-educational school, a logic which would presumably also extend to them running a single-sex school. Thus, in a question of discrimination between the sexes, the nature of the institution would also be required to be seen. The courts, like in the case of caste, seem to prioritise rights of minorities to administer their own educational institutions over arguments about sex discrimination.

This discussion also shows that often discrimination does not occur in neat binaries. For instance, a person from a historically backward caste can make a claim of discrimination not only against a person from an upper caste, but also against a person of a different faith or the speaker of a different language. This is hardly surprising because very few individuals in society have such reductive identities so as to have the effects of discrimination only in one aspect of life. We all have multiple identities with multiple axes of possible discrimination. The oppressed can easily be an oppressor and vice versa.

One particularly vexed example of the clash between group rights and individual rights in matters of equality is in the ban on the hijab. The government of Karnataka in 2022 decided to enforce a common dress code for all students, as long as the students wore 'clothes that are in the interests of unity, equality and public order'. This peculiar phrasing was really a euphemism to ban female students from wearing a hijab. A full bench of the Karnataka High Court unanimously upheld the prohibition on the hijab,[39] and the matter was taken in appeal to the Supreme Court. There, a two-judge bench heard the case and delivered a split verdict.[40] Justice Hemant Gupta ruled to uphold the ban, while Justice Sudhanshu Dhulia ruled to strike it down. In view of the disagreement between the judges, the matter was referred to a larger bench which has yet to be constituted.

The issues, at first blush, appear to relate to the right of a woman to make an autonomous decision about her clothes, versus the right of an institute to regulate its affairs, including the power to prescribe a uniform. However, one judgment of the court gave a novel twist to the argument. Justice Gupta juxtaposed the right of all students to wear the same uniform vis-à-vis the right of an individual woman to wear the clothes of her choice. A rather novel description of equality was proffered when he ruled that 'Before a student goes for higher studies in colleges, she should not grow with a specific identity, but under the umbrella of equality guaranteed under Article 14 transcending the group identity.[41] If a particular student feels that she cannot compromise with the wearing of headscarf or of any other student to wear any outwardly religious symbol, the school would be justified not to allow such student, in the larger interest of treating all the students alike as a part of mandate of Article 14, which is central to the theme of Part III of the Constitution.'[42] As per the learned judge, equality is now not an individual right, but a collective right of a group of students to force another student to conform to a specified dress code. Or perhaps the proposition can be formulated as giving the State a right under Article 14, which trumps the right of a female student to decide what to wear. While the question of legality, indeed even the morality of the hijab, is a deeply vexed one, this formulation of the test for equality is at odds with the prior jurisprudence of the court. The conflict here was not between the rights of two groups, but between members of a group, who claimed a right to choose clothes of their own choice, versus the right of another group to force the former to wear a school uniform. There may be a compelling State interest to ensure that students abide by a dress code, but to draw justification from the right to equality seems a bit farfetched. More worryingly, the right to equality has been turned on its head and now appears to be a charter for enforcing uniformity rather than celebrating differences. The right to equality allows individuals to lead their life on their own terms but mandates the government not to discriminate against her for those differences. It surely does not require the government to intervene and enforce equality by making people into clones of each other.

Graduating Confusion

This doctrinal inconsistency in relation to the meaning and purpose of equality come into sharp relief in the context of reservations in postgraduate education. Seats in postgraduate medical colleges in India are like gold dust. Admission to these institutions is usually through a competitive exam. However, to ensure that the students who take the exam have a certain calibre, the rules often provide for a minimum qualifying mark. Thus, in a case of medical colleges situated in Madhya Pradesh, the rules prescribed that the qualifying candidates would have to secure at least 50 per cent marks in the exam before they would be given a seat. However, in the case of scheduled caste and tribe candidates, this minimum was relaxed to 40 per cent. When the exams were held, it was realized that in spite of the relaxation, only eighteen SC and two ST candidates would have been appointed out of the 216 seats reserved for them. Even when the minimum was relaxed further to 35 per cent, the number of successful candidates increased only to twenty-five SC and three ST candidates. At this point, the balance seats would normally have been allotted to the general category students. However, the state government decided to completely do away with the minimum marks requirement and admitted students regardless of the marks they had scored in the exam.

This relaxation was a step too far for a young candidate, Kumari Nivedita Jain. She was a general category student who had secured the minimum qualifying marks. If the seats reserved for the SC and ST candidates had been thrown open to the general pool, she would have secured a seat in a medical college. However, because the state government decided to do away with minimum qualifying mark altogether, these seats were eventually filled up. She moved the high court asking it to strike down the decision of the court doing away with the minimum prescribed marks. The high court allowed the Nivedita Jain's petition and the matter was taken in appeal to the Supreme Court.[43]

The Supreme Court reversed the decision of the high court and held that the lowering of minimum qualifying marks was permissible since a candidate would have to ultimately clear the final exams in medical school in any case.[44] Thus reduction in the entry requirements would have no impact on the final calibre of the graduating doctor since she would have had to clear the presumably stringent graduating requirements. If a student was good enough to pass the medical exams and graduate, she was good enough to be a doctor.

After a few years the Supreme Court reversed this view and held that there cannot be a wide disparity between the minimum qualifying marks in entrance examinations for candidates from the general category versus those from the reserved category.[45] In another case arising from Madhya Pradesh, a five-judge bench of the court overruled the earlier judgment and held that:

> The final pass marks in an examination indicate that the candidate possesses the minimum requisite knowledge for passing the examination. A pass mark is not a guarantee of excellence. There is a great deal of difference between a person who qualifies with the minimum passing marks and a person who qualifies with high marks. If excellence is to be promoted at postgraduate levels the candidates qualifying should be able to secure good marks while qualifying. It may be that if the final examination standard itself is high, even a candidate with pass marks would have a reasonable standard.

This logic is slightly hard to understand. It is true that a person merely scraping through graduation may be less meritorious than a person who passes the exams with flying colours. However, this is precisely the issue. Two candidates, one from the reserved category who barely manages to get into college, and another general category candidate, who scores a high rank in the entrance test, will thereafter be taught the same courses. During medical school, the reserved category student would get quality education which will permit her to overcome the previous denial of proper instruction that she had faced. Thereafter, when both candidates were to take the final exams, they would be more evenly placed. It cannot be said that the reserved category student who made it into the college by the skin of her teeth would necessarily score less that the general category student. This logic is a result of the failure to consider why it is that reserved category students perform comparatively badly in entrance examinations and why they need additional advantages. A reserved category student who has not had access to the same training for entrance examinations as a more privileged student will obviously perform poorly.[46] However, once she secures admission and has access to the same resources as her upper caste counterpart, she might thrive in the academic environment. At the least, by passing the final exam, she would demonstrate the required competence as mandated by the competent standard setting authority.

The same judgment also held that there was no scope for reservations in super-speciality medical courses. The court held that 'at the level of admission to the supers-speciality courses, no special provisions are permissible, they being contrary to the national interest. Merit alone can be the basis of selection'.[47] At another place, the court seems to indicate that as one moves up the educational ladder, from primary education to university enrolment and postgraduate courses, the scope for reservation diminishes.[48] This logic mirrors that of the rationale for excluding the creamy layer, i.e., the idea that as a community moves socially upward, there is less need for reservations. Unfortunately, the judgment does not appear to recognize this correlation. Instead, the focus appears to be on the deleterious impact reservations have on the public at large. The starting principle is that reservations while being inherently anti-meritocratic, are something that has to be put up with.[49]

This line of reasoning reflects the ambiguous view of the courts on reservations. While there is a recognition about the need for quotas to bring the lower castes on a level-playing field, there also appears to be an unease about the lowering of standards. Thus, the court states that failure to consider 'merit' is detrimental to the national interest. There is, of course, a value judgment in this, i.e., the belief that students who enter the education system with the aid of reservations are less meritorious or less proficient. In considering the question of equality, the court has moved the focus away from discrimination between reserved and general category students. There is now a conflation of the idea that allowing unreserved category students into medical school is tantamount to encouraging merit. In other words, reservations are a dole or a handout, while open competition promotes national interest. Whether this is a fact, is unfortunately rarely discussed.

Judicial dicta thus show ambivalence towards the concept of reservations. Verdicts also contain unexamined questions about the nature of equality, possibly because the courts believe them to be in the realm of academics rather than part of the task of writing judgments. Inevitably, it is difficult to have a jurisprudence which is completely consistent ideologically. This is hardly surprising and certainly not unique to the problem of quotas. Judges author judgments shaped as they are by their own political philosophies and fashioned by the dominant thinking of the times. Just as human thought is not static and ossified, judgments which reflect the Constitutional thinking of judges, also change with time. This does not necessarily imply confusion, but it certainly points to a tension between different competing schools of thought about the nature and need for reservations. At the least, it is required that judges spell out their conceptions of equality clearly rather than hiding behind rhetoric.

Conclusion

Given the high stakes in the quest for access to education, it is not surprising that the discussion about reservations is so politically and legally vexed. Perhaps, the more important question is why we are so focused on the issue of reservations in the area of education. An excessive reliance on reservations as a panacea reflects the lack of imagination on the part of the government. Disadvantage, which is as historically deep-rooted as caste, cannot be eliminated merely by employing the politically attractive tool of reservations. Differential access to quality education for Dalit children might be responsible for their inability to gain adequate employment to an extent far more than can be addressed by providing quotas.[50]

An excessive reliance on quotas can unfortunately have the opposite effect of what they seek to do, which is improve the social standing of the most oppressed groups of people. Recent events have demonstrated the bias that exists against members of the scheduled castes in university spaces, with derogatory stereotyping, being a particular problem. As one study noted 'at every step (SC/ST students) are made aware of their quota identity, made to feel less meritorious and if they are female, subjected to sexual innuendos and harassment. If they demand their duly constituted rights to be upheld, they are labeled troublemakers and antisocial elements'.[51] Data has also shown that contrary to the popular imagination, many seats in higher education which are reserved for the oppressed castes remain vacant. Even when students are admitted, the dropout rate of the SC/ST and OBC candidates is disproportionately higher than the 'general' category candidates.[52] In such a situation, it can hardly be argued that quotas have worked to eliminate systemic social prejudices.

A case against reservations has also been made by arguing that a better way to ensure equality is to improve the quality of education. As it's said, a rising tide lifts all boats. Some say that reservations ought to wither away in an egalitarian society. Given the size of the young population of the country it is necessary to open an ever-greater number of institutions of academic excellence rather than constantly dividing the existing pie between different disadvantaged groups.

All the arguments against reservations may have some merit, but it is tough to ignore the fact that we hardly live in a just and equal society. As long as there is unequal access to educational resources, no matter what concept of equality one adopts, there is a need to level the playing field through the provisions of quotas. Further, there are few other tools in a legal arsenal to ensure an equitable system other than providing for reservations. It can only be hoped that the courts make a sincere effort to deal with the jurisprudential questions that the concept of equality poses, because that would assist in a more coherent legal regime.

The law in relation to equality in matters of education rests on a shaky, divergent and a shifting jurisprudential and philosophical basis. It seemed the court had embraced a robust understanding of equality when it upheld the Mandal Commission recommendations in the Indra Sawhney case. Backward castes as a group had faced historical disadvantage and therefore they were entitled as a group to obtain reservation. Yet, the exclusion of the creamy lawyer brought the focus back from the group to the individual. The concern of the court is not the social backwardness of the group but the 'forwardness' of the individual. One cannot but help feel that this focus on the individual reflects ambivalence towards reservations where a rich Dalit is seen to be unfairly taking the seat of a more meritorious upper caste candidate. This contradiction is further manifested in other areas of the law, including reservations in postgraduate courses. If the reason for reservations is to remedy systemic inequalities, there appears to be no reason to exclude quotas at the highest level of education, where the lowest castes are most likely to be under-represented. The language of the judgments which speak of merit and academic excellence encapsulate the lingering belief that the courts seem to harbour that, reservations are at some level anti-meritocratic and have to be viewed as an exception to the idea of equality.

4

Employment

The middle-class dream of getting a secure, well-paying and stable government job was shaken in 1990. Prime Minister V.P. Singh, who had only been elected a year earlier, was facing multiple political challenges. Possibly in an attempt to kickstart the flagging government, he issued an Office Memorandum on 13 August 1990 announcing the implementation of the Mandal Commission. That commission, named after B.P. Mandal, a former backward caste chief minister of Bihar, recommended that 27 per cent of all government jobs should be reserved for members of the backward castes. Rather than securing his position, the decision shook the government to its very foundations. While the initial reaction to the announcement was muted, things took a dramatic turn in early September when a young Delhi University student Rajiv Goswami poured kerosene and set himself ablaze in protest against the decision. This started a chain reaction across the country with multiple young men following in the footsteps of Goswami.[1] Two months later, V.P. Singh resigned as prime minister.

V.P. Singh had to resign due to several reasons, but the emotive appeal against reservations proved to be the proverbial nail in the coffin. From then to now, reservations generate strong reactions from both camps—the beneficiaries, as well as those in the 'general' category. There are also agitations by groups seeking their inclusion in the list of backward castes with counter-agitations being launched by those already in the list who fear that their share of the pie would reduce. These reactions are hardly surprising, given the importance of employment in anyone's life.

Employment is both a means to attain equality as well as a measure of equality in any society. One way to move up the social ladder is by securing a job that pays well and is valued by the public at large. Gainful and prestigious employment raises social standing and brings about parity with peers. But if a person belongs to the lowest rung of society, it is not easy to find employment which will enable such upward mobility.[2] If a society is unequal, it is all too often the case that employment opportunities are also unequal. There is a sort of a chicken-and-egg situation, with the question being, what comes first, employment or equality? To this conundrum we can add another facet, one where the self-esteem of an individual in society is deeply influenced by their vocation.[3] A stable and fulfilling career adds to the meaning and purpose of a person's life. Employment then has an intrinsic value too and is not merely a means to achieve the goal of equality.[4] Hence it is clear that there is a social, economic and a moral imperative in ensuring equal access to adequate employment.

However, securing gainful employment is not where the story stops. Employment, like marriage, must endure. Working conditions which make continued employment difficult are as much a hurdle to achieving equality as a failure to get a job, in the first place. The problem is even more acute when we realize that many discriminatory working conditions are a result of, as well a reflection of pre-existing inequalities in society. A case in point would be the unequal treatment meted out to women at the workplace. Even if a woman is able to surmount the entry barriers and obtain employment, there are a series of legal and well as structural as well as social barriers curtailing her career progression. These barriers are a result of the inherently patriarchal nature of society. Sexist attitudes act against the interests of women in matters of gaining and retaining employment.

The law thus has to deal with two separate areas of inequality so as to achieve equity at the workplace. One is to ensure access to jobs in a non-discriminatory manner and the other is to establish working conditions of employees that promote substantive equality. The former goal may be achieved by providing reservations in public employment. This would enable the socially and economically disadvantaged to achieve economic equality and would simultaneously raise the social status of the whole community. Any reservations will impinge on the competing equality claims of those excluded from the domain of consideration, i.e., the so-called 'general category' candidates. This chapter will examine how the law has dealt with this balancing exercise. In the case of quotas in education, the courts have permitted reservations in the case of employment in a fairly liberal manner. Yet, there is hesitation in permitting the reservations regime to become a crutch in perpetuity. Further, even when the court does intervene in favour of reservations for certain marginalized groups, for example, transgenders, the State in fact does not act upon the directions. Because of this non-compliance, disadvantaged groups end up being treated unequally by the law.

The second problem, i.e., the concern about workplace conditions, requires more intervention than is commonly assumed. Here, the law has kept pace with the issues of equality on a formal level but has been far more reluctant to intervene on a substantive level. Thus, the law demands the formal equality in the principle of 'equal pay for equal work' for women. But when it comes to issues like maternity leave, issues that have a real-life impact on working women, the law does not come to the aid of women to the extent it needs to.

Appointment: The Chicken and the Egg

The conundrum mentioned in the introduction, i.e., whether unemployment causes inequality or vice versa, can be illustrated by statistics. Marginalized sections of society tend to be poorer and consistently underemployed compared to the general public. Thus, almost 84 per cent of people facing multidimensional poverty come from the lower castes and tribes.[5] Of these, Dalits have an unemployment rate which is nearly twice the national average. The position of the Adivasis is even worse with unemployment levels thrice the national average. This situation has gotten worse during the Covid-19 pandemic.[6] Similarly, the labour force participation of women in India is abysmally low.[7] As in the case of the oppressed castes, women have also suffered in a loss of status during the Covid-19 pandemic. Studies show that it was women from the poorest households, whose husbands had lost jobs, who had to take up lowest paying jobs underscoring the role of women as 'insurance during low-income period by poorer households'.[8] One must also bear in mind the fact that a very significant number of people in the country are engaged in agricultural and allied activities. Thus almost 46.5 per cent of workers are engaged in agriculture even though it contributes to only 20 per cent of the total economy,[9] with a far greater proportion of women[10] and the lower castes[11] working in agriculture, than upper caste men.

There is, therefore, a clear link between the quality and extent of employment and social class, though the question of what the causal event is remains.[12] However, that is a matter for sociological experts rather than a book on the legal aspects of equality. Further, faced with this glaring inequality, the law cannot afford to stay silent awaiting an answer to these vexed philosophical questions. Indeed, there is a Constitutional imperative for the law to intervene, to ensure that 'the citizens, men and women equally, have the right to an adequate means to livelihood'.[13]

The law does this primarily through the means of reservations, at least in the case of societal inequalities due to caste. The Constitution permits reservations in matters of public employment. This power has been used to steadily increase the quotas for scheduled castes and tribes as well as the OBCs to about 49 per cent of most central jobs.[14] The courts have, over the years, generally upheld these reservations. Thus, in the case of Indra Sawhney v. Union of India,[15] the court upheld the recommendations of the Mandal commission. In explaining the rationale behind reservations and its link with the Constitutional ideal of equality, the court held that 'the concept of equality before the law contemplates minimising the inequalities in income and eliminating the inequalities in status, facilities and opportunities not only amongst individuals but also amongst groups of people, securing adequate means of livelihood to its citizens . . . Indeed, in a society where equality of status and opportunity do not obtain and where there are glaring inequalities in incomes, there is no room for equality—either equality before law or equality in any other respect'.[16]

While the law clearly permits reservations in matters of employment, the devil lies in the detail. There is a set of rules in the law relating to reservations which sheds light on how the courts view the concept of equality. Over several years, the courts have expanded and clarified these rules though not always in a consistent manner. Some of these questions include whether there is a right to reservations, what can be the extent of total reservations and who the beneficiaries of reservations may be.[17] All these queries raise extremely contentious issues and are the cause of both political and legal disagreements.

Is there a Right to Reservations?

Unlike in matters relating to education, the Constitution as drafted originally, did provide for quotas in public employment under Article 16. Article 16 (1) guaranteed the right to equality of opportunity to all citizens in matters relating to government employment. Article 16 (2) was a guarantee against discrimination promising that 'no citizen shall, on grounds only of religion, race, caste, sex, descent, place of birth, residence or any of them, be ineligible for, or discriminated against in respect or [sic of], any employment or office under the State'.

With this guarantee of non-discrimination, it would seem that the Constitution would not permit reservations of any sort. After all, reservations based on caste clearly discriminate against those who are not part of the beneficiary caste. However, at the time of drafting the Constitution, quotas for the scheduled castes and tribes were already in vogue. The members of the Constituent Assembly were keen that these should continue since the position of the lower castes was still abysmal. Accordingly, a special provision was made in the form of Article 16 (4), which stated as follows:

> Nothing in this article shall prevent the State from making any provision for the reservation of appointments or posts in favor of any backward class of citizens which, in the opinion of the State, is not adequately represented in the services under the State.

Using the powers under this Article, the government started a process of reservations of posts for members of the scheduled castes and tribes. After an initial hiccup, where the Supreme Court struck down certain caste-based reservations,[18] the governments of the day started quota regimes which were tailored to fit the Constitutional provisions. Because of the shortage of private sector jobs, there was a great demand for cushy public sector jobs synonymous with security. So, it was no surprise that any system of reservation was heavily contested. Given the ambiguity of the language of the Constitutional provisions, both legal and philosophical questions arose repeatedly before the courts.

The most basic of these questions, one that has resulted in considerable judicial discussion, is whether quotas are an exception to the general rule of equality or whether they would form part of the guarantee of equality itself. This is an important debate because it can determine the nature of how courts view equality and the relief possible in individual cases. The case law[19] of the early years after the promulgation of the Constitution as well as the discussion in the Constituent Assembly debates[20] shows that the understanding was that quotas were an exception to the idea of equality. The general principle was that any two persons were to be treated the same for the purposes of employment. However, in certain cases an exception would be made to this rule by the provision of quotas to account for the disadvantages of history and status. This is a formalistic conception of the ideal of equality. In other words, even though reservations were given to the underprivileged, the assumption was that any two persons were to be regarded as equal, regardless of their historically disadvantaged status.

Over time, this idea of quotas was given up and the court has (for now) ruled that quotas are not an exception to the idea of equality, but are part of its very concept. This shift in judicial thinking got a boost when the Supreme Court decided the case of State of Kerala v. N.M. Thomas[21] ('the N.M. Thomas case'). The case concerned members of the scheduled castes and tribes who were required to obtain certain qualifications before consideration for promotion. The government rules permitted them to be promoted on an ad hoc basis and secure the qualifications thereafter in a two-year period. The Kerala High Court struck down the rule and the matter reached the Supreme Court by way of an appeal. There, while pronouncing on the validity of the government rules, the court also opined on how it viewed the concept of equality in the context of reservations. Marking a break from the past jurisprudence, the court ruled that Article 16 (4) was not an exception to the equality of opportunity but was itself a necessary vehicle to achieve the promise of equality embodied in the Constitution. In an interesting passage, Justice K.K. Mathews held:

> The guarantee of equality before the law or the equal opportunity in matters of employment is a guarantee of something more than what is required by formal equality. It implies differential treatment of persons who are unequal . . . the emphasis in Article 16(1) is on the mandatory aspect, namely, that there shall be equality of opportunity for all citizens in matters relating to employment or appointment to any office under the State implying thereby that affirmative action by Government would be consistent with the article if it is calculated to achieve it.[22]

In effect, the judgment ruled that substantive equality disallowed treating unequally placed people similarly. As opposed to formal equality, substantive equality was not blind to the social differences between two individuals and did not automatically treat them as equals. Instead, two persons, one of who had access to far more resources than the other due to the privilege of birth, could not be said to be equal. This formulation of equality implies that the only way that such two persons can be treated similarly is by accounting for such differences through the agency of the law.

A possible implication of this argument is that there is a right to reservations. A disadvantaged person can argue that failure to get any compensatory advantages places her at an unequal pedestal from which she cannot compete with her upper-caste competitor. This would result in a violation of her fundamental rights. To avoid such an infringement, the State would be required under the Constitution to provide for reservations. In other words, Article 16 would have been transformed from an enabling provision which empowers the government to offer reservations, into a mandatory provision, where a citizen has a right to approach the court, and demand reservations. Reservations would thus be a right and not merely largesse.

The problem with right to reservations is that it is contrary to the text of Article 16, which reads like an enabling provision, i.e., one that empowers the government rather than imposing any positive duty.[23] There would also be practical problems in implying such a right. For instance, if the government were to fail to provide reservations, would that give a right to a person to move court asking for reservations? If so, would the court be able to direct the government to provide a fixed amount of quotas in a particular stream of employment? The court surely does not have the competence to determine the myriad policy implications in matters relating to reservations. Further, the question of quotas is highly divisive and would require the Courts to wade into the political thicket, something that they are reluctant to do.[24] An interpretation which might make more sense of the N.M. Thomas judgment is that the right to equality vested in a disadvantaged person does not imply a duty on the State to provide for reservations. Instead, there is a duty to undertake such acts, either political or socio-economic, which would ensure equality. Thus, there would be a duty for affirmative action and not for positive discrimination.[25]

Whether there is a duty on the State to provide for reservations or not, the N.M. Thomas case ruled decisively in favour of a substantive as opposed to a more formalistic idea of equality. It also sought to build a bridge between the ideas of equality of opportunity and equality of results. The Court held that 'Whether there is equality of opportunity can be gauged only by the equality attained in the result. Formal equality of opportunity simply enables people with more education and intelligence to capture all the posts and to win over the less fortunate in education and talent even when the competition is fair. Equality of result is the test of equality of opportunity.'[26] The implication obviously is that if there is inequality of results, there is no real equality of opportunity. This also seems to make some intuitive sense. If the top 10 per cent of the country get access to 90 per cent of the resources, it would be reasonable to assume that it would not be a very egalitarian place. Inequality of results proves, by itself, the inequality of opportunity.

'Promoting' Equality

Thus, there is now a jurisprudential basis for stating that reservations are a facet of equality and that the equality of opportunity can be assessed only by seeing whether there is equality of results. Unfortunately, this issue is as vexed and mired in contradictory judgments as in many other areas of reservation jurisprudence. For instance, the Supreme Court had ruled that there can be no reservations in matters of promotion (as opposed to initial appointment), holding that this would virtually create a separate stream of employment.[27] Members of the reserved category would vie for promotions with other members of their class and not with the general category. This would not only cause heartburn and frustration[28] to the general category, but would also be a 'serious and unacceptable inroad into the rule of equality of opportunity'.[29] Why this should be so for promotions, but not for appointments was never fully answered in the judgment. Indeed, there may be very good reasons for denying reservations in promotions, for instance to keep all employees enthused and not lethargic in the belief that they would get promotions no matter what. Studies have shown that quotas for entry-level positions do not have any impact on the overall efficiency of the bureaucracy.[30] On the other hand, there may be efficiency losses in case of reservations in promotions or jobs at higher levels. But if reservations are part of equality, and it can be empirically established that the representation of the lower castes falls as one moves up the career ladder,[31] would there not be an obligation on the State to allow for reservations in promotions as well? Unfortunately, these questions were not seriously considered by the court.

In any case, Parliament was not having any of this and responded to the judgment by amending the Constitution and allowing for reservations in promotions.[32] The amendment permitting reservations in promotions was questioned but the challenge was rejected by the Supreme Court.[33] While upholding the amendment, the court held that there was no Constitutional right to reservations and that Article 16 was merely an enabling right. The judgment held that this enabling provision sought to 'balance equality with positive discrimination',[34] even though it noted that previous judgments had held that Article 16 (1) and 16 (4) were a composite whole. At one point the court held that 'equality has two facets — "formal equality" and "proportional equality". Proportional equality is equality "in fact" whereas formal equality is equality "in law". Formal equality exists in the rule of law. In the case of proportional equality the State is expected to take affirmative steps in favour of disadvantaged sections of the society within the framework of liberal democracy'. What 'proportional equality' really means is not very clear. A court may have to ask itself whether reservations are intended to ensure representation of the lowest castes in public service or are they meant to serve as a means to guarantee an equality of outcomes. When seen as something more than a mere rhetorical flourish in a judgment, the concept of 'proportional equality' thus has clear implications for the quantum of total reservations. It implies a right to have a quota that exactly matches the share of that caste in the general population. But how does one determine the share of any caste in the population? That is a question that has a rather vexed history and an equally controversial present.

How Much is too Much?

John Henry Hutton was an Indian Civil Services officer and a self-proclaimed anthropologist who had secured a not very respectable third-class degree in History from Worcester College Oxford.[35] Naturally, the British government thought that this qualified him to become the Census Commissioner for India in 1929. Under his leadership, the last publicly available caste census was conducted in 1931. After Independence, a policy decision appears to have been taken that conducting such an exercise would entrench caste.[36] So when B.P. Mandal came up with his report recommending reservations, he only had the figures tabulated in 1931 to calculate the quantum of quotas. More recently, this absence of data has led political parties to ask for a new caste census. The State of Bihar conducted just such an exercise in 2023 and discovered that the numbers of lower castes had been severely underestimated. The survey estimated that 63 per cent of the population was OBC and 21.5 per cent belonged to the scheduled castes and tribes. The share of the 'general' castes in the population was only about 15.5 per cent.[37] This has led some politicians to start demanding proportional representation for members of various backward castes with Bihar leading the way and passing a legislation reserving 65 per cent of jobs for the lower castes.[38]

If the law requires proportional equality, it follows that the number of reserved seats must mirror the caste breakup of the population. After all, if say 70 per cent of the population are lower castes but have only 30 per cent of the jobs, there appears to be an inequality of results, constituting a breach of the equality provisions in the Constitution. Only when there is an exact identity between the enumeration of the caste and jobs, can there be true equality of opportunity. Till that happens, any member of the lower caste would have the right to approach the court asking for enforcement of the generalised right to affirmative action. So, is there a right to a particular numerical representation and what do the courts think about it?

Unsurprisingly, during the period in which the court viewed reservations as an exception to the idea of equality, there was a cap on the possible amount of permissible quotas. The reasoning of the court was that while quotas were necessary to ameliorate the disadvantages faced by the oppressed castes, they were inherently violative of the principle of equality. If the exception (of quotas) was not to swallow the main principle (of caste blindness), there had to be a limit on the amount of reservation. Thus in 1963, the Supreme Court ruled that reservations generally ought to be less than 50 per cent of the total seats holding that 'the interests of weaker sections of society which are a first charge on the States and the Centre have to be adjusted with the interests of the community as a whole'.[39]

Though there was some doubt about whether the 50 per cent limit was Constitutionally sanctioned,[40] the nine-judge bench decision of the Supreme Court in Indra Sawhney's case converted the limit to a virtual judicial axiom. Pointing out that Article 16 (4) of the Constitution only permitted 'adequate' representation and not proportional representation, the total permitted quotas could therefore not generally exceed 50 per cent. However, after holding so, the court gave an escape clause and held:

> While 50% shall be the rule, it is necessary not to put out of consideration certain extraordinary situations inherent in the great diversity of this country and the people. It might happen that in far flung and remote. areas

> the population inhabiting those areas might, on account of their being out of the mainstream of national life and in view of conditions peculiar to and characteristical to them, need to be treated in a different way, some relaxation in this strict rule may become imperative. In doing so, extreme caution is to be exercised and a special case made out.

Thus, in exceptional circumstances, the 50 per cent rule could be breached. However, what these exceptional circumstances could be were not exhaustively listed. Over a period of time an increasing number of social and caste groups started agitating for reservation. As any student of politics would anticipate, electoral compulsions forced the powers that be to start providing for more reservations and test the limits of this exception. Thus, the politically powerful Jats in the north as well as the Marathas in Maharashtra sought for, and initially obtained, quotas in jobs albeit by different methods. In each case, the matter was carried to the courts with the Supreme Court ultimately rebuffing the attempts. In the case of the former, the Jats were included in the central list of OBCs.[41] However, the court struck down this decision holding that there was insufficient evidence to show that Jats were entitled to be included in such a list.[42] The Marathas secured reservations by pushing the Maharashtra Assembly to pass a law permitting up to 16 per cent reservations in educational institutions and public employment.[43] The Bombay High Court upheld the Act,[44] but the decision was overturned by a Constitution Bench of the Supreme Court.[45] The Supreme Court ruled that there was no compelling reason which justified the breach of the 50 per cent rule established in the Indra Sawhney case.

It would have seemed that the court had finally decided that the 50 per cent limit on quotas was more or less absolute. However, this requires a sense of judicial consistency that the court has often failed to show in the recent past. It is not surprising that within a year of the judgment striking down reservations in favour of Marathas, the court had another occasion to revisit the 50 per cent ceiling in the case of quotas for the economically weaker sections of society where it ruled that the limit was not absolute.

The case arose out of the 103rd amendment to the Constitution which inserted provisions for reservations for members of the poorer sections of society. The new provisions, Articles 15 (6) and 16 (6), provided for reservations in educational institutions and public employment, respectively. The amendment was challenged on multiple grounds and was upheld by a sharply divided Supreme Court.[46] Allowing Parliament to breach the 50 per cent limit, the court noted that the threshold was only applicable in matters relating to reservations for OBCs and the SC/ST communities. The court did not appear to question the effect that the reservations would have on the persons who did not fall in any of the 'reserved' categories, and how the Constitutional guarantee of equality would be impacted. The court held that members of the backward castes could not complain if the benefit of reservations was extended to other disadvantaged groups as well. In doing so, the court did not address the issue whether the breach of the 50 per cent limit was in violation of the right to equality of the general candidates. On a more fundamental level, the court held that the reservation regime was both part of the doctrine of equality[47] and was an exception to it.[48] The judgment is thus a study in contradictions and in unanswered (and unasked) questions. However, it is clear that the 50 per cent limit is not sacrosanct, paving the way for a future court or amendment to breach it even in the case of caste quotas.

Who can be the Beneficiary of Reservations?

This judicial inconstancy is reflective of a deep-set ideological ambiguity in the minds of the judges. It is not surprising that this is reflected in other parts of the equality jurisprudence of the courts. For instance, another question that has often engaged the court is who is entitled to the benefits of reservations. As seen in the chapter on education, the courts have already excluded the 'creamy layer' from considerations for quotas on the ground that they are socially advanced and hence undeserving of additional benefits. The focus of reservation would then be the individual and not the community. This same dilemma exists in other areas too. A particularly tricky question that the courts have faced is on the issue of whether members of the lower castes who convert to religions other than Hinduism are also entitled to reservations. Thus, is a 'Dalit Christian' or a 'Dalit Muslim' a contradiction in terms since these religions do not recognize caste, or does the stigma of caste carry on even after conversion?

Shortly after the promulgation of the Constitution, the President issued an order which gave a list of all those castes which were deemed to be scheduled castes.[49] Clause 2 of the order specifically excluded non-Hindus from the list stating that 'no person who professes a religion different from Hinduism shall be deemed to be a member of a Schedule caste'. Over time, members of the Sikh and the Buddhist communities were also included in the list. However, other major religions including Christianity and Islam are still omitted from the list. Even though a report headed by a former Chief Justice of India[50] recommended the inclusion of these religions in the list in 2007, the government did not accept the suggestion. Instead, a fresh panel to look into the issue, headed by another former Chief Justice of India, has been appointed. The matter is currently pending before the Supreme Court.[51] This is not the end of the matter. In some cases, there are complex rules which hold that a convert from Hinduism may not lose her caste status on conversion. Thus, the courts have held that whether a person would cease to be a member of the scheduled caste depends on '(1) the reactions of the old body, (2) the intentions of the individual himself, and (3) the rules of the new order'.[52] The criteria for each of these three tests are varied and complex, but the net test is that if a person still identifies as a member of a scheduled caste and is considered to be part of the caste by her fellow members, she continues to remain a member of the that caste if the rules of that sub-caste permit it.

The position of law becomes even more peculiar in the case of inter-caste marriage. If an upper caste woman marries a scheduled caste man, she is not entitled to any reservations that her husband may be entitled to.[53] This would seem to rebuff the patriarchal notion of a woman taking the caste of her husband upon marriage. However, the children born out of such a marriage would likely be eligible for reservations as they are presumed to have the caste of their father. Nothing exemplifies the strangeness of this argument than the case of Rohith Vemula, the young Dalit scholar, who died by suicide and whose tragic death caused Yashica Dutt to come out as Dalit. Rohith was a member of the Ambedkar Students Association of his university and had commenced a fast to protest against the suspension of his monthly stipend and his eviction from his hostel. He camped in a tent outside the university campus and ultimately took his own life in 2016, leaving behind a poignant note where he said that 'my birth was my fatal accident'.[54] The government set up a judicial commission headed by a retired judge of the Allahabad High Court to probe the causes of his death. Rather than examining the cause of the suicide, the commission concluded that Rohith was not a Dalit, because he had been born to an OBC father.[55] His mother belonged to the Mala community, a Dalit sub-caste, and had separated from her husband. A single mother, she brought up Rohith as a Dalit, but this was of no concern to the commission. Importantly, Rohith saw himself as a Dalit. For the commission, he was born to a non-Dalit father; ergo he was not a Dalit.

In India, where women take the name of their husbands and move to his house after marriage, to pretend that she alone will retain her caste after marriage while her husband and children belong to another caste, is quite puzzling. On the other hand, a lower caste man marrying an upper caste woman does not lose the benefits of his caste upon marriage,[56] in a tacit recognition of the Indian social reality. The implication of all these rules on the doctrine of equality is bewildering. If the object of reservations is the community and not the individual, why should the status of a particular convert from Hinduism to another religion matter? And if the status of the individual should be of ultimate concern, then why is there a presumption, albeit rebuttable,[57] that Rohith Vemula was not a Dalit even though he suffered all the indignities of belonging to that caste throughout his life?

The end result is that the jurisprudence in relation to equality at the workplace is a patchwork of different rules. There does not appear to be a consistent judicial or legislative philosophy about how to erase the vice of discrimination in matters relating to employment. Another reason for this lack of coherence is the changing judicial attitudes about the roles of various employees, both at the workplace as well as in society. No place is this inconsistency more apparent for women than in the workplace.

Recruitment: The Law and the Reality

The promise of gender equality is mentioned at several places in the Constitution. Article 39 (d) of the Constitution states that 'the State shall, in particular, direct its policy towards securing that there is equal pay for equal work for both men and women'. Even though this promise is not justiciable (i.e. cannot be enforced as a matter of right by courts) the doctrine has been held to be a facet of Article 14 and 16 of the Constitution.[58] In other words, the promise of equal pay for equal work is not just part of a directive principle of State policy but also is a fundamental right. Thus, relying on the equality clauses of the Constitution, pay parity can be sought against the State. Even in the private sector, Parliament has intervened by enacting the Equal Remuneration Act, 1976. The Act provides that there should be no discrimination in matters of remuneration when a woman does the same or similar work as a man.[59] Other than salary, the Act mandates that there can be no sex discrimination in any service conditions. Section 5 of the Act reads as under:

> No discrimination to be made while recruiting men and women workers. -- On and from the commencement of this Act, no employer shall, while making recruitment for the same work or work of a similar nature, or in any condition of service subsequent to recruitment such as promotions, training or transfer, make any discrimination against women except where the employment of women in such work is prohibited or restricted by or under any law for the time being in force.

In the face of this declaration by Parliament, can it still be said that there is no equality in law for women? The answer sadly is, yes. The devil, as is so often the case with the law, lies in the details. First, the section only applies to those 'establishments and employments' that the government notifies. The one major area that escapes the scrutiny of this law is the unorganized sector, where the vast majority of women work.[60] Secondly, while the judgments of the courts establish that temporary employees performing the same work as a permanent employee are entitled to the same pay, the basic question of what counts as 'same work or work of a similar nature' is vexed and is detrimental to women. Thus, as one commentator points out, the work of a female crèche worker at a factory might require the same (or more) skill than a male machine operator.[61] Yet, since the work is different, it is possible to pay the woman less than the man, even though bringing up children might require more knowledge, experience, and skill than merely running a machine. Bringing up children is seen as the natural work of women and is hence devalued, if not altogether ignored, in the job market.

While assessing the work that women perform, it is difficult to ignore the obvious problem of stereotyping. Women are automatically seen as the 'weaker sex' needing state protection rather than the right to equal employment. One classic example of such a case arose in the context of women being unable to work in bars in Delhi. As per the provisions of the Punjab Excise Act, 1914, no woman was allowed to work in premises where liquor or other intoxicating substances were served in public.[62] The government defended this provision before the high court stating that the provision was 'meant to ensure safety and dignity of women as well as of young men of impressionable age group'.[63] Yet again, women were asked to restrain their employment opportunities because men could not control their 'impressions'.

Fortunately, the high court[64] and then the Supreme Court struck down this prohibition as being unconstitutional and contrary to the equality provisions of the Constitution.[65] What was innovative about the judgment was that it signaled that the courts were willing to move away from a formal concept of equality to a more substantive one. Quoting an academic text,[66] the court noted that 'the difference between human beings, whether perceived or real, and whether biologically or socially based, should not be permitted to make a difference in the lived-out equality of those persons'.[67] What the court was trying to say was that when the State sought to justify the prohibition on the ground of security of women, it indulged in gender stereotyping. There was a 'romantic paternalism' which meant that the State would seek to protect the hapless woman from working in an unsafe environment.[68] This was in ignorance of the fact that such a ban would detrimentally impact a woman's ability to secure gainful employment or the fact that the woman was probably quite capable of taking care of herself.

Another example of gender stereotyping that resulted in discrimination is in the recruitment of women in the armed forces. Both legislation[69] as well as the Constitution[70] gives greater leeway to the armed forces to treat men and women differently in matters relating to employment. Women were generally only allowed short service commissions,[71] in spite of a judgment of the Delhi High Court holding this to be unconstitutional.[72] Almost seventy years after Independence, the government finally issued a circular in 2019 permitting women to get permanent commissions in all the services of the army. However, even this circular contained discriminatory provisions in matters of service and recruitment. The Supreme Court struck down these discriminatory provisions and held that any policy excluding women from appointment to the armed forces was discriminatory and based on unjustified gender stereotypes.[73]

Stereotyping women typically operates at a subliminal or a cognitive level and is therefore particularly hard to eradicate.[74] Therefore, while the cases discussed above give hope for matters relating to equality in recruitment of women, it is not the complete story. Courts only step in on a case-by-case basis to remedy the defects in the law. However, given the scale of the problem, there is an urgent need of legislative intervention rather than the incremental approach the courts must necessarily adopt. As pointed out earlier in the chapter, women face discrimination not only in matters of recruitment and wages, but also in their service conditions. In some cases, legislation has been enacted to ensure that women achieve substantive equality at the workplace. Whether these interventions have succeeded is a matter of debate.

Service Conditions and the Burden of Motherhood

In the case of women, the barriers to appointment are a result of the same conditions which make continued employment difficult. One of the major grounds of discrimination is the perceived child rearing obligations of the mother. The law has stepped in and provisions have been made to secure certain maternity benefits for mothers.[75] However, such legislation does not always result in achieving the desired result. Employers are reluctant to hire women because they fear that there would be additional costs in order to comply with egalitarian laws such as maternity benefits. Paradoxically, the greater the amount of protection afforded to women to account for their unequal status, the greater the compliance costs and hence greater the disincentive to hiring women.

While one might expect this thinking from the private sector, it is unfortunate that even the government has often taken a similar position. This, in spite of the fact that the Constitution states that 'the State shall make provision for securing just and humane conditions of work and for maternity relief'.[76] One early example of this was the case of airhostesses working with Air India. The regulations provided that their services could be terminated if they got married within four years of joining the service or upon their first pregnancy. Further, the retirement age of women was thirty-five years, extendable up to forty-five years, at the discretion of the managing director of Air India. On the other hand, the retirement age for male pursers who were doing a fairly similar job was fifty-eight years. The Supreme Court struck down the provision which provided for termination of services after the first pregnancy,[77] but upheld the different retirement ages between the male and female employees.[78] The truly astounding rationale was when the court upheld the provision permitting termination if the airhostess got married within the first four years of her service. The court noted that if an airhostess joined service at nineteen, she could not get married till she was at least twenty-three, lest she lose her job. This, as per the judgment, was a good thing because 'apart from improving the health of the employee, it helps a good deal in the promotion and boosting up of our family planning programme. Secondly, if a woman marries near about the age or 20 to 23 years, she becomes fully mature and there is every chance of such a marriage proving a success, all things being equal'. Clearly, the court thought that the responsibility of family planning lay only upon women and that the requirement to be mature before marriage was also solely cast upon women!

The judgment was ultimately based on a reading of Articles 15 and 16 of the Constitution which permitted discrimination on the grounds of sex as long as that was not the only ground of distinction. If the government could show that there was any other reason along with the discrimination on account of sex, the provision would be upheld. The government had issued a notification stating that the differences were based on 'different conditions of service and not on the difference of sex' in the case of airhostesses. Relying on this, the court held that since the government had issued such a notification, it was settled that the discrimination was not only on the grounds of sex.

There are several problems with such a decision. First, deference to a government notification hardly behoved the Supreme Court of India. More importantly, to hold that there was no violation of the Constitutional promise of equality because the discrimination was on grounds of sex as well as other grounds (i.e., not solely on the grounds of sex) makes the right meaningless. A clever employer can always think of creative ways to discriminate by imagining grounds which are different from sex, but which are peculiar to one sex (or our stereotypical assumptions of that sex). Thus, in a follow-up case in the Air India matter, women were required to stop flying duties at the age of fifty after which they could continue with ground duties till the age of fifty-eight. This was disadvantageous to women as flying duties paid more than ground duties. The Supreme Court upheld this regulation holding that 'the twin Articles 15 and 16 prohibit a discriminatory treatment but not preferential or special treatment of women, which is a positive measure in their favour'.[79] Apparently the Supreme Court felt that making women retire at the age of fifty (or opt for ground duties) was a measure in their interest.

Fortunately, it seems that this line of cases is no longer good law. In Navtej Johar v. Union of India,[80] the case where Section 377 of the Indian Penal Code criminalizing homosexuality was read down, the Supreme Court disapproved of this line of reasoning. In a passage that is worth reproducing (and self-explanatory), Justice D.Y. Chandrachud held thus:

> A discriminatory act will be tested against constitutional values. A discrimination will not survive constitutional scrutiny when it is grounded in and perpetuates stereotypes about a class constituted by the grounds prohibited in Article 15(1). If any ground of discrimination, whether direct or indirect is founded on a stereotypical understanding of the role of the sex, it would not be distinguishable from the discrimination which is prohibited by Article 15 on the grounds only of sex. If certain characteristics grounded in stereotypes, are to be associated with entire classes of people constituted as groups by any of the grounds prohibited in Article 15(1), that cannot establish a permissible reason to discriminate. Such a discrimination will be in violation of the constitutional guarantee against discrimination in Article 15(1). That such a discrimination is a result of grounds rooted in sex and other considerations, can no longer be held to be a position supported by the intersectional understanding of how discrimination operates. This infuses Article 15 with true rigour to give it a complete constitutional dimension in prohibiting discrimination.

The Constitution, in essence, does not permit an employer (as long as it is the government) from making any stereotypical assumption about women and use that to discriminate against women. This was also the basis of the judgment in the case of Anuj Garg discussed above, where women were prohibited from working in bars only because of their presumed frailty.

This trend of judgments is certainly promising. Yet there are other areas in matters of motherhood where the law does not do enough to secure equality. For instance, while the law does provide for maternity leave,[81] it fails to recognize that child rearing duties fall squarely on women in our society and that these responsibilities do not end when maternity leave is over. To be able to fully participate at the workplace, women need access to childcare facilities including crèches, which are simply not available at most workplaces. There are no laws requiring employers to provide these facilities, making it tough for women to continue working.

The Proof of the Pudding

However, pregnancy and marriage are not the only concerns of women. There are other areas where the issues peculiar to women remain unaddressed. For instance, failure to give menstrual leave to women disables many from being able to fully participate at work. Sexual harassment at the workplace also largely contributes to women disproportionately leaving employment compared to men. While the law does provide some protection in the case of harassment, the application is incomplete and patchy. Possibly the greatest discrimination in an area where the law has shown reluctance to intervene, is the unregulated informal sector of the economy. This indifference to the unorganized sector is all the worse when it is seen that the sector, at least in one account, employs 94 per cent of workers but produces only 45 per cent of the output.[82] Women in this unregulated sector face a double whammy. Women not only tend to get the lowest paying jobs but also their domestic work in households is completely unpaid.[83] One consequence of this is that there is no stable market for household work which enables price valuations on such work. As a consequence, it is found that the minimum wages set under the Minimum Wages Act, 1948 for domestic work are arbitrarily lower than other equivalent unskilled work.[84]

In the light of the yawning gaps in the law providing for equality, or at least a modicum of social security for women, can we really say that they are equally placed to men? To borrow the logic of the reservations cases discussed earlier, one way to examine whether there is equality of opportunity is to determine whether there is an equality of results. On that basic smell test, it is clear to any observer that gender equality is a distant dream because for all that the law promises, the reality of Indian women is quite different. An International Labour Organization study shows that women earn 34 per cent less than men in corporate India for doing the same job.[85] Even if women do find jobs, the quality of employment and the amount of pay that they receive as compared to men is generally inferior.[86] India has the lowest pay parity amongst the BRIC countries.[87] Further, empirical evidence suggests that women are far less likely to get managerial positions than their male counterparts, even if there is greater equality in the overall unskilled workforce.[88] In turn, unequal access of women to managerial positions lowers the equilibrium wages for both men and women in non-agricultural sectors.[89] In other words, excluding women from managerial positions is both a fact as well as a clear economic drag. Things also look bleak for the future because economic growth alone will not guarantee greater female workforce participation. As a family gains greater wealth, the women of the family are less likely to work given the social stigma attached to the general idea of working women.[90]

One response that the lawmakers have to this wage gap at upper levels of governance is the familiar one of reservations. The law provides for reservations for women, albeit a miniscule one. The Companies Act, 2013 mandates that the boards of all listed companies and large public companies must have at least one female director.[91] Fortunately, this measure has not resulted in tokenism, but substantially increased the representation of women on company boards.[92] Unfortunately, the women who have come on the board are largely non-executive directors with little actual control over the management of the company. For instance, fewer than 5 per cent of all companies have female chairpersons. This lack of power is manifested not just at the board, but also in the upper management of a company. An Indian Institute of Management study reveals that female representation in senior management of a company is consistently lower than the percentage of women on its board.[93]

Horizontal Reservations

Speaking of reservations for women, we seem to have come full circle in this chapter. The discussion started with the need for quotas for the upliftment of the socially backward castes and is now about providing for reservations for women. It seems that the imagination of the law in matters of securing social justice often begins and ends with reservations. For certain communities however, even this promise of reservations is not available.

The transgender community in India has been historically marginalized. It was in 2014 in the NALSA judgment[94] that the Supreme Court definitively gave judicial recognition to the community by recognizing the right of transgendered persons to determine their own gender. The State and the Central governments were also directed to give legal recognition to their gender identity as male, female, or third gender. The governments have done this to some extent.[95] However, the judgment also contained a direction to the governments to treat the community as socially and legally backward and to provide for reservations in admissions to educational institutions as well as in public appointment. The affirmative action program was ordered so that the 'injustice done to them for centuries could be remedied'.[96] This was exactly the same logic which formed the basis for reservations in favour of the scheduled castes and tribes. What is interesting is that the nature of reservations required to be given to the transgender community is a slight departure from those given to members of the lower castes.

Reservations can be of two types—vertical or horizontal.[97] Vertical reservations are how a regime of affirmative action is traditionally understood. Thus, a fixed percentage of the total available jobs are reserved in favour of a caste or any other defined class. Therefore the 22 per cent reservation of government jobs for the scheduled castes would amount to vertical reservations. Horizontal reservations are different. Over time, different castes and groups have varying portions of reservation—the job pie, so to speak, is divided into slices of different sizes.

However, there could be disparity within these groups as well. For instance, women or the disabled as a class are likely to have been discriminated in whichever caste group they are found. Therefore, to accommodate for this kind of generalized discrimination, the law provides for horizontal reservations where a fixed percentage of each caste quota is further reserved for the discriminated class. For instance, persons with disabilities are entitled to 4 per cent of posts in irrespective of their reserved category.[98]

This distinction between the two forms of reservation has a profound effect on how inequality is viewed between sections. Horizontal reservations have been seen as part of Article 16 (1) while vertical reservations are stated to be a facet of Article 16 (4).[99] Of course, this is a slightly confusing statement of the law because as we saw earlier, the two clauses of the articles are meant to be a composite whole. However, the implication probably is that the beneficiaries of vertical reservations (i.e. the backward and scheduled castes) operate in a sphere which is an exception to the general concept of equality whereas beneficiaries of horizontal reservation (women and the physically handicapped) deserve reservations because the very concept of equality demands it. This recognizes the unique experience and the special form of discrimination faced by the beneficiaries of horizontal reservations.

The court in NALSA did not clarify whether the mandated reservations would be horizontal or vertical in nature. Members of the transgender community have urged that they should be entitled to horizontal rather than vertical reservations. An application was moved before the Supreme Court asking for clarification that the reservations mandated by the NALSA judgment were for horizontal reservations. The court dismissed the application on procedural grounds holding that the petitioners ought to have filed a substantive petition seeking horizontal reservations rather than asking for the clarification of a judgment already passed. As of the writing of this book, this issue remains unresolved.

Sadly, even though the court has directed the provision for reservations, it has largely been ignored. The Central Government has taken a stand that no reservations can be provided to the transgender community. Some state governments like Karnataka have provided for reservation, while most others have not. The Transgender (Protection of Rights) Act, 2019, which was enacted pursuant to the NALSA judgment, does not provide for reservations, in clear violation of the Supreme Court order. Being politically disempowered seems to offer a reason for the government to ignore the demands of those who most need State aid. A heart-wrenching instance is that of Ms X, a bright student in a private school in Delhi who dreamed of being a doctor. She also identified as a transwoman and eventually came out to her family. In her twenties, she felt that her family was not supportive and decided to move out of her home and support herself through giving tuitions and other part-time jobs. She was, in essence, a person who faced social stigma and yet fought on to realize her goals. Her dream was to specialize in reproductive health. In an interview to a newspaper she said, 'Since I cannot become a mother, I wanted to help others through methods such as IVF.'[100] She took the entrance test for the master's program conducted by AIIMS and secured the eleventh rank in the examination. Sadly, that rank was not enough to bag a place in her preferred course—MSc in Reproductive

Biology and Clinical Embryology. The course had seats reserved for various castes and the EWS category, but none for the transgender community. This was even though on most metrics, the transgender community performs worse than certain OBCs. Ms X has since moved the Delhi High Court seeking for implementation of the NALSA judgment. While the Centre denies and the court prevaricates, Ms X has no place to turn to—she is the child of a lesser god.

Conclusion

Ms X is not alone in our country. There are multiple axes of injustices and we are increasingly failing our youth, particularly the most disadvantaged and the disempowered. India is a young country with the median age being twenty-eight years.[101] To put it in context, the median age of a person in China is thirty-nine years and in Japan it is forty-eight years.[102] There is inevitably talk of the so-called 'demographic dividend' where a booming workforce promises to increase the net national wealth. However, having a young country is not sufficient to ensure economic growth. The alleged dividend can quickly sour if the masses of young people entering the workforce remain unemployed. Also, if India is a young country, it is also a deeply unequal country. As noted earlier, the income disparities are greatest between the haves at the top, and the have nots at the bottom of the rung—women, lower castes and religious minorities. Widespread income disparities hardly encourage a stable social set up, other than being ethically questionable. Hence, there is both a pragmatic as well as a moral imperative to ensure equal (and adequate) access to employment for all sections of society. While the law cannot assist in job creation, which is in the political and economic domain, it is an important social tool to mitigate the effects of inequality.

The courts have held that reservations and quotas are part of the doctrine of equality, albeit in a hesitating and not altogether consistent manner. In recent years, they have even moved towards an idea of proportional equality, the belief that different groups in society are entitled to a proportionate share of resources. In this, the courts seem to mirror the increasing political consensus that those in the lowest socioeconomic strata need the greatest help. The conception of equality as a robust, substantive idea appears to be universally accepted, even if not always followed in practice. It is important that at such a time, the imagination of the law should move beyond reservations and address the various underlying causes of systemic inequality faced by lower castes, women, and the transgender community. The responsibility is not just upon the courts but also on Parliament to ensure that comprehensive legislation is enacted to tackle injustices wherever they arise, both in matters of appointment and also in the conditions of service. This, and nothing less, is what the youth of this country need and deserve.

5

Business

A manufacturer and supplier of bidis, rather unimaginatively called the, 'Bidi Supply Company', had a run in with the Indian Income Tax Department in the early 1950s. While its assessment proceedings were on, it received a notice from the department that the case would be transferred from Kolkata to Ranchi, even though its head office was in Kolkata. Given the administrative inconvenience caused by such a decision, the company moved the Supreme Court. The Bidi Supply Company argued that there was no reason why it had been singled out and its assessment proceedings transferred to a far-off place while other manufacturers could continue with their cases in Kolkata. Agreeing with the petitioner's contention, one of the most celebrated judges of the court, Justice Vivian Bose, ruled that the Act which permitted such arbitrary transfers was unconstitutional.[1] But in holding this, he gave an eloquent exposition of the law when he asked, 'After all, for whose benefit was the Constitution enacted? What was the point of making all this other about fundamental rights? I am clear that the Constitution is not for the exclusive benefit governments and States; it is not only for lawyers and politicians and officials and those highly placed. It also exists for the common man, for the poor and the humble, for those who have businesses at stake, for the "butcher, the baker and the candlestick maker". It lays down for this land "a rule of law" as understood in the free democracies of the world. It constitutes India into a Sovereign Republic and guarantees in every page rights and freedom to the side by side and consistent with the overriding power of the State to act for the common good of all.'

Over years, it seems that this principle of law has been watered down, with rights themselves seen in opposition to public good. It's as though rights somehow hold back the development of the country rather than foster individual development. Constitutionally speaking, nothing could be further from the truth. A rights-based culture is often seen as an indicator of a flourishing democracy, with a variety of inalienable rights being found in Constitutions and international treaties across the world. The rights to freedom of expression, life and liberty, and equality are valued as essential attributes of a society that respects the innate dignity of every person living in that country. Indeed, these rights are often referred to as 'human' rights because it is believed that they inhere in every human regardless of 'race, sex, nationality, ethnicity, language, religion, or any other status'.[2] Every year, international conferences are held extolling these rights or lamenting their violations.

Other than being an indicator of a healthy democracy, respect for rights also has a direct bearing on the economic development of the country. While competition is necessary to ensure innovation and value, companies also need a level playing field, for instance between public and private enterprises[3]. These interests are protected under Article 14 of the Constitution. So, it is unsurprising that the right to equality has been used by people to advance their business interests as well as other loftier ideals.

This is not the only reason behind the 'constitutionalization' of business law. On a practical level, the fact that large number of judgments emerging from the court relate to businesses should not be surprising. Filing a case, engaging lawyers, summoning witnesses and domain experts to give evidence often requires substantial expenditure. Corporate entities tend to have deeper pockets than individuals and can more readily afford to undertake such expenses.

Other than this rather prosaic reason, different facets of Article 14 have a close conceptual link to business law. First, is the obligation to treat all persons equally, i.e. for the government not to claim any special privileges compared to a common citizen. The second is not to discriminate against different classes of persons. Finally, the Constitution also requires the government to act in a rational and non-arbitrary manner. These Constitutional obligations have been interpreted by the courts as requiring the State to act in a fair and transparent manner even in matters relating to its commercial dealings. While private entities can use profit maximization as a legitimate business goal, this liberty is not available to the State. Using the requirement of fairness as a central organizing principle, multiple different strands of case law have developed over time. It is this duty to act fairly that will be examined at some length in this chapter.

The Rule of Law and the Duty to Act Fairly

Article 14 prohibits the 'State' from discriminating against any 'person'. Both these terms are of wide amplitude. The courts have expanded the meaning of the 'State' to include not just the elected government but also include public sector undertakings,[4] companies incorporated by special statutes[5] and even schools,[6] universities[7] and research institutions.[8] Similarly the word 'person' in the Article means not just a citizen but also includes foreigners and corporate entities[9].

Thus, the obligations imposed by the Article act on a very wide number of people and authorities. Each of these entities are subjected to different facets of the case law relating to equality. As noted in the chapter on the Rule of Law, there is a strong connection between equality and the Rule of Law and this holds true for businesses as well in multiple ways. For instance, the minimum content of the rule of law as well as that of Article 14 is that everyone is equal before the law and that the law binds each person equally. One offshoot of this requirement is that the government is also bound to follow the same principles that apply to all private citizens and entities without any discrimination. In the context of business, this usually means that the State is as bound by contractual obligations as any other entity.[10]

However, this is not the only requirement of the rule of law. The substantive conception of the rule of law imposes an obligation on the State to act reasonably in its dealings with all persons. This is reflected in the case law where judgments impose additional obligations upon the State compared to private entities. One such obligation is the general duty cast upon the State to act fairly. While the early judgments of the Courts did not seem to impose any such obligation, the duty was read into the Constitution by judgments of the 1980s and 1990s. Perhaps the most celebrated of these cases concerned contracts between the government and its lawyers in a case titled, Kumari Shrilekha Vidyarthi v. State of Uttar Pradesh.[11] The verdict of the court in this case gives a hint on how judges viewed the obligation of the equal protection clause in the Constitution.

Indian politics was in a churn in the late 1980s. The Congress party lost power at the Center and was replaced by the Janata Dal government. This shift in politics was also mirrored in the States. In November 1989, elections took place in the state of Uttar Pradesh and the Janata Dal government led by Mulayam Singh Yadav came to power. One of the first measures of the newly installed government was to terminate the services of all district government counsels in the state and to replace them with a fresh panel of lawyers. The incumbent lawyers filed petitions in the high court, claiming that the state government had acted arbitrarily in terminating their services in one go and that too without giving them a hearing. The high court dismissed the petitions and so the matter was taken in appeal to the Supreme Court.

The Supreme Court seemed incensed by the actions of the government since the action reeked of political opportunism and vendetta. The court likened the intention behind the en masse termination of all government counsel to the adoption of a spoils system where the victor would reward its supporters with lucrative government positions and punish those who did not tow its line.[12] This, the court said was alien to our Constitutional scheme.[13] The court struck down the decision of the government to unilaterally terminate all the lawyers as being arbitrary and not based on any good reason.

Importantly, the court distinguished the position of the State and a private entity in matters relating to contracts holding that 'the State cannot claim comparison with a private individual even in the field of contract'. In effect, the court held that the State was expected to be held to a higher standard than a private entity. While the latter had the freedom to enter into a contract and thereafter be solely governed by the terms of the contract[14] and the provisions of the Contract Act, the State had no such freedom. Other than the contractual terms, it was required at all times to comply with the additional mandate of Article 14. Even if the terms of the contract entitled the State to act in a particular manner, that course of action might still be prohibited if it would result in an unfair, arbitrary or unreasonable result.

In deciding this case, the court also referred to two other verdicts which had been delivered around the same time. In one case, the court had held that even in cases of commercial tenancies, which were otherwise governed by the rent acts and the terms of the lease, the government was required to act in the interest of the public.[15] Therefore, even if the government had the power to terminate a lease, it could not end the tenancy unreasonably or for an ulterior motive. In another case, a long-time distributor of lube produced by the Indian Oil Corporation suddenly found that the IOC stopped supplying lube to it for the purposes of resale. Even though the distributor did not have a formal contract with the IOC, it moved the court complaining that they had been arbitrarily blacklisted and that too without any opportunity to put forth their defence. The Supreme Court directed that the informal blacklisting was unconstitutional and directed the reinstatement of the distributorship. The court held that the 'rule of reason and rule against arbitrariness and discrimination, rules of fair play and natural justice are part of the rule of law applicable in situation or action by State instrumentality in dealing with citizens'.[16]

These judgments, all delivered in the late 80s and early 90s, seemed to forge a new path for the interplay between Constitutional and commercial jurisprudence. This was clearly in the mind of the judges when they remarked that 'bringing the State activity in contractual matters also within the purview of judicial review is inevitable and is a logical corollary to the stage already reached in the decisions of this Court so far. Having fortunately reached this point, we should not now turn back or take a turn in a different direction or merely stop there'.[17]

The evolving jurisprudence was a clarion call for other judges to take the task of holding the government accountable in all matters, including those relating to commerce, forward. However, these judgments also sounded a note of caution. While all actions of the government were subject to judicial scrutiny, there was a fair bit of leeway that was to be afforded to the government in the commercial decisions it took. At a time before economic liberalization, government was often a competitor of private industry. To demand a higher standard of probity from the State, but not from other businesses, would be akin to asking the government to compete with one hand tied behind its back. This, the courts would not countenance.[18] The court was also conscious of Constitutional limitations and did not want to impinge on the right of the executive to take policy and business decisions. Thus, there began a long process in the evolution of law where the competing requirements of accountability were pitched against judicial deference to executive decision making. The consequence is a branch of the law which is not entirely predictable—something which is an anathema to business.

Nevertheless, the obligation of the State to act fairly in all aspects of its commercial dealings with business entities has been accepted as a cardinal principle. How it applies to different fact-situations is what causes some confusion in the law. It is therefore useful to break down different areas where the duty to act fairly can be applied and examine how that courts have dealt with them.

Equality and Government Contracts

The case law clearly establishes that the State has to be fair in its dealings with all persons. This element of fairness is required at all stages of its operations—from the formation of contracts to their execution and even their termination. Of course, while there is a general duty, its specific demands at each of these stages varies substantially. For instance, in the case of formation of contracts the question is whom the state can enter into a contract with and on what terms.[19]

In the early years of the Supreme Court, the court gave considerable freedom to the government in matters relating to formation of contracts. Thus, in a case concerning the award of a contract to supply milk to a government hospital, the court ruled that 'it is perfectly open to the Government, even as it is to a private party, to choose a person to their liking, to fulfill contracts which they wish to be performed. When one person is chosen rather than another, the aggrieved party cannot claim the protection of Article 14, because the choice of the person to fulfill a particular contract must be left to the Government'. The government could thus opt to enter into a contract with whomsoever it preferred and the courts would not transgress this freedom. The reasoning behind this conclusion was that the government was to be treated as just another party to a contract with no additional rights or burdens. It was as though the government lost its identity as a 'State' bound by the rigours of Article 14 once it entered into the commercial arena.

However, as the jurisprudence evolved, the courts refused to accept this Dr Jekyll and Mr Hyde personality of the State where Constitutional obligations would apply to the government in matters of public law but would cease to operate the moment it decided to enter into a contract.[20] This was brought out clearly in a judgment relating to the grant of government contracts by way of tenders.[21] The case related to tenders floated by the International Airports Authority (IAA) to run a canteen at the Bombay airport. One of the conditions of the tender was that the bidders were required to be 'registered IInd class hoteliers having atleast 5 years experience' of running restaurants. The tender was awarded to the proprietorship concern of a Mr Kumaria who technically did not have the required experience as he was not a registered IInd Class hotelier'. However, he did have substantial experience in the catering business as he used to run canteens in several large establishments. The IAA accepted the bid even though it did not technically comply with the eligibility conditions, by arguing that it had the freedom to negotiate with whomsoever it thought fit. A concerned citizen, Mr Shetty, moved court saying that he had not bid for the tender since he was not a registered hotelier as required under the tender conditions. He claimed that had he known that the conditions could so easily be ignored, he might well have bid for the contract. Considering the bid of Mr Kumaria while not considering his bid, even though neither party was technically qualified, amounted to a violation of the equality of opportunity and was therefore contrary to Article 14 of the Constitution.

The Supreme Court agreed with Mr Shetty and held that the action of the IAA in deviating from the terms of the tender was unconstitutional. The court ruled that it was unthinkable that in a democracy governed by the rule of law, the government could wield arbitrary power over citizens. In choosing whom it entered into a contract with, the government was required to act for good reasons and in the public interest. No person could randomly be given a contract while the same privilege was denied to another person who was otherwise identically placed. This was the mandate of the equality code as well as the general principles of administrative law. In the words of the court 'the principle of reasonableness and rationality which is legally as well as philosophically an essential element of equality or non-arbitrariness is projected by Article 14 and it must characterize every State action, whether it be under authority of law or in exercise of executive power without the making of a law. The State cannot, therefore, act arbitrarily in entering into relationship, contractual or otherwise, with a third party, but its action must conform to some standard or norm which is rational and non-discriminatory'.[22]

This justification was based on both principles of administrative law as well as the equality clause of the Constitution. Of course, the reimagining of the manifest unreasonableness test as a facet of Article 14 has to an extent merged the two concepts—administrative law and constitutional law.[23] Nevertheless, there seemed to emerge a new principle of accountability which would cover all areas of commercial activities of the State.

The non-arbitrariness doctrine crept in not only in matters relating to the formation of contracts but also to how the terms of the contracts were to be understood and how they had to be performed or even terminated. Contractual clauses that were onerous or one-sided were struck down on the ground of inequality of bargaining power. For instance, employment contracts which contained a provision for termination of an employee on the basis of a notice period, or pay in lieu of the notice period, were struck down by holding the clause to be unconscionable and arbitrary.[24] Given the might of the State as opposed to the comparatively weaker position of the employee, such a contract could not be said to be a fair and just bargain between two parties. The reasoning of the court was also that this power to unilaterally terminate employees, without even giving them an opportunity to defend themselves, gave the government arbitrary discretion to decide which employee to fire or retain.

With this line of case, the era of judicial supervision of the State's commercial activities seemed to be at hand. However, if it seemed that the courts were now holding the government to account, it was only partially true. While the courts did rule that Article 14 and the doctrine of fairness would apply to commercial activities of the State, the judgments also gave a fair bit of leeway to the government. Therefore, though the courts were now willing to examine the fairness of the terms of the contracts entered (or proposed to be entered) into, they afforded the government a measure of 'free play in the joints'.[25] Effectively, this ensured that the extent of judicial review would be fairly restrained with the government having considerable freedom in its commercial activities. As far back as 1994, the court summarized the principles of judicial review and ruled that:

(1) The modern trend points to judicial restraint in administrative action.
(2) The court does not sit as a court of appeal but merely reviews the manner in which the decision was made.
(3) The court does not have the expertise to correct the administrative decision. If a review of the administrative decision is permitted it will be substituting its own decision, without the necessary expertise, which may be fallible.
(4) The terms of the invitation to tender cannot be open to judicial scrutiny because the invitation to tender is in the realm of contract.
(5) The government must have freedom of contract. In other words, a fair play in the joints is a necessary concomitant for an administrative body functioning in an administrative sphere or quasi-administrative sphere . . .[26]

This judgment marked a retreat from the creeping judicial expansionism in the commercial sphere and henceforth the contours of judicial review became relatively conservative. The ostensible reason was that the courts were cognizant of their lack of expertise and the possible negative impact on the exchequer in case of quashing administrative decisions.[27] This position of judicial deference to the executive has carried on till date,[28] save for a few minor blips.[29]

Equity and the Rule of Law: Estoppel and Legitimate Expectation

In spite of this reticence to interfere in contract formation and execution, the fundamental tests of rationality and fairness are now firmly established in our jurisprudence. However, in law, contracts are not the only way obligations can be incurred by parties. There are cases where even prior to the execution of a formal contract, parties can incur duties and responsibilities toward one another. For instance, a sale negotiation. A prospective buyer may make a token advance payment to a seller in anticipation of a contract. If for some reason the deal falls through, the seller would normally be under an obligation to return the money to the buyer even in the absence of a concluded contract. In private law these duties are called quasi-contracts and are imposed both by the provisions of the Indian Contract Act[30] as well as general common law principles.[31] Similar obligations are also imposed under public law and are manifested in the form of two different but related doctrines—legitimate expectation and estoppel. The source of these obligations can be traced to Article 14 as understood in its expansive and substantive sense and draws from the requirements of equity and the rule of law.

The rule of law requires the state as well as a private citizen to be placed on an equal footing. The government does not, so to say, get a free pass in its dealings with the common person. As far back as 1970, the Supreme Court stated, 'If our nascent democracy is to thrive, different standards of conduct for the people and the public bodies cannot ordinarily be permitted.'[32] Thus, the State could not simply resile from the promises and assurances made to private entities, which the private person would have relied on. This was contrary to a legitimate expectation that a citizen had that the State would act fairly with it. It was also iniquitous to permit the government to avoid their obligations when a private party would be held to their end of the bargain in similar circumstances. To use a term of art, the court ruled that the government would be estopped from acting contrary to the state of affairs held out by them to be true. Of course, a term of art can best be understood with reference to actual cases so it is to one such instance that we turn.

In an effort to encourage setting up more industries, the government of Uttar Pradesh offered entrepreneurs a three-year sales tax holiday. Relying on this assurance, a company, Motilal Padampat Industries (MP Industries), started to construct a plant for the manufacture of vanaspati. Unfortunately for MP Industries, during this period, the government had a rethink about the tax holiday and issued a circular stating that the benefit would not be extended to companies setting up hydrogenation plants for the manufacture of vanaspati. The company was understandably aggrieved by this decision and moved court. It argued that it had spent large sums of money to set up a factory on the assumption that the government would comply with the assurances made by it.

Under normal law of promissory estoppel, a person who had made a representation to someone else would be bound by it. However, the government argued that this principle would not apply to it because any promise, which was not reduced into a formal contract, could 'fetter its executive action'. This claim effectively implied that the government had the freedom not to honour any representation made by it. The sovereign government was supposed to be given the freedom to take any action that it considered fit regardless of its prior conduct. As per the government, it did not matter that MP Industries had spent money based on the promises made by it.

The court strongly rejected this attempted governmental exceptionalism.[33] The court asked whether the government could 'say that it is under no obligation to act in a manner that is fair and just or that it is not bound by considerations of "honesty and good faith"? Why should the Government not be held to a high "standard of rectangular rectitude while dealing with its citizens?" There was a time when the doctrine of executive necessity was regarded as sufficient justification for the Government to repudiate even its contractual obligations ; but, let it be said to the eternal glory of this Court, this doctrine was emphatically negatived in the Indo-Afghan Agencies case[34] and the supremacy of the rule of law was established'. [35] With this pat on its own back, the court directed that the state government could not ask for the sales tax demanded by it contrary to the assurance made by it. The State and the citizen were to be place on an equal pedestal and the same equity, justice and good faith conduct that was demanded of private parties would be demanded of the State as well.[36]

If the doctrine of promissory estoppel is based upon equity, the principle of legitimate expectation can be said to be based on the idea of the rule of law. While the case law had moved towards equating the rule of law and equality by the 1970s, one manifestation of this linking was settled much later in a case relating to tenders. The Food Corporation of India (FCI) invited tenders to sell its stocks of damaged food grains. One bidder, Kamdhenu Cattle Feed Industries, submitted the highest bid and thus expected that it would be awarded the tender. However, the FCI felt that the bids were all very low. Consequently, rather than awarding the tender to the highest bidder, the FCI called all the parties for negotiations and awarded the contract to the person who had increased his offer above the price that had been offered by Kamdhenu. When the matter reached the court, Kamdhenu argued that the decision to negotiate with parties, even while its offer was under consideration, was arbitrary and contrary to the rule of law.

In its judgment, the Supreme Court held that no public authority had any unfettered discretion and that all decisions by government authorities were required to be taken only for the public good. The mandate against arbitrariness contained in Article 14 raised 'a reasonable or legitimate expectation in every citizen to be treated fairly in his interaction with the State and its instrumentalities, with this element forming a necessary component of the decision-making process in all State actions'.[37] Thus was born the rule of 'legitimate expectation' which has since been applied consistently by the courts.[38] The doctrine states that if the State deals with a citizen in a particular manner for a long period, thereby giving rise to the expectation that the same course of action will be followed even in the future, it will not be allowed to act differently without taking into account the 'legitimate expectation' that the person has that the normal course of conduct would carry on being followed. This doctrine of legitimate expectation is derived from the rule of law which requires 'required regularity, predictability and certainty in government dealings with the public, operating on procedural and substantive matters'.[39]

Fairness and Natural Justice

These principles of equity and the rule of law are not independent concepts but are part of the concept of reasonableness and non-arbitrariness which run through the whole fabric of the Constitution like a golden thread.[40] However, a decision can be unfair in two separate senses. First, the outcome of the decision may be unfair to any person. On the other hand, the way a person or her grievance is dealt with, can also be unfair. Thus, a decision taken behind ones back without any notice or hearing would immediately raise the hackles of the person whose fate is sealed. This is an instance of procedural unfairness or, to use a term used often by courts, a violation of natural justice. The rule of law requires, amongst other things, compliance with basic principles of procedure which inspires confidence in litigants that their cases are fairly dealt with.

In the early jurisprudence of the court, the principles of natural justice were seen as part of the common law,[41] in particular the rules of administrative law. Following English jurisprudence, a set of rules were developed by the courts which were expected to be obeyed by authorities. There were two rules in particular that embodied a commitment to compliance with the requirements of natural justice. These were the rules of *nemo judex in cause sua*[42] and *audi alteram partem*.[43] To put it more comprehensibly, these were the rules against bias and the requirement of hearing all parties before passing a decision. To this was added a third rule, one that required authorities to give reasons for their decisions[44] when they were exercising quasi-judicial functions.[45]

Over time, the courts ruled that the basis of these principles of natural justice was not only in the rules of common law but flowed from various Constitutional provisions, in particular the right to equality. In the Maneka Gandhi case, which has been discussed in the chapter dealing on the Rule of Law, a seven-judge bench of the Supreme Court held that the principles of natural justice arose out of the requirements of Article 14.

This general proposition of equating natural justice and the right to equality has been invoked often by businesses when they challenge government actions. This is partly because courts are reticent to intervene in matters of economic policy. However, the same courts have a different approach when it comes to allegations of violation of the principles of natural justice. There the courts hold the government to a strict standard. Thus, if any decision is taken by the government without hearing a party, the courts do not hesitate in striking down such actions.

One instance where this absence of judicial restraint is seen most often is in the case of blacklisting. This is a concept where the government can disqualify an entity from participating in tenders and other government contracts on account of previous conduct. Therefore, if a business has been found to have indulged in misdemeanours in the performance of a contract, the government can impose a penalty by disallowing that business from entering into any government contracts for a certain period. However, this blacklisting can only happen if the affected party is given a show cause notice and is heard before the order is passed. If the business is not heard before the order, such an order is almost inevitably set aside. The rationale for this, and the link with equality, has been explained in one of first cases which laid down this principle. In Erusian Equipment and Chemicals v. The State of West Bengal,[46] the Supreme Court ruled that:

> A citizen has a right to claim equal treatment to enter into a contract which may be proper, necessary and essential to his lawful calling . . . The activities of the Government have a public element and, therefore, there should be fairness and equality. The State need not enter into any contract with any one but if it does so, it must do so fairly without discrimination and without unfair procedure. . . . Exclusion of a member of the public from dealing with a State in sales transactions has the effect of preventing him from purchasing and doing a lawful trade in the goods in discriminating against him in favour of other people. Where the State is dealing with individuals in transactions of sales and purchase of goods, the two important factors are that an individual is entitled to trade with the Government and an individual is entitled to a fair and equal treatment with others. A duty to act fairly can be interpreted as

meaning a duty to observe certain aspects of rules of natural justice.

The rather lengthy extract from the judgment clearly explains the entire basis on which the right to equality has infiltrated commercial jurisprudence in matters of State contracts. When the State enters into a contract, it cannot exclude any person arbitrarily. This is a corollary of every person's right to be dealt equally by the State. Once this right to be dealt with fairly is established, all the requirements of what fair dealing requires, are also attracted. Since natural justice is part of the principles of fairness, each business has a right to compliance with these principles.

While the proposition sounds relatively simple, the jurisprudence in these matters is complex and often contradictory. While blacklisting usually entails a hearing, the form and content of the hearing is relatively unclear. In some cases, no hearing is required while in other cases a post decisional hearing (i.e., a hearing after the event) is sufficient. In some cases oral hearing is mandated while in other cases a written representation suffices. Some academics have put this confusion down to the fact that the principles of administrative law review and Constitutional law review have been conflated.[47] While that might be true, it is today a judicial dogma that the principles of natural justice flow from the chapter on fundamental rights of the Constitution.

Substantive Challenges—Legislation and Economic Policy

The State acts in two capacities when dealing with businesses. First, it engages in the conduct of business as a participant itself. The law discussed thus far related to the process of contract formation and execution when the State is directly dealing with a business. There is a second role to be played by the State. As a regulator and a law maker/enforcer, the State establishes rules and standards for businesses to comply with. Through legislation and executive action, the State is also a facilitator, regulator, and enabler. In its capacity as a regulator or an administrator, the State makes economic policies and regulations. In exercise of its legislative power, the State enacts laws which govern the commercial and financial world. The actions of the State in both these areas is subject to judicial scrutiny, which includes an examination as to whether the actions are in accord with the mandate of Article 14 of the Constitution.

While these actions are subject to judicial review, courts have generally deferred to the discretion of the government. This principle was most famously enunciated in what is known as the bearer bonds case. In the 1980s, the economy of the country was stagnant. There was a large parallel economy where black money was circulating. This black money was a largely unproductive asset as it could not be openly used for investments. In an effort to bring this tainted money into the formal economy, the government enacted a piece of legislation titled the Special Bearer Bonds (Immunities and Exemptions) Act, 1981. Under this Act, people could buy bearer bonds in cash which would carry a rate of 2 per cent simple interest redeemable after ten years. Thus, if a person was to buy a bond worth Rs 10,000 in 1981, she could redeem it for Rs 12,000 in 1991. The Act also provided immunity to the holder of the bearer bond from explaining the source of the money used to purchase the bonds. These bonds would also not be counted towards computation of wealth tax of the holder. Effectively, this was a scheme to convert black money into white money, which could then be used productively by the government to finance its deficits or for some other expenditure.

The problem lay with the benefits that the Act gave to the holders of black money, as compared to honest taxpayers who did not have such cash. The highest rate of tax during that period was around 77 per cent. A person who paid taxes honestly would be left with only 23 per cent of their income. If the money was invested in the bearer bonds, the tax paying individual would get none of the advantages that a person who had bought the bonds with black money would have had. It was argued that this amounted to hostile discrimination between honest taxpayers and tax evaders.

The majority of the court (by a four to one verdict) rejected this challenge.[48] They noticed that no sensible person who had white money would purchase the bonds which offered a measly return of 2 per cent per annum and that too after ten years. The scheme, in the view of the court, was purely one for the benefit of black money holders and there was thus a reasonable classification between the two groups. The court also held that this classification had a rational nexus with the object of the Act which was to bring black money into the formal economy.

This was an application of the well-established two-pronged test in cases of alleged violations of Article 14. However, more than the actual application of the test, the case really turned-on judicial attitudes towards matters of finance and the economy. Relying on a batch of American cases,[49] the court held that in matters of economic policy, the courts had to give the legislature the freedom to choose the course of action it thought best to follow. The judges ruled that 'the Court must defer to legislative judgment in matters relating to social and economic policies and must not interfere, unless the exercise of legislative judgment appears to be palpably arbitrary'. When it came to classification, the courts clearly stated that they would permit unequal treatment to a large extent. Interestingly, the court also noted that the immunities given to holders of black money may have been immoral. However, this was not a ground to strike down the Act because 'immorality by itself is not a ground of constitutional challenge and it obviously cannot be, because morality is essentially a subjective value, except insofar as it may be reflected in any provision of the Constitution or may have crystallised into some well-accepted norm of social behaviour'.[50] This implied that mere unequal treatment of people was not by itself immoral. In matters of economics, it was pragmatism that was more important than some form of 'fair' treatment of persons.

This policy of deference has been followed by the courts in multiple areas. From taxation[51] to decisions to disinvest,[52] judges have ruled that they do not have the expertise or the jurisdiction to decide on matters of economic policy. Unfortunately, there is no consistent application of this doctrine of judicial restraint. For instance, in many cases the Court has stopped development of infrastructure projects, which can have a beneficial economic potential, on the grounds of an adverse environmental impact.[53] Thus, as in the case of the case law in the United States, it can be said that even in India 'the most arrogant legal scholar would not claim that all of these cases applied a uniform or consistent test under equal protection principles'.[54]

Conclusion

The evolution of the equality code as a tool to further business interests has had a chequered history. While during the initial years of the republic it was the common citizen who approached the courts seeking enforcement of fundamental rights, this situation changed over time. An increasing number of corporations and businessmen began to file cases seeking to protect their business interests. The courts initially gave a wide berth to the government to conduct its business with a hands-off approach to how the government conducted its affairs. However, this changed in the seventies with the expansion of the view of what equality implied, in particular the idea that all government action should be reasonable, and that any arbitrary decision would automatically imply a violation of Article 14. Using this new stream of judicial thought, the courts began to hold the government to a higher standard of conduct than other private entities. Over time, the courts retreated, in practice if not in theory, from holding the government to account. This flip-flop has led to some amount of ambiguity in the law.

This judicial inconsistency is also the result of a polyvocal court, i.e., a court that speaks in multiple voices. The Supreme Court, with a total strength of thirty-four judges, sits in multiple benches of two, three or higher bench strengths. Given the workload and the pressure to dispose of pending cases, inadequate attention is paid to judicial consistency. Further, given the absence of appeals, judges also feel free to rule as per their own ideological considerations rather than being bound by judicial discipline. In a recent judgment of the court, without any sense of apparent irony, one judge stated that he was aware of the 'ordeals that arise from a multiplicity of judicial opinions' and yet felt compelled to deliver a separate judgment because 'it was reflective of the diversity of judicial thought'.[55]

This desire to pen judgments has led to unpredictability in commercial jurisprudence generally and in matters relating to the interaction between the law on inequality and government action particularly. Needless to say, one of the greatest needs of businesses is certainty.[56] Faced with an unpredictable legal regime, businesses have a difficult time to organize their affairs and plan for the future. To compound the problem, unscrupulous litigants take advantage of the endemic delays in the legal system by filing cases and securing a stay. The Supreme Court has frowned upon granting interim injunctions pointing out the adverse impact such orders have on the public exchequer. Perhaps what is needed is for the judiciary to introspect and ensure mechanisms whereby wildly different results do not ensue in similarly placed cases. While judgments of the courts cannot, by definition, violate Article 14,[57] contradictory verdicts foster a sense of arbitrariness. It is important to remember that a polyvocal court which creates uncertainty in the law is less a symphony and more a cacophony.

This discordance might be partly a result of the fact that the Constitution at times seems to be ambivalent towards business. The original text of the Constitution guaranteed the fundamental right to property as well as the right to do business. Yet, the directive principles of state policy exhort the State to ensure that the economic system of the country should be to serve the common good. Over time, the right to property was deleted and the word socialism was inserted in the preamble, cementing a distinctly leftward lurch. However, even though the right to do business seems to have weakened over the years, the animal spirits of the economy as well as the innovative thinking of lawyers and judges have ensured that the Constitution is used to promote free enterprise. As the chapter has shown, a novel interpretation of Article 14 of the Constitution has been used to demand accountability from the government. By repudiating arbitrariness and demanding fairness, the courts have at the least sought to infuse a degree of predictability in business. Unfortunately, the courts' own doctrinal ambivalence has often caused as much uncertainty as government action.

6

Democracy

One of the most hotly contested elections for President of the United States of America was held in the year 2000. The former vice-president and climate change activist Al Gore was standing against George Bush in what turned out to be one of the closest elections in history. The results came down to the wire with the final verdict depending on the outcome of the vote in Florida. The matter also reached the Supreme Court of the United States whose decision in favour of George Bush finally swung the decision in his favour.[1] Lost in the nail-biting drama was the fact that Gore actually secured almost half a million more votes than his competitor and yet lost the presidency.[2] It would seem that the electoral process was designed in a way that the vote of an Al Gore voter was worth less than a George Bush voter, surely an anomaly in an electoral democracy. If all persons are equal under the law, is it not essential that the worth of each vote should be the same?

This is a question that is often overlooked in most texts about equality.

When one speaks of equality under the Constitution, the immediate thought, at least for most lawyers, is of Article 14. However, that provision, powerful as it is, is not the only place where the goal of egalitarianism is located. This ideal runs like a golden thread through the entire text of the Constitution. Both the right to equality and its enforcement have multiple loci in the form of different Constitutional provisions. Fundamental rights enforced by an unelected court provides a mechanism to secure equality for citizens.[3] But another way to ensure equality is through a political process. Regular elections entitle the majority to elect a government which would presumably strive to provide equality and fairness for its electorate.[4] While not perfect, democracy is a means through which the preambular goal of 'equality of status and opportunity' could be achieved. Indeed, given the limited jurisdiction and expertise of the courts, it is likely that most social and economic interventions to make the country a more equal place would happen through a political process.[5]

Since elections have a significant role in ensuring equality, it is doubly important that the vote of each elector must count for the same. However, this may not always be the case. Given the fact that our law recognizes the right of every adult to vote, ostensibly each voter has the same right as any other voter. However, like a lot of things in the law, the devil lies in the details. For instance, a voter in a constituency comprising only ten other voters has far greater influence than a voter belonging to a constituency where there are a million voters. The two voters would have the same right to vote, but the electoral impact of their vote is completely unequal. Thus, the way a constituency is drawn up can vitally affect the worth of each vote. It is in this sense that two voters can be unequal even though they have the same right to vote.

This is not to say that there is no other way by which voting can be an unequal experience. Access to adequate information to decide the better candidate, the privilege of being able to take time off to actually cast one's ballot, and the ability to obtain identity documents mandatory for voting, are just a few ways that a voter may be placed at a disadvantage while voting. These are structural disadvantages that may be because of the socio-political and economic situation of particular voters. However, the scope of this chapter is to examine the legal provisions which regulate voting and the larger electoral system. In particular, the three fundamental aspects of elections need to be examined—the voter, the candidate and the constituencies. The concerns of equality colour each of these facets. While there is a common goal at stake, the way the different issues manifest themselves shows the diversity of how the right to equality makes claims on the democratic process.

Voting in Equality

The first way that an individual can be guaranteed equality in voting is through the mechanism of the universal adult franchise. The ability to vote is so commonplace today that it is difficult to remember that it was a hard-fought battle to achieve. During the British Raj, the already limited democratic participation of citizens was heavily circumscribed by stringent property and educational thresholds. It is estimated that under the Government of India Act, 1919, only 2.8 per cent of the population was entitled to vote. This figure went up under the Government of India Act, 1935, but was still limited to about 30 million, i.e., about one-fifth of the total population of British India.[6]

At the time of Independence the decision about how far to extend the vote lay with the Constituent Assembly. That body had been indirectly elected by members of the provincial assemblies who in turn had been elected by a limited electorate. Though generally representative of the population of the country, the assembly also suffered from a formal democratic deficit. Fortunately, or possibly to mitigate that impression, the assembly decided not to have any restrictions on voting relating to gender, wealth, or education. Indeed, there was an initial consensus in the Constituent assembly that the right to vote should be a fundamental right. K.M. Munshi drafted an article guaranteeing that, 'Every citizen has the right to choose the Government and the legislators of the Union and his State on the footing of equality in accordance with the law of the Union or the unit, as the case may be, in free, secret and periodic elections.'[7] This was duly approved by the Fundamental Rights sub-committee which was of the view that Universal Adult Franchise should be made a fundamental right for each citizen.[8] However, during the course of further deliberation, particularly in the face of opposition by C. Rajagopalachari the then Governor General,[9] the right to vote was moved from the fundamental rights chapter[10] to another place in the Constitution—Article 326. This Article states that 'the elections to the House of the People and to the Legislative Assembly of every State shall be on the basis of adult suffrage; that is to say, every person who is a citizen of India . . . shall be entitled to be registered as a voter at any such election'.

This right to vote given to all persons was progressive for its time[11] and epitomised the faith in the ideal of equality which was held by the members of the assembly. Even though there was fear that a largely illiterate electorate would not be able to cast their ballot with the sagacity deemed necessary for a voter,[12] the assembly voted to enshrine the right in the Constitution. Each citizen of India was now equal when it came to electing their representatives to the highest decision-making bodies of the country.

Over time, this commitment to electoral equality has strengthened. The idea of being a voter is central in the consciousness of the average Indian citizen.[13] However, universal adult franchise does not automatically guarantee the equality of voting. The method of election to the Lok Sabha and the state assemblies is through the 'first past the post' system. Under this system, whichever person secures more votes than other candidates is declared elected. A person may be elected if she has secured a minority of the total votes cast. It is a case of a 'winner takes it all' where the elector voting for the winning candidate gets an outsized say while those who voted for a losing candidate are effectively unrepresented in Parliament. Their votes are, to use a term that has also become common in the public imagination, wasted.

While seemingly fair, the very system of first-past-the-post appears to condone a possible violation of equality. Even though there is a formal equality of all to vote, there is no equality of representation. The voter opting for the losing candidate will not have her vote count for anything. The problem becomes even more acute because elections are held at five-year intervals. So, a voter who voted against the winning candidate is effectively ousted from having even an indirect say in Parliament for a long period of time.

In opposition to this system is the method of election through proportional representation. The aim of such a mechanism is to ensure that each voting group gets represented in Parliament. While such a system does not provide an absolute guarantee of equality,[14] it is generally considered to result in a more representative assembly.[15]

It is not as though this manner of voting is totally alien to the Constitution. Elections to the Rajya Sabha are held through this system. Article 80 (4) of the Constitution provides that 'the representatives of each State in the council of States shall be elected by the elected members of the Legislative Assembly of the State in accordance with the system of proportional representation by means of the single transferable vote'. Under this system, each voter has to rank the candidates in order of voting preference. A threshold number of votes to be secured by any successful candidate is then determined. Initially, all first preference votes are counted and the candidate who secures the threshold number of votes is declared elected. Thereafter, any additional votes secured by the elected candidate are 'transferred' in order of preference to the other candidates. The aim of this system, as pointed out by the Supreme Court, is that 'The system of voting by secret ballot on the system of proportional representation by means of the single transferable vote is adopted from the Constitution of Eire. The object of introducing proportional representation in these elections is to give each minority group an effective share as per its strength . . . Each elector has only one vote in the sense that it will be capable of electing one candidate only. But that vote will not be wasted in case the candidate whom he wishes to elect has got more than the required number of votes.'[16]

However, this mechanism has not been adopted when it comes to elections for the Lok Sabha and the legislative assemblies of the states. As a consequence, an electoral system has come into effect where it is quite common that a large number of voters have no representation of their views in the bodies that are said to govern in their name. On the opposite side of the spectrum, some voters are privileged and have an outsized say in the election. Elected representatives who are beholden only to those who voted for them can take decisions in complete violation of the wishes of the actual majority—hardly a just outcome.[17] This impacts not only on the rights of the voters, but also on the candidates being elected. For instance, the minority community of Muslims regularly get fewer representatives in Parliament or the assemblies then their numerical strength in various states would suggest.[18] Voters (or candidates), it seems, are not equal when it comes to being represented in Parliament.

The impact on equality by such a voting mechanism is immediately apparent. This fact was not lost on members of the Assembly. In particular, the link between equality, protection of minority rights, and proportional representation was recognised during the assembly debates.[19] The Muslim League mooted elections through proportional representation and was supported by Muslim members of the Constituent Assembly.[20] Kazi Syed Karimuddin argued that the 'system is also profoundly democratic for it increases the influence of thousands of those who would have no voice in the Government and it brings men more near an equality by so contriving that no vote shall be wasted and that every voter shall contribute to bring into Parliament a member of his own choice and opinion'. Even members from the majority community supported proportional representation as a means to elect MPs to the Lok Sabha.[21] One intended effect of the system of proportional representation was to reconcile the requirements of equality with the protection of communal and political minorities.[22] However, Dr Ambedkar opposed the proposal on the ground that it pre-supposed a degree of literacy where a voter would be required to mark the ballot paper in order of some preference. Given the low level of literacy in India at the time of Independence, Dr Ambedkar was not in favour of proportional representation.[23] This was also the view of the majority of the Constituent Assembly and accordingly the amendment seeking to replace the first past the post system was rejected.

In 2000, the National Democratic Alliance government appointed a committee headed by a former Chief Justice of India to examine how the Constitution was working and to suggest changes for improvement in certain areas. The report of the committee noted that given the multiplicity of political parties and the fractured political mandate, multiple candidates were elected with a minority of the votes. Such a situation challenged 'representational legitimacy' but felt unable to recommend any change from the existing system.[24]

As a consequence, the electoral imbalance continues[25]. For instance, in the 17th Lok Sabha, only twenty-six MPs were Muslim, half of who came from two states (Uttar Pradesh and West Bengal). This amounts to 4.8 per cent of the total MPs. Christian and Sikh MPs constituted a further

4 per cent of Parliament.[26] This is a severe underrepresentation of the minority community since Muslims constitute about 14.2 per cent of the population of the country.[27] Therefore, Muslims get only about a third of the number of seats than their numerical strength would suggest. While there can be no guarantee of an exact correlation between population and representation, such a dramatic difference shows that there is a case of voter inequality.

In a country with several minority groups, it is possible that their numbers may never reach the critical amount to be able to win elections. Such a community could end up being completely unrepresented in the legislature. This lack of representation is a direct violation of the precept of equality. While this problem was not addressed in the case of religious minorities, the members of the Constituent Assembly came up with another method to remedy this denial of representation for members of the scheduled castes and tribes. Rather than suggesting a proportional system of representation, the solution offered was slightly different—a provision for reservation of seats as a temporary measure.

Constituencies: Reservation and Composition

The reservation of seats in Parliament has deep historical roots. As far back as 1906, a delegation of Indian Muslims led by the Aga Khan met the Viceroy Lord Minto to demand that there be separate electorates for Muslims. This suggestion was readily accepted and the Indian Councils Act, 1909 provided for communal electorates. In this system only Muslims were allowed to vote for separate candidates in larger constituencies while also retaining the vote for the general candidates in the regular constituencies. This was the so-called double vote system and was encoded under the provisions of the Government of India Act, 1935. This legislation, based on the so-called communal award, provided for reservations to Muslims, Europeans, Sikhs, Indian Christians and Anglo-Indians, and reserved seats for Marathas in certain general constituencies in Bombay.[28]

As discussed in the earlier chapters of the book historically there was an apparent, if grudging, acceptance of reservations for members of minority religions,[29] but there was a reluctance to afford a separate electorate to the depressed castes. Paradoxically, when it came to the drafting of the Constitution, the situation was reversed. With the Partition of the country and the riots and mass migration that followed, there was a demand for constructing the identity of the Indian citizen as one who owed allegiance to the country rather than any particular religion. In this atmosphere, there was really no room for separate electorates or reserved seats for Muslims or any other religious minority.[30] Thus, the drafting committee of the Constitution recommended that there ought to be no special reservations or privileges for religious minorities. This report was placed before the Constituent Assembly and was duly adopted by it.[31]

In the case of the scheduled castes however, Dr Ambedkar and other members of the Constituent Assembly were firmer. The advisory committee of the Constituent Assembly recommended the reservation of seats for members of the scheduled castes and tribes in proportion to their population. This proposal was finally adopted by the Assembly and reserved seats found their place in Article 330 and 332 of the Constitution. The text of the Constitution required that number of reserved seats shall bear 'as nearly as may be, the same proportion to the total number of seats allotted to that State or Union territory in the House of the People as the population of the scheduled castes . . . or of the scheduled tribes in the state or Union territory . . . in respect of which seats are so reserved, bears to the total population of the state or Union territory'. In other words, if 20 per cent of the population of a state constituted scheduled castes and that state had fifty Members of Parliament in the Lok Sabha, the total number of reserved seats would be 20 per cent of fifty, i.e., a total of ten seats.

This proportionate representation is nothing but a strong form of substantive equality. It is an equality of outcomes rather than an equality of opportunities. The Supreme Court has held that these provisions confer a positive Constitutional right to have a proportional extent of reservation in Parliament holding that 'having regard to the Constitutional obligations, as contained in Articles 332, 330 and 243-D of the Constitution of India, the scheduled tribes have a right to be represented in proportion to their numbers in the different constituencies in the state'.[32]

Even though reservations were provided for, there was unease among the members of the Constituent Assembly about its extent. To assuage these concerns, the Constitution provided for a sunset clause in matters of reservations of seats. This was even as some members felt there was no need for reservations to end.[33] Article 334 provided that the reservations to the Lok Sabha and the state legislatures would only operate for a period of ten years after its promulgation. This expiration date was however repeatedly extended by Constitutional amendments. Just before the period contemplated by the Constitution was about to expire, the Constitution (Eighth Amendment) Act of 1959, was enacted. The provision in the Constitution was amended for the first time by substituting the words 'ten years' with 'twenty years' in Article 334. After this amendment, the floodgates appear to have been opened and the period for reservations were constantly extended.[34] The last such amendment was in 2019 when the 104th Amendment Act extended reservations till the year 2030. Therefore as of today, of the 543 seats in the Lok Sabha, 412 are general category, eighty-four seats are reserved for scheduled castes and forty-seven seats for the scheduled tribes.[35]

As a result of these amendments, a temporary provision in the Constitution appears to have become its permanent feature. Furthermore, the reserved seats are not changed at each election. Once designated a reserved seat, it remained that way. As a consequence, no general category candidate could contest from reserved seats as long as they were reserved. Equally, no voter in such a constituency had the possibility of voting for a non-scheduled caste candidate. As is so often the case, a system devised to ensure equality to one section of society potentially takes away the right to equality for another group. Alleging such that such a form of reservations violates the equality clause of the Constitution, a writ petition has been filed in the Supreme Court challenging the Constitutional amendments. The outcome of the case is still awaited and would probably significantly influence the jurisprudence in relation to the interplay between seat reservations and equality.[36]

Another area where the judgment would have a potential impact would on the reservation of seats for women. There has been a dismal representation of women in all levels of representative bodies. To remedy that, Parliament first provided for reservations in favour of women in Panchayati Raj institutions.[37] However, even though there appears to have been significant empowerment of women in institutions of local governance, the same does not appear to have translated to the Union and state legislatures.[38] To remedy this lack of representation, there had been a long-drawn battle seeking to reserve seats for women in the Lok Sabha and the state Assembly. A Constitutional amendment to this effect was passed by a near-unanimous Parliament in the form of the 128th Amendment Act called the Nari Shakti Vandan Adhiniyam. The amendment seeks to reserve, as nearly as may be, one third of the total seats in the Lok Sabha and legislative Assemblies for women. Though the bill has been criticized because of several conditionalities,[39] it is certainly a step forward in ensuring representation of women in the highest echelons of government.

These forms of reservation aim to ensure equality in the electoral field. The aim is that the composition of the assemblies would closely resemble the makeup of the general population. In this manner it is hoped that oppressed communities would have their voices heard in Parliament. Other than the symbolic fact of representation, an even distribution also goes a long way in ensuring equality and social justice for those communities.

Gerrymandering

Paradoxically, the process of having reserved constituencies to promote equality can be turned on its head to perpetuate inequality. After all, a reserved seat amounts to negating the right of a non-scheduled caste candidate to stand for elections or restricting the right of a voter of a general category caste. There is another way that the inequality can be perpetuated; drawing up the boundaries of constituencies result in disenfranchising certain communities. This is through the process of gerrymandering, a particularly insidious practice where the worth of a vote is altered by the inclusion (or exclusion) of certain areas as to affect the outcome of elections there.

The term gerrymandering has been used extensively in American jurisprudence and it is to the judgments in that country that one can turn to for understanding the nature of the problem. The term originated when the governor of Massachusetts Elbert Gerry drew up a constituency which was so convoluted in shape that its map looked like a salamander. The opposition, playing on the governor's name, mockingly called it the 'Gerry'mander.[40] Thus began a long series of cases where politicians sought to redraw maps of various districts with the opposition (or voters) petitioning courts against such an effort.

In the US, the initial challenges which successfully challenged gerrymandering were in relation to the exclusion of voters on the grounds of race. This would typically happen by drawing up constituencies where certain races would be deliberately put in a minority so as to lessen their voting power. For instance, Black voters could be artificially squeezed into a virtually Black majority district so that the rest of the Black voters in the state would be thinly spread across White majority constituencies. Thus, even though there might have been enough Black voters to be in a majority in more than one seat in the state, their numbers would be artificially reduced in all but one constituency so as to render them a minority. This kind of ouster would violate the 'one person one vote' rule that ensures voter equality and would thus be liable to be struck down.[41] US courts have looked at this form of gerrymandering with suspicion as it violates the equal protection clause of the Constitution. In one case, the court noted the problem of gerrymandering on account of race by pointing out that 'by perpetuating stereotypical notions about members of the same racial group—that they think alike, share the same political interests, and prefer the same candidates—a racial gerrymander may exacerbate the very patterns of racial bloc voting that majority minority districting is sometimes said to counteract. It also sends to elected representatives the message that their primary obligation is to represent only that group's members, rather than their constituency as a whole'.[42] This reasoning would of course also apply to constituencies reserved for a particular class, but the Indian Constitution permits this so there is little scope for the courts to interfere.

However, in matters relating to 'partisan gerrymandering', the American courts have been reluctant to intervene. These are cases where the boundaries of the constituencies are drawn not to disempower certain races but to promote, or suppress, the chances of any particular party (in the US context the Republican or the Democratic Party) being elected from that constituency. The court has ruled that this is an inherently a political question and not one that is amenable to judicial scrutiny.[43]

So, does gerrymandering really happen in India? There is ample evidence that it does. As far back as 1970, the ruling party in the state of Rajasthan sought to redraw districts for elections to the local bodies. The matter reached the Supreme Court which held that there had indeed been a case of gerrymandering. The court held that 'As is well known, "gerrymander" is an American expression which has taken root in the English language, meaning to arrange election districts so as to give an unfair advantage to the party in power by means of a redistribution act or to manipulate constituencies generally. The whole purpose of delimitation . . . is to ensure that every citizen should get a fair representation . . . . The result of any election under a majority system depends in fact not only on the way people vote but on the way their votes are distributed among the constituencies. It was therefore impermissible for the State Government to redistribute the constituencies . . . so as to give an unfair advantage to the party in power . . .'[44]

This case shows that gerrymandering in India occurred even in the 1970s.[45] The same trend continues today. An analysis of the electoral map of the country shows that the contours of multiple constituencies are fantastically convoluted.[46] This is prima facie evidence of gerrymandering because in normal circumstances there is no reason not to divide constituencies in roughly the same shape, of course after accounting for state borders or other natural features. As per this analysis, the most gerrymandered state in India is Assam, while the least is Madhya Pradesh. One reason for the shapes of the constituencies could be purely unintentional. This is because the constituencies are drawn up from multiple wards at the municipal level.[47] When they are put together on a larger scale to form the constituency at the level of the Assembly, it may be difficult to have mathematically precise shapes.

In other instances, there are accusations that this is not an innocent coincidence. Recently, allegations of deliberate mala fide gerrymandering have been levelled in the case of Jammu and Kashmir[48] and Assam.[49] In both cases, the allegation is that there is an attempt to reduce the voting power of the Muslims in that area, an allegation denied by the government. Whatever may be the motivating factor for this exercise, in the face of allegations of gerrymandering, the Indian Courts have adopted a policy of restraint. This is partly because in India, the act of drawing the electoral map is not done by the party in power but by an ostensibly independent body, the Delimitation Commission.

The Delimitation Commission is an expert body which is set up under an Act of Parliament and is headed by a retired judge of the Supreme Court.[50] The commission is specifically tasked with the duty to fix or limit the boundaries of territorial constituencies for the purpose of elections to the Lok Sabha and the legislative assemblies of the states. The delimitation exercise is usually done on the basis of data collected in the latest available census. The drafters of the Constitution specifically excluded the exercise of delimitation from the judicial review of the courts. Therefore, Article 329 (a) of the Constitution provides that 'Notwithstanding anything in this Constitution . . . the validity of any law relating to the delimitation of constituencies or the allotment of seats to such constituencies, made or purporting to be made under Article 327 or Article 328, shall not be called in question in any court.'

Relying on this exclusion, the Supreme Court has ruled that the delimitation exercise, at least for the Lok Sabha and the Assemblies, carries immunity and cannot be challenged in court, even if it is palpably arbitrary.[51] Therefore, the jurisprudence of the form that has developed in the US has not really been seen in India. The only exercise that the court undertakes in such a case is to examine whether the prescribed procedure has been followed in a case.

One Size Does Not Fit All

Even where there is no deliberate attempt to lessen the worth of a vote through the drawing of electoral boundaries, there can be inequality in the allocation of the number of constituencies to a particular state. This is because, as noted in the introduction, the value of a vote in a constituency with very few other voters is far greater than that in one with a very large number of voters. Generally speaking, the population of a state should be evenly divided across all the constituencies in that state. Equally, the number of seats allocated to a state should be roughly proportional to the population of that state to the total population of the country. The idea is that the vote of an elector in one constituency should not be worth more or less than that of a voter in another.

Thus the general aim of mapping constituencies is to ensure equality of voting power. When the Constitution was being drafted, there was a fair bit of discussion in this regard. The Union Constitution Committee[52] and other members of the Assembly decided that as far as the Lok Sabha was concerned, any member of Parliament would represent roughly the same number of voters across constituencies. This idea was incorporated into Article 81 of the Constitution which provided that the constituencies were to be drawn up so that there was 'not less than one member for every 750,000 of the population'. However, soon after the promulgation of the Constitution, this cap was deleted by the Constitution (Second Amendment) Act, 1952. Thus was born the possibility of having constituencies with voters in excess of 7,50,000 people. In the first elections to the Lok Sabha held in in 1952, an average MP represented about

4.32 lakh eligible voters. When elections took place in 2019, the average member of the Lok Sabha represented nearly 1.5 million voters, nearly double the maximum envisaged number originally in the Constitution.

When considering the number of seats to comprise the Rajya Sabha, the Union Constitution Committee initially decided that the number of seats would be no more than 40 per cent of the total seats of the Lok Sabha. However, this proviso was dropped by the drafters and a rough rule of thumb was adopted. One seat would be given to each state with a population between one million to five million. Thereafter, an extra seat would be given for each additional population of two million.[53] The number of seats would be roughly proportional to the population of a state, ensuring some form of equality of voting power to each citizen. Today each MP of Rajya Sabha represents on an average around 60 lakh citizens,[54] even though they are indirectly elected. This is the size of the population of many countries.[55]

While these huge numbers seem to undermine the idea of representative democracy, does it also constitute a violation of equality? By itself larger constituencies dilute the voting power of individual voters equally and there does not appear to be any violation of Article 14. However, over the course of time another source of inequality has emanated. This is not by the distribution of constituencies within a state but by the number of seats allotted to any state. In the initial years after Independence, the size of the constituencies was roughly the same. Over time, some states, particularly those in the south, had a lower rate of growth of population. Consequently, even though the number of constituencies remained fixed for each state, the number of voters per constituency started getting skewed. Normally, as per the mandate of Article 81(2) of the Constitution, the number of seats reserved for each state must be such that the ratio of the population to the number of seats is the same across the country. Therefore, in the case of a falling population, the number of seats reserved for that state ought to fall and correspondingly ought to increase for a state with a larger population.

Such a result would further the cause of equal representation but was seen as politically unpalatable. The states with a slow population growth argued that their success in family planning ought not to result in them getting less representation in Parliament. To address the concerns of these states, the Constitution was amended in 1976 and there was a freeze in altering the number of seats allotted to each state, regardless of the change in the population. This freeze has been extended from time to time and is now in place until 2026. As a consequence, a typical constituency in the Uttar Pradesh has more citizens than one in Kerala.[56] Consequently, a voter in UP can argue that this freeze has resulted in substantial dilution of voting power in comparison with a resident of Kerala. The voter would also argue that given the size of the constituency, there would be a high chance of there being a large number of people who vote for the losing candidate and would thus not have a say in Parliament. If delimitation is held after accounting for an increase of 33 per cent, pursuant to the Constitutional amendment giving reservations to women, the electoral map would be completely reconfigured. The seat for the states in the Hindi-speaking heartland would go up significantly while there would be only a meagre increase for those in the south. In such a case, states in the south would be reduced to a much smaller minority, possibly bringing into question the Constitutional compact at the time of Independence.

These discrepancies show that equality is just one additional consideration in a political compromise. There is a conflict between the claims of equality in representation and the fear of being overrun by a majority. While the status quo is in place, these issues have not yet been the subject matter of intense political debate in the public domain. How long this acquiescence lasts remains to be seen.

Candidates and Indirect Discrimination

Conflicting claims are not unusual in the area of equality, or indeed in many other rights-based claims under the Constitution. However, in the case of electoral democracy, these claims take on a greater hold in the public imagination precisely because politics is so important to the immediate lives of people. Thus far, this chapter has examined these issues in relation to the rights of a voters and in relation to drawing up of constituencies. There is another sphere where the exercise of political rights can come into conflict with claims of equality and that is the right to stand for elections as a candidate. One way to skew the electoral pitch is to make it difficult for some candidates to stand for election while making it easier for others.

A case that starkly brings out such potential is the judgment of the Supreme Court in Rajbala v. State of Haryana.[57] The case pertained to a law enacted by the legislature of Haryana which prescribed for certain disqualifications for candidates contesting for panchayat elections. In particular, the Haryana Panchayat Raj (Amendment) Act, 2015 stipulated that people who did not possess the specified educational qualification or did not have a functional toilet at their place of residence were not eligible to contest elections.[58]

This amendment was challenged before the courts arguing that the exclusion was arbitrary and violative of Article 14 of the Constitution. The petitioners urged that given the immense poverty in rural Haryana, these requirements excluded a large section of the population who would be unable to fulfil the stringent conditions. The argument in essence was that the classification between uneducated and educated persons, and those with or without toilets, had no connection with the object sought to be achieved by the Act. The purpose of the Act was to elect people's representatives to local bodies. Therefore, excluding a large number of poor people, who were the true reflection of the makeup of the rural population, was violative of the principles of equality and hence completely arbitrary.

The challenge was ultimately dismissed by the Supreme Court which upheld these amendments.[59] The court ruled that the classification on the grounds of education, financial health, and toilets in the house, was based on 'intelligible differentia'. In other words, these were grounds that were rational and well founded. In the case of educational qualifications, the court said that 'It is only education which gives a human being the power to discriminate between right and wrong, good and bad. Therefore, prescription of an educational qualification is not irrelevant for better administration of the panchayats.'[60] Similarly, the ground of disqualification for not having a functional toilet was explained by holding, 'If people still do not have a toilet it is not because of their poverty but because of their lacking the requisite will.'[61]

More importantly, faced with the possible exclusion of a huge class of people, the court adopted a problematic approach. In the view of the court, the fact that the number of excluded persons was large would make no difference to determine the Constitutionality of the scheme.[62] The court held that every person who did not have a toilet or education would be excluded. The application of the law was thus neutral—all persons who opted not to comply with the law would be excluded and those who made the effort to comply with the law would be permitted to stand for election. There was, on the face of it, no inequality of treatment by the state. However, such an argument misses the realpolitik of the situation. Such exclusions would apply disproportionately against poorer persons who would either not have the money or the social upbringing to value a toilet or perhaps even education. Thus the facially neutral measure would have a disproportionately adverse impact on poor individuals.[63] This form of discrimination has been recognised as indirect discrimination in jurisdictions across the world, and arguably even in Indian law.[64] However, the court does not seem to have applied its mind to this test, possibly because it held that arbitrariness was not a ground to test the validity of the statute. As it happens so often, the discrimination faced by the poor was hidden by Constitutional niceties.

The Citizenship Amendment Act

The exclusion of the poor from the political space is akin to the ouster of other historically oppressed communities, for instance on the grounds of race, caste, or religion.

In the case of the Haryana Act, a whole class of people belonging to the economically weaker section of society were disentitled to stand for elections. In another area, i.e. in the case of the Citizenship Amendment Act, 2019 ('CAA') certain groups within a larger group have been excluded from becoming citizens of India and therefore any voting rights or the right to stand for election.

There are multiple ways in which one can become a citizen of a country. One can be a citizen through birth, i.e., automatically acquiring the citizenship of the country where one is born.[65] Another way is to acquire citizenship through blood, i.e. by acquiring the nationality of one's parents or some defined ancestor.[66] The third common method is through naturalization, i.e. when the law of any country provides a method through which a person can become a citizen by making an application and fulfilling certain prescribed conditions. These could be the length of stay in a country[67] or after making a large investment[68] there.

The Citizenship Act, 1955 in India also provides for some of these methods for acquiring citizenship. However, by an amendment to the Foreigners Act, 1946 it was declared that children of illegal immigrants, i.e. persons who had entered India without valid documents, were not entitled to acquire citizenship through naturalization or registration. The ostensible motive of the amendment was to stem the perceived flow of illegal immigrants into India.[69] One consequence of this amendment was that refugees fleeing religious persecution in neighbouring countries were deemed ineligible from acquiring Indian citizenship. It was to remedy this perceived lacuna that the controversial CAA was enacted, to provide for an exception for a certain class of people. Specifically, the CAA permitted nationals of Afghanistan, Bangladesh or Pakistan to acquire Indian citizenship if they belonged to the Hindu, Sikh, Buddhist, Jain, Parsi or Christian community.[70] The government justified the amendment by pointing to the instances of members of religious minorities being discriminated against in the specified neighbouring countries. However, opponents of the amendment have argued that the CAA is unconstitutional and is violative of Article 14 of the Constitution.

As has been discussed earlier in the book, the law permits classification of people only if it is based in intelligible differentia which has a rational nexus with the object sought to be achieved by the law.[71] In the present case, the object of the Act was to come to the aid of people who were the victims of religious persecution in the country. A question which would therefore arise is whether the classification (i.e., inclusion of the specified countries and religions to the exclusion of others) would have any nexus with this object.

The critics of the CAA would argue that there is no such nexus. If the object is to ameliorate the effects of persecution, there is no reason to limit the religions and the countries as has been done by the amendment.[72] It can be argued that including only some religions for the purpose of the Act excludes members of other religions who also face religious persecution in their countries—for instance the Ahmadiyyas in Pakistan. There is also an exclusion of persons belonging to other neighbouring countries who also face persecution, for instance the Tamil community in Sri Lanka or the Rohingya Muslims in Myanmar.

Other than the accusation of direct discrimination, there is also a fear that permitting an exalted class of persons to become citizens ends up demeaning the status of persons who are not in that class, a problem compounded when reference is had to provisions of the Foreigners Act, 1946.[73] Thus, the effects of discrimination are not only direct, but also have a disparate impact on members of those communities who are not covered by the Act, for instance Indian Muslims.

On the other hand, the supporters of the CAA also marshal arguments in support of their claim that the Act is Constitutional. First, it can be pointed out that discrimination on the ground of religion, which is prohibited under Article 15 of the Constitution, does not apply to non-citizens. This is because the provisions of Article 15 apply only to citizens unlike the more general words of Article 14, which apply to all persons.[74] Second, it can be argued that even on the test of Article 14, the CAA passes Constitutional muster because that provision permits 'under-inclusion'. This is an well-settled concept in Constitutional law and states that 'a classification is bad as under-inclusive when a State benefits or burdens persons in a manner that furthers a legitimate purpose but does not confer the same benefit or place the same burden on others who are similarly situated'.[75] In such cases, the courts afford the legislature, a wide amplitude because 'the legislature is free to recognize degrees of harm and it may confine the restrictions to those classes of cases where the need seemed to be clearest'.[76]

The principle of law which permits under-inclusion in essence implies that not all persons who could potentially be covered by a legislation are necessarily required to be included in it. Therefore, just because Muslims or members of other religions or other countries could be included within the provisions of the CAA, it does not follow that the Act is unconstitutional. The State is permitted the freedom to extend the benefits of citizenship to those who it deems most urgently needs it. It is not the task of the court, as per this line of reasoning, to second guess the decisions that the elected representatives of the people have taken in this regard. This judicial deference to Parliamentary wisdom is even more pronounced in matters relating to the grant of citizenship since it part of the most basic and sovereign functions of government. The validity of the CAA has also reached the courts and it is only a matter of time before a decision on the Constitutionality of the Act is pronounced.[77]

Conclusion

Democracy is a system where the people have the final say in the decision-making process and is thus an inherently egalitarian concept. The discussion about equality in the realm of elections and democracy is thus ultimately a discussion about politics and Constitutionalism. Traditionally, Constitutionalism has been understood to be a negative concept, i.e., a system through which the State is kept within confined bounds. The Constitution is popularly understood to be a document that provides for an intricate system of checks and balances where different organs of the State have limited power and exercise control over different areas so as to ensure that no branch of the government can overwhelm any other. This view is intimately connected to a particular political philosophy, one of minimal-state liberalism[78] where the State is seen as a necessary evil that has to be kept in check by the Constitution.

However, this negative view of the Constitution ignores the vital positive nature of Constitutions in general and the Indian Constitution in particular. The positive version of Constitutionalism envisages a different form of the State, one that is enabling and Constitutionally required to improve the lives of its citizens. As one academic puts it 'the principles of constitutionalism are directed towards ensuring that the state possesses an institutional structure that has the capacity to effectively advance the well-being of its members'.[79] This is also the vision of those who framed the Constitution at a time when a multitude of obligations were cast upon by the State which had to ensure the wretched and the poor were uplifted.

Elections afford a potent form of ensuring that this Constitutional vision is actualised. A government answerable to the people would be one that is more likely to ensure greater justice and fairness, at least in theory.[80] Thus, political equality[81] is essential for achieving the larger Constitutional goal of equality. In the fractious debates on equality today, the subtle means by which voter inequality can creep in is often neglected. It is important to address this form of inequality for this engenders a potentially cascading series of economic and social inequalities.

7
Marriage

Images of candlelit vigils over a decade ago that followed the infamous 2012 Delhi gang rape (also known as the Nirbhaya case) still occupy public memory. The brutality of the crime coupled with the perceived middle-class origins of the victim[1] led to a sense of outrage in the media and civil society. Massive protests were held in Delhi and across the country. Yet, at the same time as the protests were happening, almost certainly some woman somewhere in India was being raped by her husband without the slightest public anger.[2] Because the law does not recognize the crime of a husband raping his wife, the so-called 'marital rape exception', such a woman has no legal recourse under criminal law[3]. Even though the rape laws were overhauled after the horrific case, the marital rape exception remained stubbornly on the statute books.

The exception then came to be challenged before the courts. In May 2022, the Delhi High Court passed a split verdict with one judge holding the exception to be unconstitutional and the other judge holding it to be valid. The learned judge who upheld the provision ruled that the exception was 'eminently in public interest' and that there was a special 'entitlement, of the marital sphere, to its own privacy'.[4] The judge was of the view that neither the court nor the executive ought to interfere with the privacy of the marital bedroom, even if that meant that a wife who had suffered sexual assault could not seek legal redress.

This reluctance to interfere with the perceived 'private' or family sphere leads one to ask whether the Constitution of India stops at the doorstep of the marital home? Or do the Constitutional mandates of equality manage to cross that Lakshman Rekha (a boundary line set by Lakshman from the Ramayana) and provide succor to all those who need it? Earlier chapters have discussed the law in relation to interactions between the State and its citizens or groups. But what happens to breaches of equality in interactions between individuals in the privacy of their homes? If the State seeks to regulate such relationships to mitigate legal and substantive inequalities, there might be a fear of overreach. After all, if the right to privacy means anything, it certainly includes the demand to keep the government out of the bedroom. On the other hand, if the State does not intervene in cases of marital inequality, it might end up perpetuating injustice. To compound matters, it may be the actions of the State which create the inequalities in the first place. In such a case, do the courts have a responsibility to step in and either direct the State to rectify its (in)action or offer remedial measures themselves?

One might think that in areas of formal inequality, a situation where the laws on the face of it discriminate between men and women, change would be easy. All the legislature would have to do is to step in and amend the law to make it gender neutral. This would entail no greater State interference in the marital bond than in any other area of family life. Even the court could rely on the provisions of the Constitution and strike down any patently discriminatory provisions. However, this is easier said than done for many reasons. The laws of marriage are deeply interconnected with religion making it politically difficult to achieve reform. The courts also feel constrained when considering matters of 'personal laws' for fear of disturbing the Constitutional balance in matters of freedom of religion. The situation gets hazier when the substantive inequalities within a marriage are analysed. The power dynamic in a typical Indian marriage clearly favours the man. Societal and cultural conditioning, economic disempowerment and religious practices and taboos act disproportionately against women. In such a situation even if the laws are facially neutral, their application in the context of extreme inequality would itself perpetuate discrimination. How should the law, or judges, deal with this imbalance?

Marriage is an ancient institution, albeit in a form that would be quite unrecognizable to most of us in the modern world. Its origins lie in the economic arrangements of groups, themselves organized around the links of religion or kinship. It is, therefore, not a coincidence that the law in relation to marriage also lies at the cusp of history, religion, culture, economics and politics. The law has to navigate all these areas with their often competing demands. Unlike other areas of the law where the courts have been increasingly progressive, marriage is an area where the courts have shown an excessive degree of deference to both tradition as well as Parliament. Whether this is a result of most judges being men and therefore steeped in a patriarchal tradition or whether a result of a genuine conflict of Constitutional values is a matter for debate. However, with the courts failing to perform their role as agents of social change, there is no doubt that the law of marriage in India remains deeply flawed and skewed against the most vulnerable of its citizens. This chapter will examine the law relating to marriage and in the process ask a more fundamental question; given its innate patriarchal nature, is the institution of marriage with all its flaws worth retaining? Perhaps nowhere is this question most brought into relief when discussing the rights of that group of people who do not have that right—non-heterosexual people. There the role of marriage, not just as a repository of a bouquet of rights but also as a public act of signaling by the State becomes significant. As noticed often in the book, it is when inequality is apparent that the role of the Constitution as an ameliorative text comes into sharper notice. Unfortunately in the case of queer marriages, it seems that the community would have to wait a bit longer to have its own tryst with destiny.

Marriage and Formal Equality

Contrary to the legislative interventions of the recent past seeking to secure greater equality for women,[5] personal laws have been stubbornly resistant to change and remain biased against women. This is partly a result of how these laws came into being. After the transfer of power from the British East India Company to the British Crown, the colonizers offered a semblance of religious freedom to the native population. Queen Victoria offered her newly minted subjects the assurance: 'We disclaim alike the right and the desire to impose our convictions on our subjects. We declare it to be our royal will and pleasure that none be in anywise favoured, none molested or disquieted, by reason of their religious faith or observances, but that all shall alike enjoy the equal and impartial protection of the law; we do strictly charge and enjoin all those who may be in authority under us that they abstain from all interference with religious belief or worship of any subjects on pain of our highest displeasure.'[6]

The ostensible effect of this promise was that customs and practices relating to marriage and matters of the family would be left untouched by the colonizers.[7] Using the well-worn distinction between the spiritual and temporal laws in the West, a similar exercise was attempted in India. Matters of commerce which enabled the British to govern their newly acquired colony were deemed matters of secular concern and were legislated upon. During the period from 1861 to 1869, over 211 laws were enacted including the Indian Contract Act, the Transfer of Property Act, and the erstwhile Penal Code.[8]

However, matters pertaining to the family were seen as areas where religious laws would be immune from governmental interference, ignoring the fact that all laws of Hindus and Muslims were religious.[9] Over time, the multiple variations in personal laws which were rooted in culture and custom, as opposed to purely in religion, were erased because of legislative interventions and the need for judicial uniformity.[10] Yet, the core idea that has persisted is of personal laws being a facet of religious freedom. This has conferred the laws with a sense of immutability since courts and legislatures are wary of intervening in these areas of freedom. The price of this consolidation of custom into religious dogma by the colonial masters has been paid by women in the form of unjust and discriminatory laws.

Instances of formal inequality abound in matters relating to marriage across religions. In Muslims, the most well-known example was the case of the instant triple *talaq* or the *talaq-e-biddat*. A man, but not a woman, could divorce his spouse by simply uttering the word talaq three times. While the practice was intrinsically grotesque, it was immediately apparent that it was also discriminatory because a woman could not so divorce her husband. It took a brave woman who had suffered immense personal injustice to bring a change to this form of divorce.

Shayara Bano was a young Muslim woman who had an MA in sociology but like many Indian wives was a homemaker and financially dependent on her husband.[11] She was subjected to demands for dowry and was forced to undergo abortions at her husband's behest. She duly complied thinking that it would save her marriage. When she was visiting her parents' home in Uttarakhand, she received *talaqnama* (divorce deed) by post proclaiming that her husband had uttered the word talaq thrice and divorced her. All that the husband offered was Rs 16,000 as *mehr* (dower). After having suffered in silence over the years, Shayara Bano challenged the constitutional validity of the practice of triple talaq before the Supreme Court.

The Supreme Court heard the matter over seven days in the summer vacations of the court. The verdict was delivered on a sweltering August morning in 2017 where a five-judge bench, by a 3:2 majority held triple talaq to be unconstitutional.[12] However, it was not struck down on the basis of discrimination against women. One judge, Justice Kurian Joseph, after analysing the Koran and other scriptures ruled that talaq-e-biddat was not a mandated religious practice and therefore had no Constitutional protection. The two other judges, Justices R.F. Nariman and Justice U.U. Lalit held that the practice was violative of Article 14 because it was manifestly arbitrary. The prime reason that the majority struck down the practice was because the ability to divorce a person was whimsical and capricious. Such a drastic exercise could be undertaken by the husband without any attempt at reconciliation or mediation. The underlying belief seems to be that the sanctity of marriage implied that marital bonds could not be extinguished in a fit of pique or for no reasonable grounds. The court ruled that 'manifest arbitrariness, therefore, must be something done by the legislature capriciously, irrationally and/or without adequate determining principle. Also, when something is done which is excessive and disproportionate, such legislation would be manifestly arbitrary'.[13]

In finding this violation, the court relied on the doctrine of unreasonableness expounded in the Royappa case[14] which states that an action can be struck down if it appears to be manifestly arbitrary. This use of the doctrine of manifest unreasonableness as a facet of Article 14 establishes a few things. First, that the test is one where value judgments of the court come front and center. Irrationality in the eyes of the judges inevitably require them to make an assessment about the merits of the law from a substantive point of view. In this case, the judges clearly valued the sanctity of marriage and hence ruled that the ease of divorce provided by triple talaq was unreasonable. However, why this is the case was never clearly spelt out. Indeed, it is difficult to provide an objective answer to a question which has its roots in the subjective opinions of the judges.

Second, there was no reason provided in the judgment as to why the traditional classification test was not applied, or what would have been the result if it had in fact been used. Using the classification test might have forced the judges to see what the two classes created by the legislation were. In the case of unilateral talaq, the two classes would have been husbands who had the right to divorce and women who did not. The court could have asked itself the question as to whether this classification was based on any intelligible differentia and then decided to uphold or strike down the law. So why was this test not used? After all, it is not as though the classification test is not good law—it has been used most recently in the marriage equality case as we shall see further in the chapter.

This brings us to the third factor, which is that even though Article 14 was pressed into service, there appears to be little discussion about the practice from a feminist perspective. Gender inequality was writ large in the provision, yet the text of the judgment is seemingly unaware of the discrimination innate in the provision. One feminist scholar was rather scathing when she notes that 'instead of developing jurisprudence based on the intersectionality of gender and religious identity, we are presented with a laboriously lengthy and impotent decision which reflects the judges' lack of knowledge on feminist jurisprudence.[15]

The Constitutional Immunity of Religious Personal Laws

A kinder reason for this abstention to consider women's rights could be because the court wanted to skirt the question about the justiciability of personal laws. This is a quirk in the law that renders the personal laws of a community immune from judicial review, even if they are patently discriminatory to women. How this came about is a study in how a measure designed to help women can end up, in the long run, being used against them.

As discussed in the first chapter of the book, the members of the Constituent Assembly had struck a compromise when it came to the promulgation of a Uniform Civil Code (UCC). This compromise permitted personal laws of all religious communities to be applicable to them. In place of a general secular law that was to be applicable to all citizens, the Directive Principles of State Policy merely provided that the State had to 'endeavour to secure for the citizens a Uniform Civil Code throughout the territory of India'[16]. Rather than imposing a general obligation upon the state to enact a UCC, the can was kicked down the road requiring its enactment at an unspecified future date. Curiously the Constitution did not explicitly state whether the personal laws had to necessarily be compliant with the fundamental rights provisions, including the right to equality. The exemption of religious personal laws from the rigors of equality was created by judges through an interpretive process rather than from the clear language of the Constitution. Interestingly, this was in a case where the challenge was to a law that had been enacted for the benefit of Hindu women.

Contemporaneously with the framing of the Constitution, there was also a move to codify and reform the family law as applied to the majority Hindu community. A Hindu Law Committee was constituted in 1944[17] which submitted its proposals to the federal Parliament in 1947. Thereafter, these recommendations were debated in Parliament from 1958 to 1951 and then again from 1951 to 1954 (after the elections to the first Parliament). The comprehensive reform bill was split into four politically manageable bills.[18] These were finally passed by Parliament after great opposition by the conservative section of Hindu society.[19]

One provision in the Hindu Marriage Act which was particularly contentious was the abolition of polygamy. A provision similar to the ban on polygamy had already been passed by the Bombay Legislature in the form of the Bombay Prevention of Hindu Bigamous Marriages Act, 1946. This legislation was challenged before the high court by a Hindu husband who claimed that the law impaired his freedom of religion and also discriminated against him on the ground of religion. He argued that Muslim men were allowed to contract polygamous marriages, and so the ban singled out Hindu men for unequal treatment.

A division bench of two judges of the Bombay High Court dismissed the case.[20] The lead judgment was authored by Chief Justice M.C. Chagla who held that personal laws could not be challenged as violating any fundamental right guaranteed under the Constitution. This was on the basis that the definition of the term law[21] in the Constitution did not include personal laws in its purview. Justice P.B. Gajendragadkar,[22] who went on to become Chief Justice of India, agreed with Chief Justice Chagla, and explained the position in starker terms.[23] He ruled that 'the rules prescribed for marriages are determined by the social and economic condition of the society. In dealing with these rules, it is also necessary to remember the obvious natural differences between the sexes themselves and considerations which may legitimately arise from these differences'.[24]

In his view, Article 15 of the Constitution prohibited discrimination against women if it was based on the ground of sex 'only'. This use of the word only, as per the learned judge, implied that if there was some other ground to differentiate between men and women, other than sex alone, the legislation would be upheld. Peering into the shastras, the judge held that taking a second wife was permitted only in certain circumstances, for instance if the first wife was unable to bear a son. Therefore, polygamy was permitted not because the man wanted a second wife, but because the first wife was unable to have progeny! The judgement held that since the scriptures mandated that a son conferred 'spiritual benefits upon his ancestors', the reason for a second marriage was merely to beget a son and not any form of discrimination against women. Though it is not certain that such reasoning would be accepted today,[25] the discussion does highlight how the interpretation of the Constitution is shaped deeply by the personal beliefs of judges.

Over the years this view of the Bombay High Court became almost an orthodoxy, conferring judicial immunity to all discriminatory aspects of personal laws. One judge of the Delhi High Court ruled that the 'Introduction of constitutional law in home is most inappropriate. It is like introducing a bull in a china shop. It will prove to be a ruthless destroyer of the institution of marriage. In the privacy of the home, neither Article 21 nor Article 14 have any place. In a sensitive sphere, which is most intimate and delicate, the introduction of the cold principles of constitutional law will have the effect of weakening the marriage bond. The introduction of constitutional law into the ordinary domestic relationship of husband and wife will strike at its very root and will be a fruitful source of dissent and quarrelling.'[26]

The court in the triple talaq case had the opportunity to exorcise the ghost of Narasu as also the mindset demonstrated in the judgment of the Delhi High Court, but it chose not to.[27] The decision did not actually determine whether the right to equality enshrined in Article 14 would trump the rights under Article 25. Given the expansive discussion in the judgment in relation to the Koran and the multi-religious constitution of the bench, it appears that at least part of the effort was to convince the Muslim community that their 'rights' were being appropriately dealt with. In doing so, however, the court sacrificed the fundamental rights of the individual at the altar of the rather more rarified perception of community interests. This also forms part of a pattern where the judges prefer to have a hands-off approach in matters deemed 'private' or personal. The discriminatory personal laws therefore seem to cock a snook at the Constitution. Given the pervasive nature of these laws, and the seeming reluctance of the legislature to step in and remedy the discrimination, laws that treat women unequally seem to have established their place in our legal framework.

Sadly inequality permeates all religious personal laws. In fact one could say that the one thing that unites all religions is the discriminatory nature of personal laws. Even though the Hindus have reformed their laws substantially, there still exist instances of formal inequality.[28] As an example, the inheritance rights of the heirs of a female Hindu who does without making a will are governed by Section 15 (2) of the Hindu Succession Act. The provision provides for different manners of succession depending on whether the woman inherited her property from her husband or her father. As a judgment of the Calcutta High Court noted 'there is discrimination apparent in the principle recognised in section 15(2) of the Act in it attaching significance to the source of the estate of a Hindu woman dying intestate though elsewhere in the Act there is no corresponding provision for the Hindu man'.[29] The very conception of a joint Hindu family, even after the reforms of 2005, has its underlying basis in gender discrimination.[30]

Elevating personal laws to an exalted status in the name of religious autonomy does grave injustice to women as well as the idea of religious freedom. Personal laws have become a 'marker of identity'[31] of religions and unjust laws are often cited to look down upon a community as regressive, even though the malaise of discrimination is spread across religions. Therefore, rather than being a force of liberation, these unequal personal laws merely provide a cover for discriminatory rhetoric.[32] Even the proposed solution of the Uniform Civil Code is often a stick to beat religious minorities and not sufficiently focused on actually reforming the aspect of gender discrimination.[33]

Substantive Inequality and What Can Be Done About It

Enshrining formal inequality in personal laws has pitted religion against gender equality. One way to cure this discrimination would be to amend the laws and make them gender neutral. Several proponents of the Uniform Civil Code have suggested just such a rationale. The flip side of the argument is that making the laws formally equal would still not be enough. This is because given how steeped in patriarchy and gender inequality Indian society is, treating men and women with formal equality would end up perpetuating the discrimination faced by women. As Flavia Agnes, a noted scholar of family law notes, 'Within the gendered institutions of marriage and family, it is not surprising that financial claims of maintenance are judged against the code of sexual purity. Women's moral character gets foregrounded in legal arguments and issues such as dispute over legitimacy and paternity are invoked to deny maintenance to women.'[34] She gives several examples how gender-neutral terminology results in a discriminatory impact on women, particularly in the field of divorce and settlement.

An area where this substantive inequality emerges in sharp relief is in the doctrine of restitution of conjugal rights. This is a legal principle by which the court can force a woman to return to the matrimonial home if she, for no reasonable excuse, has left the husband. There is substantial academic writing to conclude that this doctrine was not really part of Hindu law[35] but was imported into the canon through a misreading of the scriptures by British judges in the case of Bhikaji v. Rukhmabai.[36] Be that as it may, the doctrine now finds statutory recognition as a facet of Hindu law by virtue of Section 9 of the Hindu Marriage Act, 1955. Even though the remedy of restitution is available to both the man and the woman, most commonly it is a remedy used by the husband against the wife, often as a counterblast to her claim for maintenance.[37] While used less often in recent times, the remedy was used to force a woman to give up her job at a location different from the marital home and return to her husband's place of living.[38] In spite of the possibility of its abuse by husbands, the Supreme Court has upheld the Constitutionality of the remedy holding that it served 'a social purpose as an aid to the prevention of break up of marriage'.[39]

Another area of substantive inequality is the application of the law in matters of maintenance to the wife upon divorce. It has been argued that the ease of getting a divorce in a country is linked to better outcomes for women.[40] This has partly been explained by the 'bargaining theory' which postulates that spouses indulge in unwritten negotiations within the marital home on matters including the division of work within the home. The outcomes of these discussions reflect power balances within the family, which in turn are dictated by their choices within and outside marriage. As in any form of bargaining, different parties rely on their respective strengths and alternative options. Perhaps the most important of these is the nuclear option of divorce, something referred as the divorce threat point, i.e., 'when bargaining occurs within the context of the possibility of divorce, partners consider their alternatives if their relationship should end, and the attractiveness of their anticipated alternatives affect their negotiations'.[41] The possibility of getting out of an oppressive marriage may offer the woman some control over the subsisting one. As a corollary it cannot be denied that an inability to secure a fair divorce results in worse outcome for women as opposed to men. The ability of a woman to end a marriage in India is conditioned not only by how easy it is for her to obtain a divorce, but the settlement that she will get. A measly alimony with the added responsibility of rearing her child is hardly one where the possibility of divorce is a meaningful choice. In such a scenario, any operation of law that makes it harder for a woman to get a divorce on just terms, in effect, perpetuates inequality. Unfortunately, gender-neutral divorce laws result in substantial inequality towards women when they are applied in the real world.

The law mirrors societal norms and hence typically permits divorce on fault grounds, where a party to the marriage is seen as errant in some manner and thus her spouse is seen as a victim, deserving of a divorce. These include adultery, cruelty, desertion or unsoundness of mind. The discriminatory aspect of the criminal law on adultery was used by the Supreme Court to strike down Section 497 of the Indian Penal Code.[42] However, it continues on the statute books as a ground to obtain divorce. Under Section 125 (4) of the Code of Civil Procedure, 'no wife shall be entitled to receive an allowance from her husband under this section if she is living in adultery'. Therefore, there is great incentive for a man, who wishes to avoid payment of maintenance, to make allegations of adultery against a woman in an attempt to adhere with the exception provided by Section 125 (4). As an eminent practitioner of family law notes 'husbands routinely make the allegation of adultery. If proven, this becomes a complete defence against the claim of maintenance by the wife. So women have to endure a great deal of humiliation during litigation while claiming maintenance'.[43]

This de facto discrimination is perpetuated in other areas of divorce and maintenance as well. In cases of cruelty, some courts have held that filing of criminal cases against the husband or his family would amount to cruelty and give rise to a ground for divorce. While case laws in this area are not completely consistent, many judgments do reflect the 'stereotypical roles assigned to women within a society and judicial notions regarding women's position are important factors for determining cruelty'.[44] These examples establish that the operation of the law results in systemic unfairness to women. This can only be remedied either by legislative intervention or through a change in judicial attitudes.

This story of discrimination runs rampant in areas of alimony and maintenance. This is partly structural, since it is a policy of the law to make divorce more difficult so as to ensure that the moral fibre of society is maintained. This results in seeing the matrimonial home as the place where economic security for women can be ensured with the necessary corollary that maintenance outside of marriage is made more difficult.[45] It is not as though the legislature is unaware of the unequal effects that a facially neutral law can have on women. Several provisions of the law have been added where additional benefits have been given to women to try and balance unequal power equations with the relationship. One legislative example of this has been the enactment of the Protection of Women from Domestic violence Act, 2005. Notably this Act offers protection not just to wives, but also to relationships in the nature of marriage, expanding the scope of the law's protection to a larger set of women.

There is another reason to move beyond the standard construct of marriage, which is to address the issues of violence within a family unit. Equality, as has been argued repeatedly in the book, is an integral facet of the rule of law (or perhaps, vice versa). Failing to address systemic inequalities within the family results in impunity towards the law and an erosion of the rule of law. As a noted academic writes, 'Power relations within the family, for instance, can threaten the operation of the rule of law: domestic violence and child abuse are sometimes grounded in situations in which the perpetrator enjoys a practical immunity from the law. Not only are victims subjected to criminal acts—a violation of the rule of law in itself—they may also be unable to access the law-enforcing institutions to seek protection. And if this type of private lawlessness is common in society, these intimate violations of the rule of law can factor up to present problems at the level of the state, impairing the general capacity of the law to regulate power.'[46]

Substantive inequality can also result with judges who have not been sensitized to issues of gender dynamics applying the law relying on sexist stereotypes.[47] Further, even if judges are judicially trained to be aware of possibilities of injustice, multiple other participants (including lawyers and court staff) who form part of the justice delivery system remain fundamentally unaware. A study on the use of mediation as a substitute for litigation in cases of matrimonial discord shows that while the forum for adjudication is altered, the outcomes are still a reflection of the systemic power structures within marriage. As the author of the study points out, 'provisions regarding marriage and divorce are conceptually cast as equitable, but partners are in fact vastly differently situated with regard to their economic capacities and the cultural expectations. Altering the mode of litigation is thus not a sufficient condition either for overcoming the alienation of legal process or for transforming the differential privileges of marriage'.[48]

It has been argued by some feminist scholars that these problems with marriage, both in the law and in its judicial enforcement, is no accident.[49] This is an inevitability given the fact that the evolution of the social institution of marriage is in itself rooted in patriarchy,[50] where the work of women is made invisible and the gendered nature of marriage is used to portray a false freedom for women.[51] Some feminists are also deeply conflicted about the worth of marriage even for non-heterosexual persons pointing out that marriage equality would lead to perpetuation of the same stereotypes that haunt women in a straight marriage.[52]

If Marriage Is Patriarchal, Why Do Queer Folk Want It?

Marriage has two clear functions. First, it offers a bouquet of rights or at the least, a set of default options safeguarding the interest of a life partner. Statutes offer certain privileges to married couples which are not available to 'unmarriable' non-heterosexual people.[53] There are several tax advantages that flow to a married spouse. Retiral and other employment benefits, joint adoption by a couple, right of access in case of a medical emergency, are some of the areas that are available solely on the basis of marriage. The impact of default rules, also has an important role to ensuring the economic security of spouses. For instance, while a person can always will her self-acquired property to her same sex partner, the problem arises in case a person dies without making a will. The rules of succession under various laws relating to marriage would normally ensure that the married partner receives the assets of the deceased spouse. However, an unmarried queer spouse would not inherit anything upon the death of their partner if no will has been executed. These are clear instances of discrimination based on marriage, so it is hardly surprising that many queer persons want at least the option of being able to get married.

Other than conferring this set of rights, marriage performs an important role that of being a signal of acceptability, a need particularly felt for marginalised queer couples who face social disapproval. Even if marriage is an innately oppressive institution, ideas like 'rights, equality, and justice, represent persuasive and powerful symbols for movements for social change. These legal arguments can offer oppositional frames that may eventually resonate with the public in political debates and can have concrete material consequences, as well'.[54] In other words, the very demand for marriage equality with the attendant discussion (in public as well as by way of judgment) about equality and the worth of a queer relationship has value in reducing the stigma the community faces.

It was with this hope in mind that some litigants approached various high courts seeking marriage equality.[55] Eventually, a petition was also filed before the Supreme Court[56] which proceeded to transfer all matters pending in the various high courts and list them before a bench of five judges of the court.[57] The judgment was pronounced in the matter in October 2023, jolting the members of the LGBTQIA+ community who had begun by this point to see themselves as equal citizens of the country, or at the very least had hopes that the highest court in the land would not fail them given its progressive judgments in the recent past.[58]

The court declared that not only did queer couples not have the right to get married, but also that the Constitution did not recognize marriage as a fundamental right at all.[59] In other words, even straight people do not have the Constitutional right to marry. Effectively, the court held that two people belonging to different religions[60] or castes[61] do not have a fundamental right to get married. In doing so, the court might unwittingly have delegitimized the one tool that Dr Ambedkar thought was the most important one to annihilate caste. He said, 'the real remedy for breaking caste is intermarriage. Nothing else will serve as the solvent of caste'.[62] If marriage is not a fundamental right, future governments could well prohibit a class of intercaste marriages. However, even if the larger issue of intercaste marriage and its impact on the abolition of caste is kept aside, it is evident that denying queer couples the right to marry has a direct effect on their right to live as equal citizens under the Constitution.[63]

What the Decision Held in Relation to Equality

The five judges delivered four separate judgments, with the judgment of Justice S.R. Bhat being the majority opinion. All judges were of the unanimous view that same-sex couples faced immense and systemic discrimination. In a lengthy segment of the majority judgment authored by Justice Bhat titled 'discriminatory impact on queer couples', the learned judge laid out a litany of injustices faced by the queer community. The segment reads almost like a queer manifesto using language commonly heard in lectures and seminars on discrimination. For instance, the judgment notes: 'The constitution exists, and speaks for *all,* not the many or some . . . It is important to recognize, that while the state *ipso facto* may have no role in the choice of two free willed individuals to marry, its characterizing marriage for *various collateral and intersectional purposes,* as a permanent and binding *legal relationship, recognized as such* between heterosexual couples only (and no others) impacts queer couples adversely. The intention of the state, in framing the regulations or laws, is to confer on benefits to families, or individuals, who are married. This has the result of *adversely* impacting to exclude queer couples.'[64] Put slightly more comprehensibly, the judges appear to acknowledge that recognising straight marriages, while failing to do the same for queer persons, is discriminatory.

Paradoxically, while accepting the claim of substantive discrimination put forth by the petitioners, the court simply wrung its hands in purported dismay but failed to give any substantive relief. Remedying historic injustice belonged in the domain of the legislature and not the court. The majority judgment was of the view that since marriage was not itself a fundamental right, the court would be required to create a social institution of marriage specially for them. This, the judges ruled, was not part of the judicial function and belonged solely to the domain of Parliament.

On the issue of whether the Special Marriage Act violated the equality clause of the Constitution, the verdict of the court was split. Of the five judges, the majority ruled that the Special Marriage Act was not discriminatory because it envisaged a reasonable classification and had a nexus with the object sought to be achieved by the Act.[65] In essence, the court ruled that there was no unconstitutionality if a statute was 'under-inclusive'. What this meant was that the legislature was not required under the Constitution to legislate for all persons who could potentially be impacted by a law. Instead, Parliament could pick and choose and enact a law only for a part of the population. In such a case, the people left out could not complain that they had not been included in the law, which Parliament could possibly have enacted for them. This was because the Constitution allowed room for maneuver for the legislature to experiment providing relief only to a class of citizens rather than everyone. A consequence of this reasoning was that just because Parliament made a law for straight people it did not permit queer people to insist that a law be made for them too. Justice S.K. Kaul in his dissenting judgment disagreed. To him, the inequality of the Act was writ large on its face as there was no reasonable basis for distinguishing between straight and queer people, for the purposes of the Act. He also ruled that the object of the Act was to permit interfaith marriages and not to prohibit non-heterosexual marriages.[66] However, this being a minority judgment, it only flagged the error in the majority judgment, serving as a call to a future intelligence.

The petitioners had also challenged the provisions relating to adoption of children by a queer couple. The law permits only married couples to adopt and specifically bars people in live-in relationships from adopting children jointly. The argument in respect of indirect discrimination—that the effect of the law was more discriminatory on queer couples than straight couples—was clear. A live-in couple could always choose to get married and had a legal route to joint adoption. Given the prohibition on queer marriages, no live-in queer couple could fulfill this requirement of marriage deemed necessary for legal adoption. The majority, in what was now a tragically familiar manner, proceeded to note this discrimination and its ill effects on both queer parents as well as their children, but did nothing about it. In the words of the court 'the underlying assumption in the law as it exists, that such unmarried heterosexual or queer couples should not adopt needs to be closely examined'.[67] Continuing with this 'close' examination, the court detailed multiple instances of discrimination and also noticed the negative impact that the law had on vulnerable children. Having examined the issue closely, the court closed the issue without further ado.

Appealing to the very government that had drafted the discriminatory law, the court expressed the pious hope that the authorities would intervene and give 'equal concern and consideration having regard to the larger interest of the largest number of children and their development'. To quote the author Samuel Johnson, this was a 'triumph of hope over experience'.[68]

You Show me the Problem, I'll Show you the Test

The majority judgment appears to have tied itself in knots—recognizing discrimination at multiple places and yet failing to give relief. The court noted that failure to recognize queer marriages was unequal, yet upheld the provisions of the Special Marriage Act. It held that the law permitted under-inclusiveness by relying on the classification test but just a few weeks earlier ruled that the classification test could not be pushed so as to render the 'precious guarantee of equality "a mere rope of sand"'.[69]

These are some of the multiple examples of the contradictions in the judgment. It is possible that this is a result of the rather confused state of the law in relation to Article 14. There is, for instance, no clarity as to why the judge applied the classification test and not the manifest arbitrariness test. The latter test would have enabled the court to see the impact of failure to recognize marriage equality on the queer community, and also its disproportionate impact. Perhaps this is what happens when faced with a bewildering array of possibly conflicting precedent. The other manner of looking at the problem is that it offers a judge the possibility to choose his or her interpretation of the law with a sub-conscious element of reverse engineering where the outcome is justified by choosing one as opposed to another test. The government is held to a higher standard in some cases and is let off relatively easily qua others.

Good, bad, or indifferent, marriage inequality is here to stay because the Indian Supreme Court has permitted it. As of today, some alternatives to remedy the ensuing injustice can be contemplated, of which the most recent one is the proposal of executing a 'deed of familial association'[70]. Under this deed two persons may enter into a contract giving each other rights over the property, decision-making in case of emergencies and nomination for employment benefits. The move is away from status as conferred by law to contract, as opted for voluntarily by parties.[71] However, even though some aspects of discrimination could be covered through this route (and it is yet not clear whether the States would adopt such an option) the underlying inequality remains. Shorn of all legal niceties, two straight people can get married, while their non-heterosexual co-citizens cannot. This, the courts seem to have no problem with.

Conclusion

The family is probably the only area where laws are comprehensively and explicitly gendered. It is also the one sphere where judicial intervention, or rather abstention from failing to remedy discrimination in personal laws to recognizing marriage equality, has created the most controversy. This reluctance to intervene and remedy injustice stems partly because of the religious nature of the personal laws governing the citizens of the country. But it also has to do with the imbalance of power that lies between the genders and the reluctance of the courts to exercise their judicial powers to peer into the family home. There is a feeling that the 'private' is out of bounds. Sadly, this non-intervention perpetuates an unjust status quo that almost always acts contrary to the interests of the already disadvantaged.

The question is also about the power and jurisdiction of the court. Having found discrimination, can the courts simply wring their hands with anxious concern or are they Constitutionally entitled, indeed obliged, to do something about it? The same activist court which marches in to decide all manner of public interest litigation, from midday meals to corruption in government, suddenly exercises self-restraint when asked to intervene on behalf of the most oppressed.

The reasons cited, is of institutional competence—the belief that the courts have no role in complex matters of policy. Ignoring the fact that such concerns are often brushed aside in other areas, there remains the problem of unremedied Constitutional infractions. A violation of Article 14 of the Constitution requires the judiciary to act, not as a matter of choice but as a matter of constitutional principle. To permit wanton Constitutional discrimination to persist is hardly conducive to the rule of law. It encourages impunity and allows the oppressor to get away with Constitutional crimes. It also limits the freedom of those discriminated against by limiting their choices, or at the very least restricting the autonomous and free exercise of their choices. A woman cannot be said to be free when her choices are either to stay in a loveless and oppressive marriage or face the Herculean task of getting a divorce where her rights will be overridden by an uncaring legal system. And all this in the name of privacy and autonomy of the home.

It is said that an Englishman's home is his castle. But it seems that the castle only belongs to the man and not the woman with members of sexual minorities being halted at the gates. This vision of equality is surely not compatible with the jurisprudence of the court in other areas discussed in the book.

Epilogue

> 'When I use a word,' Humpty Dumpty said in rather a scornful tone, 'it means just what I choose it to mean, neither more nor less.'
>
> 'The question is,' said Alice, 'whether you can make words mean so many different things.'
>
> 'The question is,' said Humpty Dumpty, 'which is to be master — that's all.'
>
> (Lewis Carroll: *Through the Looking Glass*)

This iconic exchange was referred to in an English judgment where the dissenting judge accused his colleagues of twisting the meaning of words to deliver a judgment that mirrored their political and ideological views.[1] Closer home, the survey of the jurisprudence of the courts leaves one with a sneaking suspicion that something similar is happening in India. The general and ambiguous meaning of the words in the Constitution and the principles of interpretation which view it as an organic document capable of changing over time, have conferred great power on judges of the superior courts. By claiming the power to be the ultimate arbiters of what the Constitution means, they have the ability to shape discourse about equality in an outsized way.

Given this power, it is only natural to ask: have they delivered? Here, the answer becomes a bit complex. In matters of gender, the record is decidedly mixed. While generally moving past initially regressive judgments, the courts have batted for greater gender equity in matters of employment. However, when it comes to the family, the courts have exercised greater discretion than perhaps warranted, leaving the decidedly patriarchal status quo intact. This has gone to an extreme in the cases of sexual minorities where the judges seem almost fearful of exercising the power that they clearly possess.

Matters of religion have also forced judges to confront the ideas of competing claims of different groups and well as tensions between the individual and the community. The questions that come up before the court are in the context of employment (is a Dalit Christian entitled to reservations?) as well as education (can minority schools be compelled to admit Dalit students?). While the law does not recognize caste-based reservations for members of religious minorities, it also does not require minority institutions to admit members of the lower castes. In terms of hierarchical ordering, perhaps this means that the rights of the minorities trump that of caste. The price of this is the exclusion from the benefits of reservation. In matters of marriage, however, the courts suddenly become circumspect adopting a non-interventionist approach in matters of religious personal laws.

Perhaps the one area where the courts have been fairly proactive is in the area of caste. Judges have consistently upheld provisions for reservations and in doing so called out the arguments of 'merit' and 'efficiency' for what they are—a cloak for privilege. To the opponents of quotas, the words in the Constitution which refer to the efficiency of services, ring loudly. The argument goes that merit is being sacrificed at the altar of political expediency. Some further lament of that the focus on caste is unnecessary because in their personal experience caste has stopped mattering, at least in larger cities and for the urban elite. The naysayers are almost always from the upper castes and fail to recognize discrimination when they themselves have been the beneficiaries of it. Having cemented their educational and social dominance through the use of caste over centuries of oppression, they now claim that there is no place for it in modern society. This hypocrisy has been called out by the sociologist Satish Deshpande when he writes that 'as a modern republic, India felt duty bound to "abolish" caste, and this led the State to pursue the conflicting policies of social justice and caste-blindness'. 'As a consequence, the privileged upper castes are enabled to think of themselves as "casteless", while the disprivileged lower castes are forced to intensify their caste identities'. 'This asymmetrical division has truncated the effective meaning of caste, thus leaving the upper castes free to monopolize the "general category" by posing as "casteless citizens".'[2]

While this book has discussed caste, gender, and religion as the main areas of discrimination, it is not as though there are no other groups who don't regularly have to deal with the problems of inequality. Two prominent groups that come to mind straightway are the disabled and the poor. Discrimination on the grounds of disability first captured the imagination of the courts in the mid 1990s after the enactment of the Persons with Disabilities (Equal Opportunities, Protection of Rights and Full Participation) Act, 1995. The Act as well as the ensuing jurisprudence was criticized on the ground that it 'medicalized' disability, handing power to a presumably objective medical profession who would dole out certificates 'scientifically' quantifying the amount of disability faced by a person.[3] The law has since been substituted by other legislation[4] and has given rise to a large number of interesting concepts, including the idea of reasonable accommodation. The Act defines reasonable accommodation as requiring 'necessary and appropriate modification and adjustments, without imposing a disproportionate or undue burden in a particular case, to ensure to persons with disabilities the enjoyment or exercise of rights equally with others'.[5] The focus of the action shifts from enforcement of a black letter law to ensuring the 'creation of an appropriate environment in which the disabled can pursue the full range of entitlements which are encompassed within human liberty and is enforceable in law'.[6] However, even in the area of disability law a large amount of the litigation has been in the field of reservations given that the Rights of Persons with Disablities Act, 2016 provides for reservations in both institutions of higher education[7] as well as in public employment.[8]

An extension of reservations for the disabled is in the area of 'economic disability'. While the term may seem strange, misidentifying disability, as well as poverty, the terminology has been used in the judgment of the court upholding the 103rd amendment to the Constitution which provides for reservations for the economically backward classes.[9] This judgment has been discussed in the earlier chapters of the book in the context of excluding the scheduled castes and tribes from the benefit of 10 per cent reservations for the Economically Weaker Sections ('EWS'). While the court was split on that issue, there was unanimity in the view that amending the constitution to include the EWS, as a group entitled to reservations, did not per se offend the basic structure of the Constitution. This was the first time that the court accepted the EWS to be a group, going contrary to the reason most commonly offered for reservation, i.e. quotas as a tool for remedying historic injustice. On this point, there was a slight divergence of opinion within the bench. While the majority held that quotas could be provided for in matters of employment as well as education, the minority disagreed. The minority judgment pointed out that the purpose of reservations in education was to ensure even access to common goods, and therefore reservations could be provided under Article 15 of the Constitution. When it came to matters of public employment, the reason to provide for quotas was to ensure representation of historically disadvantaged groups. This, the minority held, was not the case for the EWS. While they were certainly pecuniarily disadvantaged, they were not so socially disadvantaged as to warrant a departure from the normal rule of equality in public employment.[10] The majority disagreed and permitted reservations even in employment pointing to the fact that the document was effectively a socialist document with multiple references to the obligation of the State to ensure the upliftment of the poor.

The majority did express some doubts while upholding the reservations. One member of the bench ruled that 'thus, reservation is not an end but a means—a means to secure social and economic justice. Reservation should not be allowed to become a vested interest. The real solution, however, lies in eliminating the causes that have led to the social, educational and economic backwardness of the weaker sections of the community'.[11] While some might say that this statement reflects the privilege of the judges, it does capture one fault with our jurisprudence—an excessive reliance on reservations as a panacea for all ills.

The multiple axes of inequality discussed in the book have their roots in different forms of structural disadvantage. One would presume that they would also be required to be addressed through multiple kinds of interventions. Unfortunately, the imagination of the law appears to stop largely at reservations. It is perhaps time to look beyond quotas and seek to remedy systemic injustices through legislative interventions, most importantly through the enactment of a general anti-discrimination law.

Some moves towards this direction have already happened after the enactment of the Civil Rights Act, 1955. The Civil Rights Act can be traced to Article 17 of the Constitution which provides that 'the enforcement of any disability arising out of "untouchability" shall be an offence punishable in accordance with law'. This Article is unusual inasmuch as it requires the State to enact a legislation prohibiting discrimination by members of the public against the scheduled castes. It is an instance of a horizontal application of a fundamental right, i.e. a case where the Constitution imposes an obligation on members of the public, as opposed to State, not to discriminate against a citizen. Unlike Article 17, Article 14 of the Constitution does not have a horizontal application. Therefore, it is necessary for legislature to enact laws in this regard since the provisions under the Constitution are not 'self-executing'. This, the legislature has not done so far. While some pieces of legislation have been passed in specific instances,[12] it is surprising that Parliament or state legislatures have not passed any anti-discrimination legislation.

As a consequence, a large portion of the current anti-discrimination law is essentially shaped by judges with all the limitations that such an exercise entails. The views of the courts are atomized and decided solely in the context of the parties before the court rather than with reference to broader principles (including consideration of the impact of the judgments on other groups not before the court). A large amount of discussion in the courts is about reservations which jurisprudence is like a banyan tree, not allowing other areas of anti-discrimination law to flourish. Also, such an exercise cannot address the issues of structural discrimination in a satisfactory manner because the nature of interventions required in such a case go beyond the traditional legal tools which are striking down arbitrary actions or (with some reluctance) reading up an affirmative action provision to an otherwise excluded group. State interventions in capacity building[13] etc., are often required to remedy discrimination, which cannot be done by the court.

Further, traditional tests applied by the courts are not always satisfactory. Arbitrariness is not a test that can address discrimination as it is not focused on difference but the substantive justification of an action. The twin test embodied in Article 14 is also unsatisfactory for addressing systemic discrimination. A comprehensive anti-discrimination law ought to examine 'disadvantage' as a systemic organizing principle[14]. Rather than focusing on justifications for state action, it would ask whether the action has any relation to historical or structural handicaps. This would send a powerful signal to the community that all citizens are equal and deserve to be treated with equal concern and respect by both the State and their fellow citizens. Such a framing of the Act would also have an instrumental value—if the aim of equality is to end discrimination one cannot but be alive to the manner in which discrimination is suffered by the disadvantaged.

The manner of remedying the discrimination would be to target the peculiar manner that the disadvantage is suffered. For instance, the object of ending caste discrimination is the elimination of caste itself. However, in the case of religion, the attempt is not to end religion. Instead, it is to ensure that the inevitable differences, which are to be celebrated in a heterogeneous community, do not lead to perpetuation of disadvantage to the minority community. Therefore, in the case of caste, the law would mandate citizens not to consider the caste of a person in matters of access to public buildings, employment etc. However, in the case of religion, the law would require members of a community to respect the traditions, values and culture of another religion. Perhaps, in such a case, the law would specifically permit a Sikh to wear a headgear or a Muslim girl to wear a hijab, to school.

Such an approach would also require judges to move away from their traditional modes of thinking and adopt novel legal tools that could address the disadvantage.

For instance, the court could press the doctrine of 'reasonable accommodation' in areas other than disability discrimination. The two tests of Article 14—the intelligible differentia test and the arbitrariness standard—may have to be replaced by new forms of testing legislation and government/private action. One possible test could be the application of a variable scale of judicial review. In the case of the listed grounds of Article 15, the courts would be required to strictly scrutinize the impugned action. In the case of other grounds of discrimination which deal with historic or systemic disadvantage, a proportionality test could be applied. Here, the court would ask itself whether the infraction of the right of a disadvantaged person is commensurate to the interest of the State in causing the discrimination. As in other tests of proportionality, the court would only permit action that would least violate the right of the individual. Thus, if another course of action which does not restrict the right of an individual is possible, the court would strike down the action as unconstitutional. Finally, in cases of no systemic disadvantage (like economic policy) a more deferential test could be applied. There will be, so to say, a sliding scale of scrutiny where the aim would be to end the culture of discrimination.

Like other laws, an anti-discrimination law would only be as effective as its enforcement and its implementation. This would require the law to be comprehensively drafted and uniformly applied. These two basic conditions also reflect the fundamental principles of the rule of law including generality, clarity and consistency. The anti-discrimination law would have to be accessible to common people. The law (the text of the legislation as well as that of the judgments) need to be simple.

Of course, mere comprehensibility of the law alone will not result in empowerment; knowledge is also necessary. There are people in India who are not even aware about the basic provisions of the Constitution, let alone their rights. To remedy this, there must be a campaign to inform the general public about their rights. This campaign of awareness must also be extended to the judges applying the law. What is needed are judges with empathy who can recognize disadvantage when they see it. Therefore, other than education, even the appointment of judges would have to be seriously examined. After all, what disadvantage means is also hotly contested as is the nature and quality of evidence required to establish it. Only judges who have a variety of lived experiences would offer a pool of persons who could determine the existence of oppressive societal structures.

In the end, with all the talk about Parliament and the courts, it is important to remember that the law is but one social tool. If we wish to bring about a more equal society, we cannot simply legislate away discrimination or eradicate injustice with a judgment. Unfortunately, just as equality appears to be an innate human desire, inequality also appears to be an entrenched human condition. A hierarchical ordering of people is both reflective of power dynamics of a society and is also a mechanism to reinforce the prejudices that cause the discrimination in the first place. Inequality, peculiarly, is used to justify itself. One possible reason for this may lie in the normal human characteristic to envy those who are better off than us and scorn those who are worse off.[15]

Envy eats away at the envious, diverting time and resources from productive endeavours to feelings of self-pity or outrage. More dangerously, scorn for people who are worse off than us brings out our worst human reactions. One effect is to dehumanize the person lower in the social strata, in particular the worst off. In an interesting study, the medial pre-frontal cortex, a part of the brain which effectively governs our capacity to assess the feelings and emotions of other persons, was recorded by MRI.[16] The study showed that the participants tended to view the people in the lowest strata of society with disgust. In particular, they saw the most marginalized groups as less than human.

People at the lowest rungs of society are dehumanized and deemed unworthy of assistance, further disabling them from being able to uplift themselves. This is a self-reinforcing cycle which ensures that those at the margins of society face a virtually impossible task of trying to move up the social ladder. Inequality, over generations, becomes entrenched. The flip side of this is that those at the highest echelons are somehow seen as deserving of their success, rather than attributing their success to fortuitous circumstances. There is a high degree of correlation between perceived status of an individual and their perceived competence.[17] In other words, we appear to believe that people get what they deserve.

To break this vicious cycle requires empathy.[18] One way to generate empathy is to break down social barriers which prohibit the weakest groups from occupying the same space as those above them. This space could be economic, societal or literally physical. Greater interaction between groups allows people to see each other and, as a consequence, see each other as equal humans. In a country with a vast and diverse population like India, this is not an easy task. As seen in the chapter on marriage, Dr

Ambedkar thought that intercaste marriage was one way to share space and eradicate caste. Yet, most marriages in India happen within the same caste. Inertia, patriarchy, traditions, unequal power and many other reasons make society reluctant to change. It is for this reason that law and culture must function symbiotically, with the Constitution acting as an instrument of social change. Judges, precisely because of their being removed from the day-to-day rough and tumble of politics and cultural considerations have the power to bring about social catharsis using the guiding principles of the Constitution. We, the citizens of the country, must be able to judge whether they have succeeded in this task. The first step for this is to educate ourselves of the law. It is hoped that this book has gone at least some way in achieving that.

Notes

Introduction

1 This story has been chronicled in the memoir *Coming Out as Dalit*, Yashica Dutt, Aleph Book Company, 2019.

2 Preamble to the Constitution.

3 The first proposed preamble drafted by Dr Amedkar had an 'inequality clause' which stated that the aim of the Constitution was 'to remove social, political and economic inequality by providing better opportunities to the submerged classes'. For a discussion on the framing of the preamble see *Ambedkar's Preamble: A Secret History of the Constitution of India*, Aakash Singh Rathore, Vintage Books, 2020.

4 These grounds—religion, caste, sex (which has been interpreted to include gender)—find specific mention in Article 15 of the Constitution. Other potential areas of discrimination have been mentioned in other constitutional provisions. For instance, the newly emerging head of Economic status has been included in multiple places in the Constitution, most notably in Article 46, which reads that: 'The State shall promote with special care the educational and economic interests of the weaker sections of the people,

and, in particular, of the Scheduled Castes and the Scheduled Tribes, and shall protect them from social injustice and all forms of exploitation.'

5 For instance, disability and mental health. These concerns have been sought to be addressed by Parliament by two separate Acts, namely the Rights of Persons with Disabilities Act, 2016 and the Mental Healthcare Act, 2017.

6 Aloysius Irudayam, S.J. Jayshree, P. Mangubhai and Joel G. Lee, *Dalit Women Speak Out—Caste, Class and Gender Violence in India*, Zubaan, 2011.

7 Bhanwari Devi was raped for trying to stop a child marriage in 1992. 'I curse her daily,' says a bride. Jyoti Yadav, *ThePrint*, 18 September 2023 and also Saurabh Kirpal, *Women in the Workplace in Fifteen Judgments*, Penguin, 2022.

8 Intersectionality has its roots in Black feminist philosophy and the term was first used by Kimberlé Crenshaw in 'Mapping the margins: Intersectionality, Identity Politics and Violence against Women of Color', 43 *Stanford Law Review* 1241, 1991.

9 Other than the title, Article 14 is only twenty-four-words long. Of course, it is further expanded in Articles 15–18 of the Constitution, but the phrasing of the provision is surprisingly short for one of the longest Constitutions in the world.

10 Suresh Kumar Koushal v. Naz Foundation 1 SCC 1, 2014, para 60.

11 Navtej Singh Johar v. UOI, 10 SCC 1, 2018, para 458.

12 This mode of reasoning has been taken to an extreme in American jurisprudence through the doctrine of originalism where the meaning of the words of the Constitution is allegedly frozen at the time of the drafting of the provisions of Constitutionalism. The term originalism was coined in 1980 by Paul Brest in *The Misconceived Quest for the Original Understanding*, 60 BU L Rev 2 (1980). In India, there is a general consensus that the meaning of the words of the text change over time; that the document is an organic one. However, even in India, judgments frequently refer

to discussions in the Constituent Assembly to shed light on ambiguities in the provisions. Though there was some dispute in the early jurisprudence of the court, an eleven-judge bench in the case of Golak Nath v. State of Punjab (1967) 2 SCR 762 settled the issue. Perhaps unwittingly, the judges adopt a semi 'original intent' doctrine through this method.

13 This is the test explained in the early jurisprudence of the Supreme Court, for instance in Charanjit Lal Chaudhary v. Union of India, SCR 869, 1950.

14 Charanjit Lal Chadhary, para 38–40.

15 State of Kerala v. N.M. Thomas, 2 SCC 310, 1976.

16 E.P. Royappa v. State of Tamil Nadu (1974) 4 SCC 3.

17 Though multiple such declarations can be found in cases, reference need only be made to the following statement in the case of Dalmia Cement (Bharat) Ltd. v. Union of India, 10 SCC 104, 1996. 'Social democracy means a way of life which recognises liberty, equality and fraternity as principles of life. They are the trinity. . . . Social and economic justice in the context of our Indian Constitution must, therefore, be understood in a comprehensive sense to remove every inequality and to provide equal opportunity to all citizens in social as well as economic activities and in every part of life . . . it means to establish a democratic way of life built upon socio-economic structure of the society to make the rule of law dynamic.'

18 Article 335 of the Constitution also addresses these concerns when it stipulates that, 'The claims of the members of the Scheduled Castes and the Scheduled Tribes shall be taken into consideration, consistently with the maintenance of efficiency of administration, in the making of appointments to services and posts in connection with the affairs of the Union or of a State.'

19 'Citing basic structure doctrine, Vice President Jagdeep Dhankhar asks, "are we a democratic nation"', *Indian Express*, 12 January 2023.

20 The doctrine of the basic structure of the Constitution was first established by a thirteen-judge bench of the Supreme Court in the case of H.H. Kesavananda Bharti v. State of Kerala, 4 SCC 225, 1973.

21 Over the years the courts have held that secularism, independence of the judiciary and federalism are part of the basic structure of the Constitution. See for instance S.R. Bommai v. UOI, 3 SCC 1, 1994.

22 Minerva Mills v. Union of India (1980) 3 SCC 625, Para 74. This awakening to individual rights was only four years after the learned judge had delivered the infamous judgment of ADM Jabalpur v. UOI, 2 SCC 521, 1976, which permitted the government to suspend basic rights during the Emergency.

23 However, it is not as though the Constitution is oblivious of group identities. In fact, one of the aims of the Constitution is to eliminate oppressive social structures like untouchability. In doing so, it aims to strengthen individual rights so that they can act as counter ballast to potentially regressive demands of the community. On the other hand, it also secures certain rights and freedoms to social and religious groups because to live a meaningful life, an individual needs thriving communities.

24 Constituent Assembly Debates, 25 November 1949.

Chapter 1: What of Equality

1 Elizabeth Kolbert, 'The Psychology of Inequality', *New Yorker*, 8 January 2018.

2 Experiments have shown that people are willing to establish expensive mechanisms to ensure that those violating principles of equality are punished. Ernst Fehr and Urs Fischbacher, 'Third Party Punishment and Social Norms', Evolution *and Human Behavior*, 25 (2004), pp. 63–87. Joseph Henrich , et al, 'Working Paper No. 106' and 'Costly Punishment across Human societies', *Science*, Vol. 312, 23 June 2006, issue 5781: pp. 1767–70.

3 Stephanie Sloane, Renée Baillargeon, David Premack, 'Do Infants Have a Sense of Fairness?', *Psychological Science*, Vol. 23, No. 2, 2012, pp. 196-204. In fact, experiments suggest that children will demand a relatively equal distribution of resources to other children including themselves. However, it seems that our primate ancestors, the chimpanzees are even more demanding of equality than humans. See, Esther Herrmann, Lou M. Haux, Henriette Zeidler and Jan M. Engelmann, 'Human children but not chimpanzees make irrational decisions driven by social comparison', *Proceedings: Biological Sciences,* Vol. 286, No. 1894 2 January, 2019, pp. 1–6

4 Almost 85 per cent of the world's Constitutions prohibit discrimination on the ground of sex or gender, and 75 per cent, prohibit discrimination on the grounds of religion, race or ethnicity. However, only 5 per cent ban discrimination on the ground of sexual orientation. This shows that while there exists a general commitment to equality, at least on paper, there is a normative hierarchy even amongst different forms of discrimination. World Policy Centre, https://www.worldpolicycenter.org/how-constitutions-around-the-world-address-the-rights-to-equality-education-and-health.

5 Jarlath Clifford, 'Locating Equality: from Historical Philosophical Thought to Modern Legal Norms', *The Equal Rights Review*, 1, 2008.

6 An argument against equality would be that it is not intrinsically worthwhile and that it is merely a foundational value that conditions how we understand other goals in society.

7 In fact, social research seems to indicate that people prefer an unequal society to a more equal one, provided that the extent of inequality is not extreme. Michael I. Norton, *Unequality: Who Gets What and Why It Matters*, Vol. 1(1), 2014, *Policy Insights from the Behavioral and Brain Sciences*, pp. 151–155.

8 This philosophy also substantially underpins the 'law and economic' theory albeit with a modification which focuses

on the maximisation of wealth rather than utilitarianism per se. See Richard Posner, 'Utilitarianism, Economics and Legal Theory', 1979, The Journal of Legal Studies 103. At least one judge of the Supreme Court has consistently advocated utilitarian philosophy to be considered in matters relating to the economic effects of the law. See the judgments of Sikri J. in Shivashakti Sugars Ltd. v. Shree Renuka Sugar Ltd., 7 SCC 729, 2017, Common Cause v. UOI, 5 SCC 1, 2018, and Arjun Gopal v. UOI, 13 SCC 523, 2018.

9 Dyble et. Al., 'Sex equality can explain the unique social structure of hunter-gatherer bands', *Science*, Vol. 348, May 2015, Issue 6236. As the study noted 'the shift from an ancestral hierarchical, female-dispersal system to a multilocal, *egalitarian* one would provide the selective context for expanded social networks, cumulative culture, and cooperation among un-related individuals'.

10 Ulrich Orth, Richard W. Robins, 'The Development of Self-Esteem, Current Directions in Psychological Science', Vol. 23, No. 5, October 2014, pp. 381–387.

11 Eszter Kollar, Daniele Santoro, 'Not by Bread Alone: Inequality, Relative Deprivation and Self-Respect', *Philosophical Topics*, Vol. 40, No. 1, Rethinking Inequality, Spring 2012, pp. 79–96.

12 This point postulates a diverse society rather one so ridden by caste and/or class hierarchies that there is virtually no interaction between the groups. In such an ossified society, it may be possible for members of an oppressed caste to have high self-esteem compared to other members of their peer group.

13 The use of terminology, borrowed from Hobbes' 'Leviathan' (1660) does not imply that the social contract thesis posited by him is the correct political philosophy. For a greater discussion on this aspect, see the chapter dealing with the 'Rule of Law' in this book.

14 Amartya Sen, *Inequality Reexamined,* Oxford University Press, 1995, pp. 17.

15 Christina Starmans, Mark Sheskin and Paul Bloom, 'Why people prefer unequal societies', *Nature Human Behaviour,* Vol.1, Article number: 0082, 2017.

16 Such a test would require that any resource must be first given to that person who has the least of it. In the context of housing, it has been argued that a single mother who was most in need of government housing was entitled to accommodation rather than members of the Orthodox Jewish community which ran a housing association. This argument was rejected by the UK Supreme Court, albeit in the framework of the Equality Act, 2010. See R (Z) v Hackney London Borough Council, 1 WLR 4327, 2020.

17 Okun, Arthur M., *Equality and Efficiency: The Big Tradeoff*, Washington: The Brookings Institution, 1975.

18 For empirical research in support of this proposition, reference may be had to, 'The Spirit Level: Why greater equality makes societies stronger', Wilkinson and Pickett, Bloomsbury 2011. The authors seek to establish that an unequal society is bad for all its members and not just for the poor.

19 Paradoxically, countries with a high degree of income inequality seem to attract authoritarian regimes. See Inglehart, R., and Norris, P., 2016, 'Trump, Brexit and the Rise of Populism: Economic Have-Nots and Cultural Backlash', Faculty Research Working Paper RW16-06, Cambridge, Massachusetts: Harvard Kennedy School.

20 Shekhar Aiyar and Christian Ebeke, 'Inequality of Opportunity, Inequality of Income and Economic Growth', *IMF Working Paper*, European Department, February 2019.

21 John Rawls, *A theory of Justice*, Harvard University Press, Revised Edn., 2020.

22 It has been argued that Rawlsian political theory would support the idea of affirmative action (even though Rawls wrote very little in that regard himself). See 'John Rawls and Affirmative Action', Thomas Nagel, *The Journal of Blacks in Higher Education*, No. 39, Spring 2003, pp. 82–84.

23 See, *Anarchy, State, and Utopia*, Robert Nozick, Basic Books, 1974.

24 Even a libertarian philosophy is, at its core, one that believes in some form of equality. It believes, at the least, in the idea of formal equality where everyone has the same shot at resources regardless of their initial starting positions.

25 There are multiple reasons for these disagreements including political and economic beliefs. Another potent cause is incommensurability, i.e. a situation where reasons simply cannot be compared. See the introduction in *Incommensurability, Incomparability and Practical Reason,* ed. Ruth Chang, Harvard University Press, 1997 and *Does Incommensurability Matter? Incommensurability and Public Policy,* Richard Warner, Vol. 146 , 1998, University of Pennsylvania Law Review, p. 1287.

26 See *The Tyranny of Merit*, Sandel.

27 On the history of caste-based inequality in India, see, *Buddhist Revolution and Counter-revolution in Ancient India*, B.R. Ambedkar, B.R. Publishing Corporation, 2011. In the book Dr Ambedkar hypothesizes that the Varna system in ancient India was not dependent on birth. However, after the adoption of the Manu Smriti as the canonical text, the caste system was rigidified and was dependent solely on birth.

28 To an extent this may seem question begging. After all, do we have a right not to be treated as second-class citizens? One answer lies in the doctrine of 'equal care and respect' which postulates that individuals are entitled to be treated as equals by the State (as opposed to merely being entitled to equality of some metric—welfare, resources etc.). The second limb is that the State must equally respect the choices made by individuals about their own life. Colonization typically violated both these precepts. Concern through prioritizing the interests of the colonial masters and respect through an imposition of a morality extrinsic to the community. The foremost exponent of this doctrine of equal concern and respect is Ronald Dworkin. For an interesting analysis of

the relation between his philosophy and the jurisprudence of the Indian Courts see, Abhishek Sudhir, *Discovering Dworkin in the Supreme Court of India—a comparative excursus*, 7 NUJS L Rev 13, 2014.

29 A.K. Bagchi, *The Political Economy of Underdevelopment*, Cambridge University Press,1982, and Irfan Habib, *Essays in Indian History: Towards a Marxist Perception*, Anthem, 2002. For a slightly contrary opinion, see *Inequality in Colonial India*, Tirthankar Roy, LSE Economic History Working Papers September 2018. Worryingly, we seem to be heading back to the colonial position, at least in matters relating to income distribution —see 'Indian income inequality, 1922–2015: From British Raj to Billionaire Raj?' Lucas Chancel and Thomas Piketty Working Paper Series, No. 2017/11 World Inequality Lab.

30 Sapru was a renowned freedom fighter and a lawyer. He is perhaps better known for the 'Sapru Report' that was drafted in 1942 and was quoted extensively during discussions before the Constituent Assembly.

31 Clause 7 (g) of the National Convention Report. https://www.constitutionofindia.net/historical-constitution/the-commonwealth-of-india-bill-national-convention-india-1925/

32 Clause 4 (ix) of the Report. https://www.constitutionofindia.net/historical-constitution/nehru-report-motilal-nehru1928/

33 Nirmala Banerjee, 'Whatever Happened to the Dreams of Modernity? The Nehruvian Era and Woman's Position', *Economic and Political Weekly*, Vol. 33, No. 17 (25 April–1 May 1998), pp. WS2–WS7.

34 'Woman's role in planned economy', National Planning Committee, 1947, http://14.139.60.153/bitstream/123456789/8963/1/0038_Woman%27s%20Role%20In%20Planned%20Economy.pdf

35 Pages 29 and 30 of the report.

36 This view of the natural role of women was shared by a large number of freedom fighters, including Mahatma

Gandhi. However, even while pointing out the 'natural difference', the fundamental equality between the sexes was stressed. Thus, Gandhi wrote 'but I am uncompromising in the matter of woman's rights. In my opinion she should labour under no legal disability not suffered by man. I should treat the daughters and sons on a footing of perfect equality. As women begin to realize their strength, as they must in proportion to the education they receive, they will naturally resent the glaring inequalities to which they are subjected'. *Young India*, 17 October 1929, reproduced in *The Makers of Modern India*, Ramachandra Guha, Viking, 2010, p. 181.

37 See the dissent note of Kapila Khandwalla in the report.

38 The Nehru report stated that 'no person shall by reason of his religion, caste or creed be prejudiced in any way in regard to public employment, office of power or honour and the exercise of any trade or calling' and that 'freedom of conscience and free profession and practice of religion are, subject to public order or morality, hereby guaranteed to every person'.

39 The demand for separate electorates was part of a consensus among the Muslim community and was most famously detailed in the fourteen points drafted by Jinnah in response to the Nehru Report of 1928. 'The Communal Award of 1932 and Its Implications in Bengal', Bidyut Chakrabarty, Modern Asian Studies, Vol. 23, No. 3, 1989, pp. 493–523.

40 Indian Councils Act, 1909. This Act was part of what are known as the Minto-Morley reforms, so named after the Secretary of State, Lord Morley and the Viceroy of India, Lord Minto.

41 Prior to the Act, the councils only had nominated members.

42 D.N., 'Gandhi, Ambedkar and Separate Electorates Issue', *Economic and Political Weekly,* Vol. 26, No. 21, 25 May 1991, pp. 1328–1330.

43 Dr Ambedkar, *What Congress and Gandhi have done to Untouchables,* p. 88. See also *The Poona Pact and the History of Dalit Representation*, Swaraj Basu, Proceedings

of the Indian History Congress, Vol. 61, Part One: Millennium, 2000–2001, pp. 986–998.

44 Dr Ambedkar, *What Congress and Gandhi have done to Untouchables*, pp. 90.

45 Resolution No F 14/17-B 33 dated 4 July 1934, Gazette of India, part I, 7 July 1934.

46 Jose Kalapura John, *Dalit Struggle for Equality: A Study of Three Movements in the 1930s*, Proceedings of the Indian History Congress, Vol. 62, 2001, pp. 668–684.

47 Charu Gupta, *Sexuality, Obscenity and Community: Women, Muslims, and the Hindu Public in Colonial India*, Palgrave Macmillan, 2002.

48 This is what the old parliament house was called after its inauguration by Lord Irwin. *Old Indian Parliament:* 'An Odyssey of Colonialism, Independence and Protest', *Outlook*, 27 May 2023, Swati Shikha.

49 'A Text without Author' in *Politics and ethics of the Indian Constitution,* ed. Bhargava OUP, 2008.

50 This system requires the voter to rank the various candidates in order of preference. If the preferred candidate of the voter has already been elected or eliminated, the vote goes to the second ranked candidate and so on. This measure allows a form of proportional representation as most votes result in the election of a candidate.

51 Shiva Rao, Vol. V, pp. 745.

52 For a compelling critique of the caste system and its distinction from the concept of race see, *Annihilation of Caste: the annotated critical edition,* Dr B.R. Ambekar, Navayana, 2014.

53 Madhav Khosla, *India's Founding Moment*, Harvard University Press, 2020, p. 146–151.

54 Marc Gallanter, *Competing Equalities: Law and the Backward Classes in India*, p. 158–160 and *These Seats are Reserved*, Abhinav Chandrachud, Penguin, 2023.

55 Per K.M. Munshi, *Constituent Assembly Debates*, Vol. 5, p. 227–228.

56 *Constituent Assembly Debates*, 30 November 1948.

57 *Constituent Assembly Debates*, 30 November 1948. That Mr Channaih had strong opinions on this issue is clear from the fact that the debates record that he refused to take his seat and had to be asked by the Vice-President of the Assembly to return to his seat.

58 Rochana Bajpai, 'Constituent Assembly Debates and Minority Rights', *Economic and Political Weekly*, Vol. 35, No. 21/22, 27 May–2 June 2000, pp. 1837–1845. She points out that, reservations to Parliament, in the Cabinet as well as public services 'were incorporated under "special provisions relating to minorities" in the draft Constitution published in February 1948. But amendments were adopted to negate each of these articles during discussions of the draft in October 1949. The amendments effectively removed religious minorities from the purview of these safeguards and restricted the scope of these articles mainly to the scheduled castes and the scheduled tribes'.

59 Constituent Assembly Debates, vol. VII, p 1057.

60 The Framing of India's Constitution, Select Documents Volume II Shiva Rao, B. Delhi: Indian Institute of Public Administration, 1967, p. 687.

61 'Make us your equal partners, then there will be no majority or minority communities in India', Tajamul Husain. CAD, vol. VIII, 25–26, May 1949, p. 337.

62 'Between inequality and identity: The Indian Constituent Assembly Debates and religious difference, 1946–50', Shabnum Tejani, in 'The Indian Constituent Assembly', Ed. Udit Bhatia, Routledge 2018.

63 Constituent Assembly Debates, vol. XI, 24 November 1949, p. 877 quoted in Tejani above.

64 'Minority Rights versus Caste Claims: Indian Christians and Predicaments of Law', Rowena Robinson, Vol. 49, No. 14 (5 April 2014), *Economic and Political Weekly*, p. 82.

65 *Founding Mothers of the Indian Republic: Gender Politics of the Framing of the Constitution*, Achyut Chetan, Cambridge University Press, 2022.

66 Annie Devenish, *Debating Women's Citizenship in India 1930-1950*, Bloomsbury, 2019, p. 149.
67 Achyut Chetan above, Chapter 6.
68 'Framing of India's Constitution', Shiva Rao, pp. 332–333.
69 Granville Austin, *The Indian Constitution: A Cornerstone of Nation*, Oxford, 1999, p. 52.
70 Ed. Udit Bhatia, *The Indian Constituent Assembly*, Routledge, 2018, p. 19.
71 Thomas Piketty, *A Brief History of Equality*, Harvard University Press, 2022.
72 Thomas Piketty, *A Brief History of Equality*, Harvard University Press, 2022.
73 Gautam Bhatia, *The Transformative Constitution: A Radical Biography in Nine Acts*, HarperCollins, 2019. See also the case of BK Pavitra v. UOI (2019) 16 SCC 129 where the Court notes that 'the Constitution is a transformative document. The realisation of its transformative potential rests ultimately in its ability to breathe life and meaning into its abstract concepts. For, above all, the Constitution was intended by its draftspersons to be a significant instrument of bringing about social change in a caste-based feudal society witnessed by centuries of oppression of and discrimination against the marginalised. As our constitutional jurisprudence has evolved, the realisation of the transformative potential of the Constitution has been founded on the evolution of equality away from its formal underpinnings to its substantive potential'.

Chapter 2: Rule of Law

1 Gouriet v. Union of Post Office Workers (1977) 2 WLR 310. This judgment was however overturned in appeal by the House of Lords in Gouriet v. Attorney General, 3 WLR 300, 1977.
2 Reproduce section 58.
3 Thomas Fuller, a British physician, published a book of proverbs called *Gnomologia* in 1732, which first used the phrase without referring to its origin.

4 A rough search on a leading legal research website (SCC Online) returned almost 180 hits where this phrase has been used in judgments of the Supreme Court as well as the high courts.

5 Article 14 has been used in this chapter as a short form for the entire 'equality code' contained in Article 14–18 of the Constitution.

6 Joseph Raz has noted a tendency to use 'the Rule of Law' as a general stand-in for everything nice one could ever want to say about a political system, or everything good one could want from it'. Jeremy Waldron, 'Is the Rule of Law an Essentially Contested Concept (in Florida)?', in ed. R. Bellamy, *The Rule of Law and the Separation of Powers* (Aldershot).

7 Such a system would require members of that society to obey even laws that they thought to be unjust or follow laws that they thought were just but inherently immoral (for instance there were many in the apartheid era in South Africa who though that the racial segregation laws were just). To some such a system may not appear to be one that follows the rule of law in a basic intuitive sense. It has been suggested that the obligation might be better phrased that 'the rule of law requires that the law make the differences it purports to make' rather than imposing any generalised obligation to obey the law. See 'The Principles of Constitutionalism', N.W. Barber, p. 86, OUP, 2018.

8 There is a strong link between this form of equality and the idea of equality as an obligation upon the State to display equal concern and respect for all its citizens. For a particular exposition of this formulation of equality, see the chapter on equality in 'Justice for hedgehogs', Ronald Dworkin, Harvard University Press, 2013.

9 *Politics, Aristotle,* translated by Benjamin Jowett, Book IV, Part IV, https://classics.mit.edu/Aristotle/politics.4.four.html.

10 Jeremy Waldron, 'The Rule of Law', *The Stanford Encyclopaedia of Philosophy,* Fall 2023 Edition, Edward N. Zalta & Uri Nodelman (eds.), forthcoming.

11 Lon Fuller, *The Morality of Law*, Yale University Press, 1965.

12 However, Fuller did argue that these rules imply a certain 'inner morality' of the law. This view led to the famous, Fuller–Hart debate. 'Positivism and the Separation of Law and Morals', HLA Hart 1958 Vol. 71 *Harvard Law Review* 593 and 'Positivism and fidelity to law: A Reply to Professor Hart', Lon Fuller, Vol. 71, 1958, *Harvard Law Review* 630.

13 See, *Natural Law and Natural Rights*, Finnis, Clarendon Press, 1980 and 'Law's Republic', Frank Michelman, *The Yale Law Journal,* Vol. 97, No. 8, 'Symposium: The Republican Civic Tradition', (July, 1988), pp. 1493–1537. This view of the rule of law seems to dovetail rather neatly with the view that Finnis has about the nature of law itself. For Finnis, a proponent of natural law, law itself is not a mere sterile set of technical rules or a technique to achieve a legal outcome. Instead as an ideal the 'law' embodies a set of self-evident values (typically based on virtue ethics) and therefore cannot be judged independent of its content.

14 For usage of this term in Indian Jurisprudence see BPCL v. Maddula Ratnavalli, 6 SCC 81, 2007.

15 Richard Bellamy, 'The rule of law', in *Political Concepts*, ed. Richard Bellamy and Andrew Mason. Manchester University Press.

16 'A substantive conception of the rule of law: non-arbitrary treatment and the limit of procedure', Corey Brettschneider, *Nomos,* Vol. 50, Getting to the Rule of Law, 2011, pp. 52–63.

17 Tom Bingham, 'The Rule of Law', Allen Lane, 2010, p. 67.

18 Jeremy Waldon, 'The Rule of Law and the Importance of Procedure', *Nomos,* Vol. 50, Getting to the Rule of Law, 2011, pp. 3–31.

19 Waldron (Stanford article above). This has been adapted from a list prepared by Justice Tashima in 'The War on Terror and the Rule of Law', *Asian American Law Journal*,

15: 245–65. Interestingly, Judge Tashima also includes principles (e.g., no review or rehearing) which Waldron does not include in his list and vice versa (e.g. Waldron requires reasons for judgment which Tashima does not). This shows that even the procedural conception is not free from disagreements.

20 The procedural aspect has both instrumental as well as intrinsic worth. A legal system which follows well established norms of procedure is likely to be one where legally sound outcomes are common. The presumption is that these procedures lead to a fair result, though that is not guaranteed. The other sense is where fair procedures are intrinsically valuable. To most of us, any legal regime where the judge is biased, or where an unreasoned decision is rendered without hearing the affected parties would be antithetical to the rule of law. This infirmity would remain even if the outcome itself is correct. This view of the intrinsic merit of the procedural fairness also draws from an idea of human dignity. See for instance Waldron.

21 For a discussion on the possible way to 'unite' these different views, see 'The Rule of Law as a Concept in Constitutional Discourse', Richard H. Fallon, 97 *Columbia Law Review*, 1997, pp. 1–56. The author notes that 'the Rule of Law is best conceived as comprising multiple strands, including values and considerations to which each of the four competing ideal types calls attention. It is a mistake to think of particular criteria as necessary in all contexts for the Rule of Law. Rather, we should recognize that the strands of the Rule of Law are complexly interwoven, and we should begin to consider which values or Criteria are presumptively primary under which conditions'.

22 'The Rule of Law and Equality', *Law and Philosophy*, 2013, pp. 565–618.

23 'Chief Justice S.R. Das and Equality Before the Law', Justice P.B. Mukherjee, Vol 2 No. 2/3, 1960, *Journal of the Indian Law Institute* 161. Even though this article was

written almost sixty years ago, there is not a lot of extra material since that date.

24 *In Re Special Courts Bill* (1979) 1 SCC 380 it was held that 'the first part of Article 14, which was adopted from the Irish Constitution, is a declaration of equality of the civil rights of all persons within the territories of India. It enshrines a basic principle of republicanism'.

25 Sri Srinivasa Theatre v. Govt. of Tamil Nadu, 2 SCC 643, 1992. Interestingly, the judgment went on to hold that 'it appears to us that the word "law" in the former expression is used in a generic sense—a philosophic sense—whereas the word "laws" in the latter expression denotes specific laws in force'. It is difficult to comprehend the exact import of the statement because a fundamental right is supposed to be justiciable, i.e. give a right for a person to approach the court and complain of a violation of the right. It is slightly hard to imagine how any person can complain of the violation of a 'philosophic sense'.

26 Part of the reason that there are varied ideas about what the rule of law requires, stems from the disagreements as to the nature of law itself. To some, law may be just a set of rules or a technique for achieving conclusions from a set of legal principles independent of any content. This view of the rule of law would readily accommodate a more formal idea of the rule of law. For others though, the idea of the law cannot be independent from its content. In other words, law intrinsically has certain substantive features and content which are required to be fulfilled before it can be adequately termed as law. This view, closely mirroring the opinions of natural law theorists, would dovetail more neatly with a substantive version of the rule of law.

27 Rohit De, *A People's Constitution*, p. 9, Princeton University Press, 2018.

28 Article 47 of the Constitution.

29 Para 1 of the Bombay High Court judgment in F.N. Balsara v. State of Bombay AIR 1951 Bom 210. This judgment was by a three-judge panel which comprised of Chief Justice

M.C. Chagla, Justice Gajendragadkar (who went on to become the Chief Justice of India) and Justice Tendolkar (in whose name one of the most famous cases on Article 14 has been delivered by the Supreme Court—see Ramkrishna Dalmia v. S.R. Tendolkar 1959 SCR 279. Interestingly, the judgment dealt with a commission of enquiry headed by a retired judge of the Bombay High Court, Justice Tendolkar, who was part of the bench that struck down the Bombay Prohibition Act.

30 Charanjit Lal Chowdhury v. Union of India, SCR 869,1950.

31 The special exemption was not only on the battlefield, but also in military canteen and messes, i.e. the clubs where the personnel would socialize. Section 39 of the BPA.

32 State of West Bengal v. Anwar Ali Sarkar, SCR 284, 1952. This classic interpretation of the equality clause stems from American Jurisprudence. It should be remembered that when this judgment was delivered in India in the early 1950s the due process doctrine had undergone significant upheavals in the US. After zealously upholding the laissez faire theory, the courts there became reluctant to strike down legislation on these grounds. Accordingly, they adopted a more deferential standard, one that Indian courts seemingly borrowed. Academics have posited that the American courts adopted the liberal approach in an 'effort to maintain one of the central distinctions in nineteenth-century constitutional law — the distinction between valid economic regulation' calculated to serve the general good and invalid "class" legislation designed to extend special privileges to a favoured class of beneficiaries'. See 'In Search of Laissez-Faire Constitutionalism', Matthew J Lindsay, (2010), 123 *Harvard Law Review* F 55

33 Concise Oxford English Dictionary, 11th Edn, OUP, 2004.

34 Ameerunissa Begum v. Mahboob Begum SCR 404, 1953.

35 However, there is no absolute bar against single person laws. If a person is placed in a unique position due to some circumstance, she can be treated differently from everyone else on that ground.

36 The stature or colour of the hair would surely constitute specific identifiable grounds for making a class and therefore would be based on 'intelligible' differentia. However, the court holds that such a class would not pass Constitutional muster. This appears to be a case where the judges have implicitly incorporated a value judgment that certain grounds of discrimination are presumptively unfair. Academics have argued that such an analysis ought to be part of the 'intelligible differentia' test. See 'Re-writing State of West Bengal v Anwar Ali Sarkar: The Possibility of an Anti-Colonial Jurisprudence', Tarunabh Khaitan, Forthcoming: World Comparative Law/VRU, 2023.

37 Khaitan notes that 'as part of this inquiry, judges have often inquired into the over- inclusiveness and under- inclusiveness of the measure in seeking the stated objective, although they have generally been tolerant of a considerable degree of misfit'. Oxford Handbook, p. 708. However, under and over inclusiveness, other than being a consequence of the rational nexus test, also considerably overlaps with the test for intelligible differentia. Therefore, wrongfully excluding people from a class (i.e. under-inclusive) or adding them erroneously to a class to which they do not belong (over-inclusive) also suffers from the vice of arbitrarily classifying people with no regard to intelligible differentia. See for instance, Shree Meenakshi Mills v. Visvanatha Sastri 1 SCR 787, 1955.

38 This failure to demand a robust link results in courts permitting a fair bit of leeway to the State in permitting over and under inclusive classification. However, in cases of categories covered by Article 15 the courts generally exercise a stronger degree of review. See for instance the judgment of Malhotra J. in Navtej Johar.

39 R.K. Garg v. UOI 4 SCC 675, 1981, para 18. For a trenchant criticism of this judgment, see, Seervai pp. 484–496.

40 Academics have suggested that this mode of determining an Article 14 violation can be polished to include other relevant consideration including a form of proportionality

between the adverse impact on the affected rights and the necessity of the undertaken measures. See Khaitan, (Oxford Handbook).

41 Khaitan, Oxford Handbook, p. 711 citing the judgment of the court in Subramanian Swamy v. CBI 8 SCC 682, 2014.

42 Another means might have been to reform the classification test itself by the adoption of substantive criteria. There is nothing in the Constitution which mandates the formal application of the test and therefore there was considerable leeway to reform, In fact, Justice Bose in the case of Anwar Ali Sarkar did hold that 'what I am concerned to see is not whether there is absolute equality in any academical sense of the term but whether the collective conscience of a sovereign democratic republic can regard the impugned law, contrasted with the ordinary law of the land, as the sort of substantially equal treatment which men of resolute minds and unbiased views can regard as right and proper in a democracy of the kind we have proclaimed ourselves to be'. Para 55. This application of the classification test was fairly substantive. In Navtej Johar v. UOI (2018) 10 SCC 1 too, the court criticised the classification test, (Chandrachud J. in para 409), yet in later judgments went on to apply the same test.

43 E.P. Royappa v. State of Tamil Nadu (1974) 4 SCC 3, para 85.

44 State of A.P. v. McDowell & Co., 3 SCC 709, 1996, and Raj Bala v. State of Haryana 2 SCC 445, 2016.

45 Shayara Bano v. Union of India 9 SCC 1, 2017.

46 Khaitan, Oxford Handbook, p. 712.

47 H.M. Seervai, 'Constitutional Law of India', Vol. I, 438, 1991, *Law & Justice Publishing Co.* 4th *Edn.*

48 This is not to argue that dignity simply collapses into equality but rather that the concepts are interconnected and give meaning and content to each other. As Khaitan explains, one way to understand dignity is as an expressive norm which reaches out to the meaning behind an action. 'Dignity as an Expressive Norm: Neither Vacuous Nor

a Panacea', Tarunabh Khaitan, Vol. 32, 2012, *Oxford Journal of Legal Studies*, pp. 1–19.
If such meaning aims to perpetuate prejudice or stereotyping, such action would also be violative of the principle of equality.

49 State of Tamil Nadu v. National South Indian River Interlinking Agriculturalist Association, 15 SCC 534, 2021.

50 To add to the confusion, there is also a concept of substantive due process. However, that lies in the domain of Article 21 rather than 14. For a discussion on how this concept, borrowed from American jurisprudence, developed in India see *Liberty after Freedom: A history of Article 21, Due Process and the Constitution of India*, Rohan Alva, Harper Collins, 2022.

51 Justice P.B. Mukherjee, 'Chief Justice S.R. Das and Equality Before the Law', Vol 2 No. 2/3, 1960, *Journal of the Indian Law Institute* 161, where he states that, 'It is enough to say here that the constitution is necessarily rooted in the tradition and legal history of a nation and not a plant of exotic growth and to look for neatness and semantic brevity of a past century in the complexities of a modern democracy is not a fruitful pursuit.'

52 Ranbir Singh, 'The March of Law in India: The Long Road from Oppression to Justice', *Journal of the Indian Law Institute,* Vol. 59, No. 3, 2017, p. 288.

53 Kasturi Lal Lakshmi Reddy v. State of J&K,1980, 4 SCC 1 referring to Royappa's case.

54 Maneka Gandhi v. UOI 1 SCC 248, 1978.

55 Union of India v. Tulsiram Patel, 3 SCC 398, 1985.

56 James B. Peterson, 'The Forms of the Syllogism', Vol. 8, No. 4, July 1899, The *Philosophical Review,* pp. 371–385.

57 Ranjit Thakur v. UOI 4 SCC 611, 1987.

58 Siemens Engineering and Manufacturing v. UOI 2 SCC 981, 1976.

59 DTC v. Mazdoor Congress, Supp 1 SCC 600, 1991.

60 Article 141 of the Constitution declares that the 'Law declared by Supreme Court to be binding on all courts

within the territory of India' while Article 144 states that 'all authorities, civil and judicial, in the territory of India shall act in aid of the Supreme Court'. These and other provisions of the Constitution have been used to assert the supremacy of the court to be the final arbiters of what the Constitution means.

Chapter 3: Education

1 'Felicity Huffman awoke to FBI agents with guns drawn at her LA home in the college cheating raid', *Los Angeles Times,* 12 March 2019.

2 Priyanka Omprakash Panwar v. State of Maharashtra, 2 Bom CR 100, 2008, affirmed in Food Corporation of India v. Jagadish Balaram Bahira, 8 SCC 670, 2017.

3 Jody Heymann, Aleta Sprague, Amy Raub, 'Advancing Equality: How Constitutional Rights Can Make a Difference Worldwide', University of California Press, 2020, pp. 199–224.

4 In fact, evidence suggests that focusing on separate aspects of disadvantage fails to see the negative effect on educational outcomes as opposed to seeing race, gender and social class cumulatively. See, 'Race, Class, and Gender in Education Research: An Argument for Integrative Analysis', Carl A. Grant, Christine E. Sleeter, *Review of Educational Research*, Vol. 56, No. 2, pp. 195–211. While race is more problematic in the American as opposed to the Indian context, some authors have drawn parallels between the two forms of discrimination. See *Caste: The Origins of Our Discontent*, Isabel Wilkinson, Random House, 2020.

5 The fact that access to education to minorities and women is less than those of upper caste Hindu men is not a surprise. What is less obvious is that the debates about reservations, at least in the popular imagination, tend to ignore the need for quotas (or immunity from quotas) for these groups.

6 Reservations were also made for public employment.

7 See also 'The Making of Adi Dravida Politics in Early Twentieth Century Tamil Nadu', Raj Sekhar Basu, *Social Scientist*, Vol. 39, No. 7/8, July–August 2011, pp. 9–41.
8 Champakam Dorairajan v. State of Madras, 63 LW 895 at p. 905, 1950.
9 Champakam, p. 918.
10 SCR 525, 1951.
11 A detailed discussion of the history and politics of the first amendment, which also diluted rights relating to free speech and the right to property can be found in *Sixteen Stormy Days: The Story of the First Amendment to the Constitution of India*, Tripurdaman Singh, Vintage Books, 2020.
12 Article 15 (4). Though judgment did generate outrage, it is curious to note that the very Constituent Assembly which amended the Constitution had refused to insert a similar position in the original Constitution. See 'Protective Discrimination for Backward Classes in India', Marc Galanter, *Journal of the Indian Law Institute*, Vol. 3, No. 1, January–March 1961, pp. 39–70 at p. 40.
13 Article 16 (4) of the Constitution.
14 Jawaharlal Nehru's speech in Parliament, 29 May 1951.
15 There is controversy even about which castes are backward and how that determination is to be made. For instance, are Marathas a backward caste? The Supreme Court, while reversing a judgment of the Bombay High Court has held not. See Jaishri Laxmanrao Patil v. State of Maharashtra, 8 SCC 1, 2021. However, a detailed discussion would be beyond the scope of this book.
16 Indra Sawhney v. UOI 1992 Supp (3) SCC 217.
17 'A caste can be and quite often is a social class in India'. Paragraph 796 of Indra Sawhney. It is important to remember though that the case concerned public employment rather than education, so the court also held 'of course, social, educational and economic backwardness are closely intertwined in the Indian context. The classes

contemplated by Article 16(4) may be wider than those contemplated by Article 15(4)'.

18 Paragraph 792 of Indra Sawhney.

19 Jarnail Singh v. Lacchmi Narain Gupta, 10 SCC 396, 2018. The judgment is an interesting one because it holds another judgment of five judges—M. Nagaraj v. UOI 8 SCC 212, 2006, to be wrong law when it requires data to be produced to establish the social and economic backwardness of the scheduled castes and tribes. While the court was probably right in Jarnail Singh that the Nagraj judgment was contrary to a larger binding judgment in Indra Sawhney, perhaps the proper course of action was to refer the matter to a bench of seven judges for an authoritative ruling in the matter.

20 In para 792 of Indra Sawhney judgement, the court held that 'it is pointed out that clause (4) of Article 16 aims at group backwardness and not individual backwardness. While we agree that clause (4) aims at group backwardness, we feel that exclusion of such socially advanced members will make the 'class' a truly backward class and would more appropriately serve the purpose and object of clause (4)'.

21 This is particularly so because evidence suggests that regardless of all else, there is a strong correlation between caste and class. See 'The Caste-Class Association in India: An Empirical Analysis', Divya Vaid, *Asian Survey*, Vol. 52, No. 2, March/April 2012, pp. 395.

22 8 SCC 481, 2002.

23 6 SCC 537, 2005. The bench of seven judges was constituted to consider the correctness of another judgment of a bench of five judges of the court in the case of Islamic Academy of Education v. Union of India, 6 SCC 697, 2003.

24 While the conventional view is that most fundamental rights have a vertical application, some recent pronouncements by the court have doubted that view. See Kaushal Kishor v. State of UP, 4 SCC 1, 2023.

25 Students for Fair Admission v. Harvard 600 US 181, 2023.

26 Students for Fair Admissions v. President and Fellows of Harvard College 600 US 181, 2023.

27 Saurabh Kirpal, 'Dissent, Democracy and the Rule of Law', 2023, *Quarterly Bar Review* 56.

28 Pramati Educational and Cultural Trust v. Union of India 8 SCC 1 at para 22, 2014. The portion of the amendment, insofar as it dealt with reservations in private institutions which received aid from the government had been upheld by a Constitution Bench of the Supreme Court in Ashok Kumar Thakur v. Union of India 6 SCC 1, 2008.

29 However, after the 103rd Amendment to the Constitution whereby reservations for the economically weaker section of society have been permitted, the immunity of minority institutions from the reservations regime has been undone to some extent.

30 It is therefore no surprise that alliances are often made between disparate minorities in the face of potential majoritarian hegemony. This political fact has a strong historical tradition. Prior to Independence and the decision to form Pakistan as a separate country, the Muslim League and the Scheduled Caste Federation (SCF) run by Dr Ambedkar were in alliance. In fact, Dr Ambedkar was elected to the Constituent Assembly as an independent member with the support of the Muslim League. It was only when he lost his seat due to Partition that he was nominated as a Congress member from Bombay. See *Dr Ambedkar and Untouchability: Fighting the Indian Caste System*, Christophe Jaffrelot, Columbia University Press, 2005 at p. 100.

31 For instance, Article 25 gives persons the freedom of conscience and the right to free profession, practice and propagation of their religion.

32 The words 'set of citizens' shows that thus right inheres in a community as opposed to an individual.

33 Article 30 (2) also has a prohibition against discrimination, but that is a restriction on the power of the State. The Article reads that 'the State shall not, in granting aid to educational institutions, discriminate against any educational institution

on the ground that it is under the management of a minority, whether based on religion or language'.

34 Pramati Educational Society, para 34.

35 Rosemary C. Salomone, Cornelius Riordan, Janice Weinman, 'Single-Sex Schooling: Law, Policy, and Research', *Brookings Papers on Education Policy*, No. 2, 1999, pp. 231–297.

36 Committee of Management, Anglo Vaidyik Balika Inter College v. Board of Highschool and Intermediate Exam, UP 2002 SCC Online All 1676. This judgment purported to follow earlier judgments of the Kerala (Joseph Thomas v. State of Kerala AIR 1958 Ker 33) and Madras High Courts (University of Madras v. Shantha Bai AIR 1954 Mad 67).

37 A single judge of the Allahabad High Court has taken the view that such a prohibition would be void. See Rama Nath Tewari *v.* Committee of Management, Allahabad Intermediate College, 1993 (21) ALR 85. This view has been affirmed by a Division Bench of the same court. The decision of the Calcutta High Court in the case of Anjali Roy v. State of West Bengal AIR 1952 Cal 1952 seems to imply to the contrary, but it is doubtful whether the judgment is good law, partly because certain observations of the single judge were not affirmed in appeal and partly because the judgment relies of other verdicts which were subsequently overruled. For a particular view on the law see, 'Same Sex Schools and Gender Discrimination under the Constitution', Anindita Pattanayak, https://indconlawphil.wordpress.com/2015/05/18/guest-post-same-sex-schools-and-gender-discrimination-under-the-constitution-i/

38 Rt. Rvd. Mark Netto v. State of Kerala 1 SCC 23, 1979. See also Christian Inter College v. State of UP 2005 (2) ESC 828.

39 Resham v. State of Karnataka ILR 2022 Kar 1477.

40 Aishat Shifa v. State of Karnataka 2 SCC 1, 2023.

41 Aishat Shifa, para 170.

42 Aishat Shifa, para 201.

43 Nivedita Jain v. State of Madhya Pradesh AIR 1981 MP 129.

44 State of MP v. Nivedita Jain, 4 SCC 296, 1981.

45 Dr. Preeti Srivastava v. State of MP 7 SCC 120, 1999.

46 The Supreme Court, in the case of B.K. Pavitra v. UOI (2019) 16 SCC 129 notes that 'merit' in competitive exams also requires resources, including economic, social and cultural resources. These are something a candidate from a backward caste lacks.

47 Para 62 of Dr Preeti Srivastava.

48 Para 22 of Dr Preeti Srivastava. See also Dr. Jagdish Saran v. UOI 2 SCC 768, 1980, and Dr Pradip Jain v. UOI 3 SCC 654, 1984.

49 In Faculty Association of AIIMS v. UOI, (2013) 11 SCC 246, the court referred to its earlier judgment in the Indra Sawhney case and held 'that while the relevance and significance of merit at the stage of initial recruitment cannot be ignored, it cannot also be ignored that the same idea of reservation implies selection of a less meritorious person. It was also observed that at the same time such a price would have to be paid if the Constitutional promise of social justice was to be redeemed'. (Para 24).

50 Vani K. Borooah, 'Social Exclusion and Jobs Reservation in India', Vol. 45, 2010, *Economic and Political Weekly*, p. 31.

51 N. Sukumar, 'Caste Discrimination and Exclusion in Indian Universities: A Critical Reflection', Routledge, 2023, p. 173.

52 Sukumar, p. 176.

Chapter 4: Employment

1 'Storm created by Mandal Commission poses serious threat to V.P. Singh's political survival', *Indian Today*, https://www.indiatoday.in/magazine/cover-story/story/19901015-storm-created-by-mandal-commission-poses-serious-threat-to-vp-singh-political-survival-813100-1990-10-14.

2 Studies show that even after accounting for educational differences, SC families get fewer well-paid jobs and have lower consumption than non-SC/ST households. See 'Caste

and Tribe Inequality: Evidence from India, 1983–1999', Yoko Kijima, *Economic Development and Cultural Change*, Vol. 54, No. 2, January 2006, pp. 369–404.

3 S. Krauss and U. Orth, 'Work Experiences and Self-Esteem Development: A Meta-Analysis of Longitudinal Studies'. *European Journal of Personality*, 36(6), 2022, pp. 849–869. This paper also shows that while self-esteem and employment are symbiotic, the effect of employment on self-esteem is greater than the other way round.

4 Robert Jense, 'Do Labour Market Opportunities Affect Young Women's Work and Family Decisions? Experimental Evidence from India', The Quarterly Journal of Economics 753, 2012.

5 'Dalit Adivasi Budget Analysis 2023–24', National Campaign for Dalit Human Rights – Dalit Arthik Adhikar Andolan.

6 Amit Thorat and Sukhadeo Thorat, 'Employment and the Dalit Equation', Outlookindia.com, 11 February 2022.

7 'Growth in Female Labour Force Participation in India Now Seems to Be Stagnating', Wire, 20 March 2023.

8 Ishaan Bansal, IDinsight, Kanika Mahajan, 'COVID-19, Income Shocks and Female Employment', Ashoka University Economics Discussion, paper 69, November 2022.

9 Ramesh Chand, 'Changes in Labour force and Employment in Rural and Urban India: 2017–18 to 2020–21', Indian Economic Association, Bengaluru, 27 December 2022.

10 '62 per cent of all women workers in the country are employed in agriculture, 16 per cent in industry and 22 per cent in the service sector. In the case of male workers, 40 per cent are employed in agriculture, 27 per cent in industry and one third in the services sector.' See 'Changes in Labour force and Employment in Rural and Urban India: 2017–18 to 2020–21' Ramesh Chand, Indian Economic Association, Bengaluru, 27 December 2022.

11 Only 20 per cent of Dalits and 10 per cent of Adivasis work outside the agricultural sector.

12 One interesting study examines applications for employment where the only family information revealed was caste and religion. An analysis of the responses to the applications even prior to an interview shows that Dalits and Muslims had far worse outcomes than upper-caste men. See 'The Legacy of Social Exclusion: A Correspondence Study of Job Discrimination in India', Sukhadeo Thorat, Paul Attewell, *Economic and Political Weekly*, 13 October 2007.

13 Article 39 (a) of the Constitution.

14 The 103rd amendment to the Constitution breaches this 49 per cent limit by providing for 10 per cent reservation for the economically weaker sections of society.

15 Supp 2 SCC 217, 1992.

16 Para 643, Indra Sawhney.

17 Caste/religion/economics.

18 Venkataramana v. State of Madras AIR 1951 SC 229. The government had permitted fixed reservations of posts for different sections, including posts of Brahmins, Muslims, backward Hindus and Harijans. The Supreme Court would have upheld the reservations for Harijans and backward castes, but the government order was struck down because it permitted discrimination in favour of non-backward groups such as Brahmins.

19 M.R. Balaji v. State of Mysore Supp 1 SCR 439, 1963.

20 Speaking on the floor of the Constituent Assembly, Dr Ambedkar said, 'If honourable Members understand this position that we have to safeguard two things namely, the principle of equality of opportunity and at the same time satisfy the demand of communities which have not had so far representation in the State, then, I am sure they will agree that unless you use some such qualifying phrase as "backward" the exception made in favour of reservation will ultimately eat up the rule altogether.' Vol VII (30 November 1948), *Constituent Assembly Debates*.

21 2 SCC 310, 1976.

22 Para 66, N.N. Thomas.

23 If there were a duty on the State, Article 16 (4) might have read as 'the State shall provide for reservations' rather than its current language which is 'Nothing in this article shall prevent the State from making any provision for the reservation.'
24 See S.R. Bommai v. UOI (1994) 3 SCC 1.
25 I am grateful to Rahul Bajaj for pointing this out.
26 Para 75, N.M. Thomas.
27 Indra Sawhney. This judgment overruled an almost thirty-year-old precedent which had held that there could be reservations in promotions. See General Manager, S Rly v. Rangachari 2 SCR 586, 1962.
28 Para 546 of Indra Sawhney, per J. Sawant.
29 Para 828 of Indra Sawhney, per B.P. Jeevan Reddy J.
30 Rikhil R. Bhavnani, Alexander Lee, 'Does Affirmative Action Worsen Bureaucratic Performance? Evidence from the Indian Administrative Service', Vol. 65, *American Journal of Political Science*, 2021, pp. 5–20.
An interesting observation made in the study is that reservations merely neutralize the cognitive bias against members of the oppressed castes at the stage of an interview in the hiring process.
31 The one area with the greatest angst about reservations is in the civil services, and yet India has not ever had a scheduled caste cabinet secretary.
32 The 77th Amendment to the Constitution introduced Article 16 (4A) and
33 M. Nagaraj v. UOI (2006) 8 SCC 212.
34 Para 106, Nagaraj.
35 'John Henry Hutton Biography at the Pitt Rivers Museum History, 1884 – 1945', http://history.prm.ox.ac.uk/collector_hutton.html.
36 Noel Mariam George, 'Tracing the Long, Complex History of Debate on Caste Census', Wire, 22 November 2023.
37 Amarnath Tewary, 'Bihar Caste Survey | OBCs, EBCs Comprise More Than 63% of State's Population', *The Hindu*, 2 October 2023. Adding 10 per cent EWS quota

would imply that almost 75 per cent of government jobs in Bihar are reserved.

38 'Bihar assembly approves hike in caste quota from 50 per cent to 65 per cent, overall reservation now at 75 per cent', *Print*, 9 November 2023.

39 Balaji, para 34.

40 This view was doubted in Akhil Bharatiya Soshit Samaj Karamchari Sangh v. Union of India (1981) 4 SCC 246 as well as the (minority) view of Chinappa Reddy J. in K.C. Vasantha Kumar v. State of Karnataka Supp SCC 714, 1985.

41 This notification was issued on 4 March 2014 when the general elections were approaching, lending credence to the belief that the decision was based more on politics than on data.

42 Ram Singh v. Union of India 4 SCC 697, 2015.

43 Maharashtra State Reservation (of Seats for Admission in Educational Institutions in the State and for Appointments in the Public Services and Posts under the State) for Socially and Educationally Backward Classes (SEBC) Act, 2018.

44 Jaishri Laxmanrao Patil v. State of Maharashtra 4 Bom CR 481, 2019.

45 Jaishri Laxmanrao Patil v. State of Maharashtra 8 SCC 1, 2021.

46 Janhit Abhiyan v. UOI (2023) 5 SCC 1. The verdict was a 3:2 split. The minority verdict was authored by Ravindra Bhat J who had penned the majority judgment in the Maratha reservation case.

47 Para 161.3 'The other learned judges did not specifically deal with the 50 per cent rule but the majority judges agreed that Article 16(4) was not an exception to Article 16(1).'

48 Para 183, 'This is essentially for the reason that the provisions contained in Articles 15 and 16 of the Constitution of India, providing for reservation by way of affirmative action, being of exception to the general rule of equality, cannot be treated as a basic feature.'

49 Constitution (schedule caste) Order, 1950 issued under Article 341 of the Constitution.

50 'Report of the National Commission for Religious and Linguistic Minorities' headed by Justice Ranganath Misra, https://www.minorityaffairs.gov.in/WriteReadData/RTF1984/1658830363.pdf.
51 Ghazi Saaduddin v. State of Maharashtra C.A. No. 329-330/2004.
52 AIR 1954 SCR 817, para 50. A good discussion of these complex rules can be found in 'These Seats are Reserved', Chandrachud, pp. 122–126.
53 Valsamma Paul v. Cochin University 3 SCC 545, 1996.
54 'Full text: Dalit scholar Rohith Vemula's suicide note', *Times of India*, 19 January 2016, https://timesofindia.indiatimes.com/city/hyderabad/full-text-dalit-scholar-rohith-vemulas-suicide-note/articleshow/50634646.cms.
55 Anand Teltumbde, 'Robbing Rohith of his Dalitness', Vol. 52, No. 9, 2017, *Economic and Political Weekly* 10.
56 K.P. Manu v. Chairman, Scrutiny Committee 4 SCC 1, 2015.
57 There is a rebuttable presumption that a child will take the caste of her father. See Rameshbhai Dabhai Naika v. State of Gujarat 3 SCC 400, 2012, which holds that this presumption is one of fact and not a matter of law.
58 State of MP v. Pramod Bhartiya 1 SCC 539, 1993.
59 Section 4 of the Act.
60 This fact was noted even at the time of the enactment of the Equal Remuneration Act, 1976. See 'State and Subordination of Women', Padmini Swaminathan, Vol 22, No. 44, 31 October 1987, *Economic and Political Weekly* 34.
61 Rishika Sahgal, 'Equal Pay for Equal Work? Flaws in the Indian Law', OxHRH Blog, 6 December 2019, <https://ohrh.law.ox.ac.uk/equal-pay-for-equal-work-flaws-in-the-indian-law>
62 Section 30 of the Punjab Excise Act, 1914 was applicable in the National Capital Territory of Delhi.
63 'SC Reserves verdict on women's right to work in Delhi bars', *Times of India,* 22 August 2007.
64 Hotel Association of India v. UOI 86 DRJ 668, 2006.

65 Anuj Garg v. Hotel Association of India 3 SCC 1, 2008.
66 *Reconstructing Sexual Equality*, Professor Christine A. Littleton 75 CALR 1279, July 1987
67 Anuj Garg, para 48.
68 Para 44, Anuj Garg
69 Section 12 of the Army Act states that 'No female shall be eligible for enrolment or employment in the regular Army, except in such corps, department, branch or other body forming part of, or attached to any portion of, the regular Army as the Central Government may, by notification in the Official Gazette, specifying this behalf.'
70 Article 33 of the Constitution states that 'Parliament may, by law, determine to what extent any of the rights conferred by this Part shall, in their application to . . . the members of the Armed Forces be restricted or abrogated so as to ensure the proper discharge of their duties and the maintenance of discipline among them.'
71 On 26 September 2008, the Ministry of Defence issued a circular permitting women to get permanent commissions on only two of the services in the army—Judge Advocate General and the Army Education Corps.
72 Babita Puniya v. Ministry of Defence 168 DLT 115, 2010.
73 Secretary, Ministry of Defence v. Babita Puniya 7 SCC 469, 2020.
74 'The Proximate Causes of Employment Discrimination', Barbara F. Reskin, Contemporary Sociology, Vol. 29, No. 2, March 2000, pp. 319–328.
75 Maternity Benefit Act, 1961.
76 Article 42 of the Constitution.
77 Air India v. Nergesh Meerza, SCC 335, 1981. This was also largely because the airline conceded that the regulation would be amended and the airhostess fired after her third pregnancy! Not that any man had his services terminated on the ground of being the father to three children.
78 Air India, para 60–63.
79 Air India Cabin Crew Assn. v. Yeshaswinee Merchant, 6 SCC 277, para 42, 2003.

80 Navtej Singh Johar v. Union of India 10 SCC 1, 2018, para 438.
81 Section 50 of the Employee State Insurance Act, 1948 and The Maternity Benefits Act 1961.
82 'India's Unorganised Sector Is Being Engulfed, Further Marginalised', Arun Kumar, *Wire*, 18 November, 2022.
83 'Unfolding unpaid domestic work in India: women's constraints, choices, and career', Pushpendra Singh and Falguni Pattanaik.
84 'Domestic Work, Unpaid Work and Wage Rates', Kamala Sankaran, *Economic and Political Weekly*, Vol. 48, No. 43, 26 October 2013, pp. 85–89.
85 Sarahbeth George, 'Why is a woman's salary less than a man's? A gaze down the gap', 23 April 2023, *ETOnline*.
86 Soumyajit Chakraborty, 'Occupational Sex Segregation: An Inquiry into Indian Job Market', *Journal of Regional Development and Planning*, Vol. 5, Issue 2, 2016.
87 For a discussion on the literature, see 'Gender Pay Gap in India: A Reality and the Way Forward—An Empirical Approach Using Quantile Regression Technique' Pooja Sengupta and Roma Puri, 2021, Studies in Microeconomics, pp. 1–32.
88 Of course, even if there is greater equality in hiring in the unskilled sector between men and women, there still is a large pay gap in the lower paying sectors of the economy. 'Gender Pay Gap in India: Evidence from Urban Labour Market', Shamim Ara, 64, *The Indian Journal of Labour Economics* 415, 2021. Paradoxically, the greater the pay, the less likely women are to be hired, but once employed in such jobs, they are likely to receive more equal pay compared to their male peers. Of course, this is also a contested position—some data suggests that wage inequality increases with greater skill. See 'Gender pay gap in the formal sector: 2006 to 2012 Preliminary Evidences from Paycheck India Data', Biju Varkkey and Rupa Kordey.
89 Christine Lagarde, Jonathan D. Ostry, 'Gender Discrimination and Growth: Theory and Evidence from

India', Berta Esteve-Volart and 'Economic Gains from Gender Inclusion: Even Greater than You Thought', IMF Blog, 28 November 2018.

90 'The U-Shaped Female Labor Force Function in Economic Development and Economic History', Claudia Goldin, 1994, Working Paper No. 4707, *National Bureau of Economic Research*.

91 Section 149 (1) of the Companies Act, 2013.

92 Women's representation on boards has increased from 6 per cent in 2013 to 13 per cent in 2017and to 18 per cent in 2022. 'Diversity in the Boardroom: Progress and the way forward', *EY Report*, 2022.

93 Sarahbeth George, 'Why is a woman's salary less than a man's? A gaze down the gap', *Economic Times*, 2 April 2023.

94 National Legal Services Authority v. Union of India 5 SC 438, 2014.

95 The right to determine gender and have legal recognition is now codified in The Transgender (Protection of Rights) Act, 2019. This Act has been trenchantly criticized for not adhering to the judgment of the court and is currently subject to challenge before the Supreme Court. Swati Bidhan Baruah v. Union of India WP (Civil) 51/2020.

96 NALSA, para 67.

97 How the two forms of reservation operate in practice has been explained in Saurav Yadav v. State of UP 4 SCC 542, 2021. See also UOI v. M. Selvakumar (2017) 3 SCC 504.

98 Rights of Persons with Disabilities Act, 2016, Section 34. Reservation in educational institutions is provided in Section 32 of the Act.

99 This was so held in Indra Sawhney, para 812.

100 Ashna Butani, 'Transgender Reservation: Delhi Transwoman blazes trail', 12 October 2023, *Hindustan Times*.

101 'World population data: Average Indian 10 years younger than Chinese', *Hindustan Times*, 20 April 2023.

102 'Japan: Demographic Shift Opens Door to Reforms', IMF, 10 February 2020, https://www.imf.org/en/News/

Articles/2020/02/10/na021020-japan-demographic-shift-opens-door-to-reforms.

Chapter 5: Business

1 Bidi Supply Company v. Union of India 1956 SCR 267.
2 This is the language to be found on the website of the United Nations. See https://www.un.org/en/global-issues/human-rights.
3 'Competitive Neutrality: Maintaining a level playing field between public and private business', OECD 2012.
4 Mohan Mahto v. Central Coal Fields Ltd. 8 SCC 549, 2007.
5 Ramana Dayaram Shetty v. Airport Authority of India, 3 SCC 489, 1979.
6 All India Sainik Schools Employees' Association v. Defence Minister, Supp 1 SCC 205, 1989.
7 Anand Vardhan Chandel v. University of Delhi, 1978 SCC Online Del 74.
8 Pradeep kumar Biswas v. Indian Institute of Chemical Biology, 5 SCC 111, 2002.
9 Case law suggests that corporations cannot be citizens and hence cannot claim rights under Article 15 and 19. See State Trading Corporation of India v. CTO, 4 SCR 99, 1964.
10 Glock Asia-Pacific Ltd. v. UOI (2023) 8 SCC 226.
11 1 SCC 212, 1991.
12 The spoils system was a patronage system first employed by US President Andrew Jackson. It was reviled for venality while being simultaneously venerated for the democratization of the civil service. See 'Patronage Regimes and American Party Development from *The Age of Jackson' to the Progressive Era*, Scott C. James Vol. 36, No. 1, *British Journal of Political Science*, pp. 39–60, January, 2006.
13 Para 2 and 45 of the Shrilekha Vidyarthi judgment.
14 Contract law is an area where the rights and liabilities are fixed by consent, i.e. by parties themselves. This is in contradistinction to tort law (which is the closest analogy

to an injury suffered by a Constitutional wrong) where the liability is fixed by the operation of law. See Jay Laxmi Salt Works v. State of Gujarat 4 SCC 1, 1994.

15 Dwarkadas Marfatia v. Board of Trustees of the Port of Bombay (1989) 3 SCC 393 'whatever be the activity of the public authority, it should meet the test of Article 14', para 25.

16 Mahabir Auto Stores v. IOC 3 SCC 752, 1990, para 12.

17 Para 48 Shrilekha Vidyarthi.

18 Tata Motors Ltd. v. BEST 2023 SCC Online SC 671.

19 In the case of government contracts, there are additional requirements of formality imposed by Article 299 of the Constitution. For a discussion, see 'Government Contracts', Umakanth Varottil, *Oxford Handbook of the Indian Constitution*, ed. Mehta, Khosla, OUP, 2016.

20 Shrilekha Vidyarthi 'the personality of the State, requiring regulation of its conduct in all spheres by requirements of Article 14, does not undergo such a radical change after the making of a contract merely because some contractual rights accrue to the other party in addition', para 20.

21 Ramana Dayaram Shetty v. International Airport Authority 3 SCC 489, 1979.

22 Shetty, para 21.

23 See the chapter on the Rule of Law for an analysis.

24 Central Inland Water Supply v. Brojo Nath Ganguly, 3 SCC 156, 1986, followed in Delhi Transport Corporation v. DTC Mazdoor Congress Supp 1 SCC 600, 1991.

25 New Horizons v. UOI, 1 SCC 478, 1995.

26 Tata Cellular v. UOI, 6 SCC 651, 1994.

27 Raunaq International v. IVR Construction (1999) 1 SCC 492.

28 In cases of award of tenders, the courts have now gone to the extent of holding that 'judicial review of such contractual matters has its own limitations. . . . In evaluating tenders and awarding contracts, the parties are to be governed by principles of commercial prudence. To that extent, principles of equity and natural justice have to stay at a

distance'. UFlex Ltd. v. State of Tamil Nadu, 1 SCC 165, 2022.

29 See for instance the decision to strike down the grant of 2G licenses to telecom companies. Centre for Public Interest Litigation v. UOI, 3 SCC 104, 2012.

30 Section 65 of the Contract Act.

31 The doctrine of restitution and unjust enrichment require any party which has gained an unfair advantage to disgorge the benefits. See Indian Council for Enviro-legal Action v. UOI, 6 SCC 215, 2011.

32 Century Spinning and manufacturing Company Ltd. v. Ulhasnagar Municipal Council, 1 SCC 582, 1970.

33 Motilal Padampat Sugar Mills Co. Ltd. v. State of UP, 2 SCC 409, 1979.

34 UOI v. Indo-Afghan Agencies Ltd. 2 SCR 366, 1968.

35 Motilal, para 24.

36 For an analysis of the doctrine of promissory estoppel, see 'Principles of Estoppel and Ultra Vires in their Application to the Discharge pf Public Duties by Public Authorities', A.K. Ganguly, *Journal of the Indian Law Institute*, 335, 1999.

37 Food Corporation of India v. Kamdhenu Cattle Feed Industries, 1 SCC 71, 1993. Interestingly, the Supreme Court in the facts of the case decided that adequate consideration had been given to the legitimate expectation of Kamdhenu by keeping its offer alive and therefore proceeded to dismiss its challenge to the tendering process.

38 For an exposition of the relevant principles, albeit in the context of service law, see Kerala State Beverages (M&M) Corpn. Ltd. v. P.P. Suresh 9 SCC 710, 2019.

39 Babita Puniya v. Secretary, 168 DLT 115, 2010, affirmed in A.U. Tayyaba v. Union of India, 5 SCC 688, 2023.

40 Ajay Hasia v. Khalid Mujib Sehravardi, 1 SCC 722, 1981, para 16.

41 Common law is a set of principles derived from judge made law in England. George Burton Adams, 'The Origin of the Common Law', Vol. 34, 1924, *Yale Law Journal*, 115.

These rules have been made applicable to India by virtue of Article 372 of the Constitution.

42 No person shall be a judge in their own cause.

43 The literal translation of the phrase is 'listen to the other side'.

44 Siemens Engineering and Manufacturing v. UOI (1976) 2 SCC 981.

45 Quasi-judicial functions are those where a tribunal decides some issue between two parties rather than taking a policy or some other general decision. See State of Gujarat v. Gujarat Revenue Tribunal Bar Assn, 10 SCC 353, 2012.

46 1 SCC 70, 1975.

47 Raeesa Vakil, 'Constitutionalizing administrative law in the Indian Supreme Court: Natural justice and fundamental rights', 16 International J. Const. L., 475, 2018.

48 R.K. Garg v. UOI 4 SCC 675, 1981.

49 Munn v. Illinois 94 US 13 and Metropolis Theater Company v. City of Chicago 228 US 61.

50 R.K. Garg, para 18.

51 As far back as in 1960 the Supreme Court ruled that taxation statutes were also amenable to an Article 14 challenge. See Kunnathat Thatehunni Moopil Nair v. State of Kerala. However, this power has been used very sparingly. See 'Constitutional law of India', H.M. Seervai, Vol I, p. 479 onwards, *Universal Law Publishing*.

52 BALCO Employees Union v. UOI, 2 SCC 333, 2002.

53 Goa Foundation v. Sesa Sterlite, 4 SCC 218, 2018.

54 United States R. Retirement Bd. v. Fritz, 449 US 166, 1980.

55 Supriyo v. UOI WP (Civil) 1011/2022 per J. Narasimha.

56 Rex Ahdar, 'Contract doctrine, Predictability and the Nebulous Exception', Vol. 73, 2014, *Cambridge Law Journal* 39.

57 Naresh Shridhar Mirajkar v. State of Maharashtra, 3 SCR 744, 1966.

Chapter 6: Democracy

1 Bush v. Gore 531 US 98, 2000.

2 https://web.archive.org/web/20120912083944/http://www.fec.gov/pubrec/2000presgeresults.htm

3 Fundamental rights guaranteed to minorities are an example of how even an electorally insignificant person is offered the same protection as a member of a majority community. Judicial intervention is necessary only when the equality provisions are violated. This is akin to a tort-based system where the jurisprudence of the court is corrective rather than constructive built on a case-by-case basis. For a criticism of this approach in the US, see 'Discrimination Law: The New Franken-Tort', Sandra F. Sperino, University of Cincinnati College of Law University of Cincinnati College of Law Scholarship and Publications, 2016. Of course, in India in the course of 'correction' of an injustice, the court can also issue directions which appear to be legislative. See Vishaka v. State of Rajasthan (1997) 6 SCC 241.

4 It is important not to conflate majoritarianism with democracy as understood in current liberal democracies. As for their connection with equality as represented by the Rule of Law, see 'Democracy, populism, and the rule of law: A reconsideration of their interconnectedness', Vasileios Adamidis, https://doi.org/10.1177/02633957211041444.

5 For instance, this obligation is recognized in the various, Directive Principles of State Policy, which are missives to the elected government to ensure equality. While these principles have been used by the courts in different ways, they are not judicially enforceable and instead cast a general obligation on the State. Article 37 states that 'the provisions contained in this part shall not be enforceable by any court, but the principles therein laid down are nevertheless fundamental in the governance of the country and it shall be the duty of the State to apply these principles in making laws'.

6 Ornit Shani, *How India Became Democratic*, p. 3, Penguin Viking, 2018.

7 Ed. B. Shiva Rao, 'The Framing of India's Constitution: Select Documents', Volume II, p. 76, *Law & Justice Publishing Co.*, 1967.

8 Ed. B. Shiva Rao, 'The Framing of India's Constitution: Select Documents', Volume II, p. 13, *Law & Justice Publishing* Co., 1967.

9 Shiva Rao, 'Framing of India's Constitution: A Study', p. 461, *The Indian Institute of Public Administration*, 1968.

10 Regardless of the intention of the Constitution makers, at least one judgment of the Supreme Court holds that the right to vote is a fundamental right. See the judgment of Rastogi J. in Anoop Baranwal v. UOI (2023) 6 SCC 161. However, an earlier unanimous decision of the Constitution Bench in Kuldip Nayar v. UOI (2006) 7 SCC 1 has held that the Constitution does not guarantee a fundamental right to vote.

11 The Swiss Canton of Appenzell Innerhoden only gave women the right to vote in 1990.

12 Pandit H.N. Kunzru, a renowned Parliamentarian, was in favour of a gradual expansion of the vote thinking that it would take time to educate an electorate. Constituent Assembly Debates, Vol. XI, p. 785.

13 Interestingly, the first ever list of voters was prepared even prior to the adoption of the Constitution leading one author to comment that 'Indians became voters before they became citizens'. See Ornit Shani, p. 5.

14 Orit Kedar, Liran Harsgor and Raz A. Sheinerman, 'Are Voters Equal under Proportional Representation?', Vol. 60, 2016, *American Journal of Political Science*, p. 676.

15 Jeffrey A. Karp and Susan A. Banducci, 'Political Efficacy and Participation in Twenty-Seven Democracies: How Electoral Systems Shape Political Behaviour', Vol. 38, 2008, *British Journal of Political Science*, p. 311.

16 Ananga Uday Singh Deo v. Ranga Nath Mishra, 1 SCC 499, 2002, p. 516.

17 In an interesting study it has been asserted that the apartheid system in South Africa was adopted because even though the National Conservative Party got less votes that the more liberal United Party, it got more seats in a first, past post-election. The National Party went on to impose

apartheid in 1948, a system that lasted for many decades after that. Owen Winter, 'How a Broken Voting System Gave South Africa Apartheid in 1948', Huffington Post, https://www.huffingtonpost.co.uk/owen-winter/south-africa-apartheid_b_11662272.html.

18 Abdullah Nasir and Priya Anuragini, 'Debate: First Past the Post Means India is Only a Namesake Democracy', *Wire*, 14 May 2018

19 Shefali Jha, 'Representation and Its Epiphanies: A Reading of Constituent Assembly Debates', September 25–October 1, 2004, *Economic and Political Weekly*, 4357.

20 See a discussion in 'A text without an Author', Aditya Nigam, pp.128–129 in *Politics and Ethics of the Indian Constitution*, Bhargava.

21 KT Shah, CAD Vol. VII, p. 1236.

22 CAD Vol. VII, p. 1233.

23 CAD Vol. VII, p. 1261.

24 Report of the National Commission to Review the Working of the Constitution, Vol. I, Chapter 4, para 4.16.

25 This is not to suggest that the first past the post system is solely responsible for minority under-representation. However, it certainly forms a large part of the problem.

26 Gilles Verniers, 'Verdict 2019 in charts and maps: Nearly half of India's Muslim MPs come from only two states', Scroll, June 2, 2019.

27 'Muslim population in 2023 estimated to be 20 crore: Lok Sabha', *Times of India*, 21 July 2023.

28 Gwyer & Appadorai, *Speeches and Documents on the Indian Constitution (1921–47)*, Vol. I, pp. 244–5, 261–5, Oxford University Press, 1957 as quoted in Shiva Rao, p. 467.

29 The Congress Working Committee denounced the communal award as anti-national but nevertheless stated that 'a change in or supersession of the communal decision should only be brought about by the mutual agreement of the parties concerned'. 'The History of the Indian National Congress', Vol. II, pp. 66–8. B. Pattabhi Sitaramayya. S. Chand & Sons, 1969.

30 See 'Minority Rights and in Colonial India and the Constituent Assembly', in *Debating Difference*, Rochana Bajpai, Oxford India Paperbacks, 2016.
31 *Constituent Assembly Debates*, Vol. VIII, pp. 269–355.
32 Virendra Pratap v. Union of India, (2012) 11 SCC 764.
33 *Constituent Assembly Debates*, Vol. IX, p. 677 and 682. Dr Amebdkar was of the view that should the members of the scheduled castes want reservation even after this period 'it would not be beyond their capacity or their intelligence to invent new ways of getting the same protection which they were promised here', Constituent Assembly Debates Deb., Vol. IX, p. 696.
34 By the 23rd Amendment Act in 1969, 45th Amendment Act in 1979, 62nd Amendment Act in 1989, 79th Amendment Act in 1999 and the 95th Amendment Act in 2009 the period for reservations was extended ten years at a time.
35 This is as per the order issued by the Delimitation Commission in 2008. https://www.mea.gov.in/Uploads/PublicationDocs/19167_State_wise_seats_in_Lok_Sabha_18-03-2009.pdf.
36 Ashok Kumar Jain v. UoI W.P. (C) No.546/2000 (Now renamed as 'In Re: Article 334 of the Constitution').
37 By the 73rd Amendment to the Constitution it was provided that least one-third of the total seats at all levels shall be reserved for women of whom one-third shall be from the scheduled castes and scheduled tribes.
38 One study in the context of the 73rd Amendment found that 'reservation introduced as a tool to ensure adequate representation also assists in adequate delivery of local public goods to disadvantaged groups'. See 'Impact of Reservation in Panchayati Raj Evidence from a Nationwide Randomised Experiment', Raghabendra Chattopadhyay, Esther Duflo, Vol. 39, No. 9, 28 February– 5 March 2004, *Economic and Political Weekly*, pp. 979.
39 Aneesha Mathur and Sanjay Sharma, 'A close look at the women's reservation bill: Legal aspects and debates', *India Today*, 22 September 2023.

40 Erick Trickey, 'Where Did the Term "Gerrymander" Come From?', *Smithsonian Magazine*, 2017, https://www.smithsonianmag.com/history/where-did-term-gerrymander-come-180964118/.
41 Allen v. Milligan 599 US 1.
42 Shaw v. Reno 509 US 630.
43 Rucho v. Common Cause 139 S. Ct. 2484 (2019). For a criticism of the reasoning of the court, see the case comment at 139, Harvard LR 252, 2019.
44 State of M.P. v. Devilal (1986) 1 SCC 657.
45 The case related to the drawing up the constituencies of local government bodies. Therefore, the bar contained in Article 329, discussed later in the chapter, did not apply in such a case.
46 Karthik Shashidhar, 'Forbes India Investigation: India's most gerrymandered constituencies', *Forbes* India, April 2019.
47 Of course, there could be a micro-level of gerrymandering at the level of the wards too. As Justice White of the US Supreme Court noted 'it requires no special genius to recognize the political consequences of drawing a district down one street rather than another'. Gaffney v. Cummings 412 U.S. 735.
48 Haseeb A. Drabu, 'J&K delimitation exercise sets a dangerous precedent', *Indian Express*, 31 December 2021. This delimitation exercise has also been challenged before the courts.
49 Sangeeta Barooah Pisharoty, 'BJP's Gerrymandering of Assam Districts Puts Identity Politics at the Centre of Its 2024 Strategy', , *Wire*, 7 January 2023.
50 In the history of Independent India, such a commission has been set up four times. In 1952 under the Delimitation Commission Act, 1952; in 1963 under Delimitation Commission Act, 1962; in 1973 under Delimitation Act, 1972, and in 2002 under Delimitation Act, 2002.
51 Association of Residents of Mhow v. Delimitation Commission of India (2009) 5 SCC 404 and Meghraj

Kothari v. Delimitation Commission of India (1967) 1 SCR 400.

52 Select Documents II, IS(ii), pp. 479–85.

53 CA Debates Vol. X, pp. 407–410.

54 The figure is calculated by dividing the total population of India (140 crore) by the total number of elected MPs (233) in the Rajya Sabha.

55 For instance, Singapore and Denmark both have populations around six million. https://www.worldometers.info/world-population/population-by-country/.

56 The number of constituencies in UP is eighty while those in Kerala is twenty. The population of UP as per the 2011 census is estimated to be around 200 million meaning that the average number of people per constituency is about 2.5 million. On the other hand, the population of Kerala is 33.4 million meaning that the average size of a constituency is 1.67 million.

57 2 SCC 445, 2016.

58 Section 175 of the Haryana Panchayati Raj Act, 1994 as amended by the 2015 Act.

59 Interestingly, the Court ruled that manifest arbitrariness was not a ground to challenge the provisions of a statute. However, this reasoning has been specifically overruled in the case of Shayara Bano v. UOI, 9 SCC 1, 2017.

60 Para 80 of Rajbala.

61 Para 91 of Rajbala.

62 Para 81 of Rajbala.

63 As held in the case of Janhit Abhiyan v. UOI (2023) 5 SCC 1, economic status is a valid ground for the State to classify individuals.

64 Dhruva Gandhi, 'Rethinking "Manifest Arbitrariness" in Article 14: Part II – Disparate Impact and Indirect Discrimination', 21 May 2020 https://indconlawphil.wordpress.com/.

65 This is the case in the US whereby virtue of the 14th Amendment to their Constitution, the concept of citizenship through birth was introduced. This was seen as a facet of

equality since one purpose was also to endow slaves in that country with the full rights of citizenship, thus showing the strong link between equality and citizenship. See also 'The Birthright Citizenship Amendment: A Threat to Equality', Vol. 107, No. 5 (March 1994), *Harvard Law Review* 1026.

66 See for instance Section 4 of the Citizenship Act, 1955.

67 A foreign national is permitted to apply for Indian citizenship after residing in India for 11 years in the preceding fourteen years, Section 6 read with the 3rd Schedule of the Citizenship Act, 1955.

68 'Golden Visas: Facts and Figures', *Transparency International Report*, October 2018.

69 This appears from the 175th report of the Law Commission which formed the basis of the Amendment.

70 Section 2 of the CAA reads thus 'In the Citizenship Act, 1955 (hereinafter referred to as the principal Act), in section 2, in sub-section (1), in clause (b), the following proviso shall be inserted, namely:—

'Provided that any person belonging to Hindu, Sikh, Buddhist, Jain, Parsi or Christian community from Afghanistan, Bangladesh or Pakistan, who entered into India on or before the 31st day of December, 2014 and who has been exempted by the Central Government by or under clause (c) of sub-section (2) of section 3 of the Passport (Entry into India) Act, 1920 or from the application of the provisions of the Foreigners Act, 1946 or any rule or order made thereunder, shall not be treated as illegal migrant for the purposes of this Act.'

71 See the Chapter on the Rule of Law.

72 See for instance 'Secularism and the Citizenship Amendment Act', Abhinav Chandrachud, SSRN, posted on 27 January 2020.

73 The Foreigners Act is a triple whammy on non-citizens (or indeed citizens who are often arbitrarily asked to prove their citizenship. First, they are politically powerless as they have no voting rights and are therefore not a 'vote bank' to any party. Second, they have no protection of any

international conventions as India is not a signatory to the refugee convention. Finally, even moving court is a fraught exercise as it requires the non-citizen to declare her status as a foreign national and risk having action taken against her on that very ground.

74 In State of Gujarat v. Shri Ambica Mills (1974) 4 SCC 656, it was held that 'Nor would this proposition violate any principle of equality before the law because citizens and non-citizens are not similarly situated a-. the citizens have certain fundamental rights which non-citizens have not.'

75 State of Gujarat v. Shri Ambica Mills, para 45

76 State of Gujarat v. Shri Ambica Mills, para 61

77 One matter that has reached the court and in which the judgment has been reserved is the question of the Constitutional validity of Section 6A of the Citizenship Act. This was an amendment meant to enforce the Assam Accord entered into between the Government of India and agitationists in Assam in 1985.

78 'Constitutionalism— A Skeptical View', Jeremy Waldron, in T. Christiano and J. Christman (eds), Contemporary Debates in Political Philosophy (Wiley-Blackwell 2009).

79 'The Principles of Constitutionalism', N.W. Barber, p. 10, (OUP 2018).

80 Professor Amartya Sen famously said that 'Democratic governments, in contrast, have to win elections and face public criticism, and have strong incentives to undertake measures to avert famines and other such catastrophes. It is not surprising that no famine has ever taken place in the history of the world in a functioning democracy', in *Development as Freedom* Amartya Sen, p. 44 (Anchor Books, 1999).

81 Other than the issues flagged in this chapter, there are multiple other facets of political equality. See for instance 'Political Equality and Election Systems', Jonathan W. Stills, (1981) Vol. 91 No. 3 Ethics 375.

Chapter 7: Marriage

1. Other than the victim, it has been argued that 'rather than representing a new self-realization in men over the need for gender equality, the protests are a reaction of the Indian middle classes to an existential angst arising from the rapid transition from pre- to post-modernity that it has experienced over the past decade". 'Understanding issues raised by the Delhi gang-rape case', Dr. Rajesh Tembarai Krishnamachari, South Asia Analysis Group, paper no. 5262, https://web.archive.org/web/20130117060325/http://www.southasiaanalysis.org/node/1130.
2. 'Nearly one in three women have suffered spousal sexual, physical violence: Family health survey', *Times of India*, 11 May 2022.
3. Explanation II to Section 375 provides that 'sexual intercourse or sexual acts with his own wife, the wife not being under fifteen years of age, is not rape'.
4. RIT Foundation v. UOI 2022 SCC Online Del1404, Paragraph 618. The learned judge, without giving any evidence for the view, further went on to hold that 'a woman who is waylaid by a stranger, and suffers sexual assault — even if it were to fall short of actual rape — sustains much more physical, emotional and psychological trauma than a wife who has, on one, or even more than one, occasion, to have sex with her husband despite her unwillingness'.
5. For instance, The Protection of Women from Domestic Violence Act, 2005.
6. C.H. Philips et al., eds., *The Evolution of India and Pakistan, 1857–1947. Select Documents*, Oxford University Press, 1962, pp. 10–11.
7. Of course, nothing could be further from the truth because the British project was to ensure the civilizational upliftment of the barbaric locals and the reform of Indian laws in the image of the English common law. 'The revision of the laws of India by a body sitting in London . . . implied that the real or at least the ultimate Legislature of India was

to be the Secretary of State with home advisers and with no more resistance or interference than Indian officials or non-officials could apply from afar', in *Background to India Law*, George C Rankin, p. 66 (Cambridge University Press, 1946). Even laws governing Christians in India, which clearly would not have been a case of reforming the 'native' religions were given a uniquely Indian spin where laws were also catering to race as opposed to just religion. 'Religious change, social conflict and legal competition: the emergence of Christian personal law in colonial India', Nandini Chatterjee, Vol. 44, 2010, *Modern Asian Studies*, p. 1147.

8 Rankin p. 74.

9 This fact was noted in the 1781 Burke's Act which stated that matters of contract were to be regulated by Hindu or Muslim law. It was only in the case of a transaction between a Hindu and a Muslim that the dispute had to be resolved 'by the laws and usages of the defendant'.

10 *Law and Gender Equality: The Politics of Women's Rights in India*, Flavia Agnes (Oxford University Press, 1999).

11 'Triple Talaq: How Shayara Bano's one step brought historic change in the lives of Indian Muslim Women', *India Today*, 29 December 2017.

12 Shayara Bano v. UOI (2017) 9 SCC 1. For a commentary on the judgment see 'Triple Talaq' by Madhavi Divan in *Sex and the Supreme Court*, ed. Saurabh Kirpal, Hachette, 2020.

13 Paragraph 101 Shayara Bano.

14 See the chapter on the Rule of Law for further discussion of these concepts.

15 'Triple Talaq Verdict: Wherein Lies the Much Hailed Victory?', Ratna Kapur, *Wire*, 28 August2017.

16 Article 44 of the Constitution.

17 The Government of India by a resolution dated 20 January 1944, constituted the Hindu Law Committee which then consisted of Justice B.N. Rau, Dwarka Nath Mitter, J.R. Gharpure and T.R. Venkatarama Sastri. See 'The Story of

the Hindu Code', G.R. Rajagopaul, Vol. 17, 1975, *Journal of the Indian Law Institute* 537.

18 The Hindu Marriage and Divorce Bill 1952, the Hindu Succession Bill 1952, the Hindu Minority and Guardianship Bill 1953 and the Hindu Adoptions and Maintenance Bill 1956.

19 Akshaya Mukul, 'How Gita Press shaped the orthodox challenge to the Hindu Code', *Caravan*, August 2015.

20 The State of Bombay v. Narasau Appa Mali AIR 1952 Bom, 72.

21 Article 13 (3) states that 'In this article, unless the context otherwise requires law includes any Ordinance, order, bye law, rule, regulation, notification, custom or usages having in the territory of India the force of law; laws in force includes laws passed or made by Legislature or other competent authority in the territory of India before the commencement of this Constitution and not previously repealed, notwithstanding that any such law or any part thereof may not be then in operation either at all or in particular areas.'

22 The learned judge ruled extensively on matters of religion during his tenure as a judge in the Supreme Court and was almost singlehandedly responsible for the development of the Essential Practices Test—a test that arguably permits greater judicial intervention in matters of religion. See 'Judging Religion: A Nehruvian in Court', in 'Articles of Faith', Rononjoy Sen, Oxford University Press, 2010. This makes his judgment in the Narasu Apa case all the more surprising.

23 Chief Justice Chagla also held the same view, but his reasoning was expressed in slightly less colourful language when he said that 'Polygamy is justified, if at all, on social, economic and religious grounds and hardly ever on grounds of sex. In the modern world polygamy may seem to be an anachronism and may seem to be based on outdated and outworn ideas. When, however, it is found recognised in any personal law, it is based on considerations which were

very vital and compelling to those who believed and who still believe in the sanctity of their personal law. Therefore, it would be difficult to say that the institution of polygamy would constitute a discrimination against members of one sex only on the ground of their sex', para 17.

24 Para 30 of Narasau Apa.

25 In fact, the judgment of Justice Gajendragadkar was specifically overruled by Justice Chandrachud in the Sabarimala Case 11 SCC 1, 2019, at para 386, though not on the ground of his interpretation of Article 15. However, the gradual abandonment of reliance on the word 'only' by the Supreme Court also lends credence to the belief that the judgment of Justice Gajendragadkar is no longer good law. See Anu Garg v. Hotel Association of India (2008) 3 SCC 1.

26 Harvinder Kaur v. Harminder Singh AIR 1984 Del 66.

27 'The Ghost of Narasu Appal Mali is Stalking the Supreme Court', Indira Jaisingh, *Leaflet*, 28 May 2018.

28 Saumya Uma, 'Lesser than equal? A feminist analysis of Hindu family law in India', Vol. 28, 2022, *The African Journal of Gender and Religion,* p. 1.

29 'Smt. Jayasri Guha Nee Ghosh v. Smt. Shukla Ghosh and Another', 2008 SCC Online Cal 839. The provision has been held to be unconstitutional by a single judge of the Bombay High Court in Mamta Dinesh Vakil vs Bansi S. Wadhwa (2012) 6 Bom CR 767, but the matter is still pending adjudication before a Division bench of that court. On the contrary, the same high court had held the provision to be Constitutional in an earlier decision, Sonubai Yeshwant Jadhay vs. Bala Govinda Yadav AIR 1983 Bom 156.

30 Mytheli Srinivas, 'Conjugality and Capital: Gender, Families, and Property under Colonial Law in India', Vol. 63, 2004, *Journal of Asian Studies* 937.

31 Archana Parashar, 'Gender Inequality and Religious Personal Laws in India', Vol. 14, No. 2, 2008, *Brown Journal of World Affairs*, 103.

32 Coupled with this is the argument that personal law within themselves carry the capacity for reform without

legislative intervention, see 'Understanding Muslim Law in the Modern Context', Justice B.D. Ahmad, in *Sex and the Supreme Court*, Ed. Saurabh Kirpal, and 'Ain't Women Religious: Critiquing the Muslim Personal Law from an Intersectional Feminist Perspective', Farhan Zia, Vol. V, *NLIU Law Review* 23.

33 Nivedita Menon, 'It isn't about women', *The Hindu*, 15 July 2016.

34 *Family Law*, Vol. 2, Flavia Agnes, Oxford University Press, 2011.

35 Agnes Vol. II, p. 22.

36 There were wildly divergent views about the case with the Anglo-Indian press lauding the single judge's judgment and the native press expressing alarm. See 'Rukhmabai: Debate over Woman's Right to Her Person', Sudhir Chandra, Vol. 31, No. 44, 2 November 1996, *Economic and Political Weekly*, p. 2937.

37 Agnes Vol II, p. 169

38 Paras Diwan, 'Weekend Marriages and the Restitution of Conjugal Rights', Vol. 20, 1978, *Journal of the Indian Law Institute* 1.

39 Saroj Rani v. Sudarshan Kumar Chadha 4 SCC 90, 1984, para17.

40 Shelly Lundberg and Robert A Pollak, 'Bargaining and distribution in marriage', 1996, *Journal of Economic Perspectives* 139.

41 Carrie Yodanis, 'Divorce Culture and Marital Gender Equality: A Cross-National Study', 2005 Vol. 19, *Gender and Society*, p. 644.

42 Joseph Shine v. UOI (2019) 3 SCC 39.

43 Agnes Vol. 2, p. 34.

44 Agnes Vol. 2, p. 37.

45 Flavia Agnes, 'Maintenance for Women Rhetoric of Equality', Vol. 27, No. 41, 10 October 1992, *Economic and Political Weekly* 2233.

46 Nick Barber, 'Principles of Constitutionalism', p. 90, OUP, 2018.

47 Namita Bhandare and Surbhi Karwa, 'How Indian Courts define a married woman's place', Article 14, https://article-14.com/post/how-indian-courts-define-a-married-woman-s-rightful-place

48 Srimati Basu, 'Judges of Normality: Mediating Marriage in the Family Courts of Kolkata, India', Vol. 37, No. 2, 2012, ed. Philip Rothwell, *Signs, Unfinished Revolutions: A Special issue*, p. 469.

49 This is not a universal opinion with some feminists seeking a reform of the institution than its abandonment. See 'Marriage, Autonomy, and the Feminine Protest', Debra B. Bergoffen, Vol. 14., 1999 Hypatia, *The Philosophy of Simone de Beauvoir*, p. 18.

50 Clare Chambers, 'The Marriage-Free State', Vol. 113, 2013, *Proceedings of the Aristotelian Society,* p. 123

51 Marth Albertson Fineman, 'Cracking the Foundational Myths: Independence, Autonomy, and Self Sufficiency', Vol. 8, 2000, *American University Journal of Gender, Social Policy and the Law*, p. 13, where the author notes that 'the gendered nature of this assumed family is essential to the maintenance and continuance of our foundational myths of individual independence, autonomy, and self-sufficiency'.

52 Ann Ferguson, 'Gay Marriage: An American and Feminist Dilemma', Vol. 22, 2000, *Hypatia, Writing Against Heterosexism*, p.39, and Mary Anne Case, 'What Feminists Have to Lose in Same-Sex Marriage Litigation', Vol. 57, 2010, *UCLA Law Review* 1199. Of course, this is not a position unique to feminists. Several queer theorists also oppose marriage equality not only on the grounds of its sexist nature but also on the normative superiority of the social hierarchies that it cements.

53 These 'bouquet of rights' have been detailed in the petitioners submissions in the Supriyo case. See Annexure three and four of the rejoinder submissions of Dr A.M. Singhvi, Supriyo, pp. 14–16.

54 'The challenge of law: Sexual orientation, gender identity, and social movements in queer mobilizations', *LGBT Activists Confront the Law* (1–20), ed. Scott Barclay, Mary Bernstein, Anna-Maria Marshall, New York University Press, 2009. On the other hand, there is still a feminist critique of same-sex marriage, not on the ground of inequality, but on the same grounds on which marriage is viewed negatively for straight couples, i.e. patriarchy and forced gender identities. Susan B. Boyd, 'Marriage is More Than Just a Piece of Paper: Feminist Critiques of Same Sex Marriage', Vol. 8, 2013, *National Taiwan U L Rev* 263.

55 Matters were, among other places, filed in the Kerala High Court and the Delhi High Court. https://www.ndtv.com/india-news/delhi-high-court-seeks-centres-stand-on-pleas-by-same-sex-couples-for-recognition-of-marriage-2309937.

56 Writ Petition (Civil) No. 1011 of 2022.

57 Order dated 6 January 2023 in Writ Petition (Civil) No. 1011 of 2022.

58 Surbhi Sachdeva, 'Why Supreme Court's same-sex marriage verdict opens no doors for queer people', Aditya Prasanna Bhattacharya, *Indian Express*, 20 October 2023.

59 Supriyo Alias Supriya Charaborty v. Union of India 2023 SCC Online SC 1348 ('Supriyo').

60 Inter-religious marriages are allowed only under the Special Marriage Act 1954 (and its predecessor Acts), rather than under the personal laws. Therefore, in the absence of enabling legislation, there is no way for two people of different religions to wed. Thus, if the Special Marriage Act were to be repealed (or never have been enacted), inter-religious couples would be in the same position as queer couples—devoid of Constitutional protection. This point has not been discussed in the judgment of the court.

61 Under the Hindu personal law, the marriage between a man from an inferior caste to a woman of a superior caste is 'pratiloma', and invalid. Valsamma Paul v. Cochin University (1996) 3 SCC 545.

62 Dr B.R. Ambedkar, *Annihilation of Caste*, Annotated Critical Edition, Navayana, 2014, p. 285.
63 The errors of the judgment in relation to the right to marry have been detailed in 'The Supreme Court's Marriage Equality Judgment – I: On the Right to Marry and a Case of Abstention through Delegitimisation', Kartik Kalra, https://indconlawphil.wordpress.com/2023/10/21/the-supreme-courts-marriage-equality-judgment-i-on-the-right-to-marry-and-a-case-of-abstention-through-delegitimisation-guest-post/
64 Supriyo, paragraph 526–527, p. 929.
65 Justice Kaul points out in his dissenting judgment that this was the result of conflating the differentia with the object of the Act (para 382 of Supriyo). If such a conflation is permitted, it would render Article 14 meaningless as every discriminatory statute would be justified by arguing that its object is to discriminate.
66 Supriyo Paragraph 382—384, p.
67 Supriyo, Paragraph 548, p. 932.
68 James Boswell, *The Life of Samuel Johnson*, Vol. II, p. 182.
69 Dev Gupta v. PEC University of Technology SCC Online SC 960, para 18. This point has also been discussed by Hardik Choubey in https://indconlawphil.wordpress.com/2023/11/08/the-supreme-courts-marriage-equality-judgment-v-on-discrimination-judicial-remedies-and-judicial-abnegation-guest-post/
70 N. Anand Venkatesh et al., 'W.M.P.No.31112 of 2023 in W.P.No.7284 of 2021', Live Law, 17 November 2023, https://www.livelaw.in/pdf_upload/deed-of-familial-association-lgbtqia-504482-504576.pdf.
71 Contract is a basis for marriage in many personal laws including the Shariat. However, that system of law has non-derogable rules which mutate the 'contract' into 'status'. On the other hand, this form of marriage allows parties to completely negotiate their relationship. Jeremy R. Garrett 2009, 'Marriage Unhitched from the State: A Defense', Vol. 23, *Public Affairs Quarterly*, p. 161.

Epilogue

1 Liversidge v. Anderson (1942) per Lord Atkin.
2 Satish Deshpande, 'Caste and Castelessness: Towards a Biography of the "General Category"', *Economic and Political Weekly*, Vol. 48, No. 15 (13 April 2013), pp. 32–39.
3 Renu Addlakha and Satish Deshpande, 'Disability Law in India: Paradigm Shift or Evolving Discourse', Vol. 44, No. 41/42, October 2009, *Economic and Political Weekly*, p. 62. See also 'The Future of Disability Law in India: A Critical Analysis of the Persons with Disabilities (Equal Opportunities, Protection of Rights and Full Participation) Act 1995', Jayna Kothari, OUP, 2012.
4 Rights of Persons with Disabilities Act, 2016 and the Mental Healthcare Act, 2017. The 2017 Act provides
5 Section 2 (y) of the Rights of Persons with Disabilities Act, 2016.
6 Vikash Kumar v. UPSC, (2021) 5 SCC 370, Para 60.
7 Section 32 of the Rights of Persons with Disabilities Act, 2016.
8 Section 34 of the Rights of Persons with Disabilities Act, 2016.
9 Janhit Abhiyan v. UOI (2023) 5 SCC 1, para 81.
10 Janhit Abhiyan, per Justice Bhat and Lalit, Para 561, where the court held that 'the introduction of reservations for economically weaker sections of the society is not premised on their lack of representation (unlike backward classes); the absence of this condition implies that persons who benefit from the EWS reservations can, and in all probability do belong to classes or castes, which are "forward" and are represented in public service, adequately. This additional reservation, by which a section of the population who are not socially backward, and whose communities are represented in public employment—violates the equality of opportunity which the Preamble assures, and Article 16(1) guarantees'.
11 Janhit Abhiyan, Per Justice Pardiwala, para 416.

12 For example, Rights of Persons with Disabilities Act, 2016 and the Scheduled Caste and Tribes (Prevention of Atrocities) Act, 1989.

13 For instance, more schools, regulatory agencies like an equal opportunities commission.

14 See 'Foundations of Indirect Discrimination Law', Hugh Collins and Tarunabh Khaitan, Bloomsbury, 2018, for discussion of disadvantage and other bases for possible laws relating to discrimination.

15 'Envy Up and Scorn Down: How Status Divides Us', Susan T. Fiske, *Russell Sage Foundation* (2012).

16 Lasana T. Harris and Susan T. Fiske, 'Dehumanizing the Lowest of the Low: Neuroimaging Responses to Extreme Out-Groups', *Psychological Science*, Vol. 17, No. 10, October 2006, pp. 847.

17 Susan T. Fiske, 'Divided by Status: Upward Envy and Downward Scorn', Proceedings of the American Philosophical Society, Vol. 157, No. 3, September 2013, p. 261.

18 Susan T. Fiske, 'Divided by Status: Upward Envy and Downward Scorn', ibid.

Scan QR code to access the
Penguin Random House India website